The Unexpected Gift

God's Biblical Perspective on Singleness

Joëlle Andre-Marié Kabamba

Space Between Publications

Copyright © 2021 by Joëlle Marie-André Kabamba
The Unexpected Gift; *God's Biblical Perspective on Singleness*
Published by Space Between Publications in Australia

Space Between Publications
Parcel Locker 1021607003
50 Flemington Road
Parkville VIC 3052
www.thespacebetweenpublications.com

Editor: Sue J. Bruce
Cover designer: Annie K. Kabamba
Typesetter: Self-PublishingLab.com

ISBN:
978-0-6488656-7-4 (paperback)
978-0-6488656-6-7 (hardback)
978-0-6488656-4-3 (eBook)

All rights reserved. No part of this book may be reproduced in any manner or form without permission in writing from the publisher.

All Scripture quotations, unless otherwise indicated, are taken from the Holy Bible, New International Version®, NIV®. Copyright ©1973, 1978, 1984, 2011 by Biblica, Inc.™ Used by permission of Zondervan. All rights reserved worldwide. www.zondervan.com. The "NIV" and "New International Version" are trademarks registered in the United States Patent and Trademark Office by Biblica, Inc.™

Scripture quotations marked MSG are taken from *THE MESSAGE*, copyright © 1993, 2002, 2018 by Eugene H. Peterson. Used by permission of NavPress. All rights reserved. Represented by Tyndale House Publishers, a Division of Tyndale House Ministries.

ENDORSEMENTS

Joëlle's book is a needed and timely voice to the church today. She captures the often times unarticulated struggles and sentiments of singleness and yet directs us towards a vision of flourishing in a God honouring way. For pastors it is a helpful resource to equip leaders to better disciple a growing proportion of their community. Personally, it has helped me learn to minister to myself in this new season as a single again widowed man in Christ.

Pastor Chee Fah
Senior Pastor of Clayton Church of Christ, Melbourne Australia

It is my pleasure to encourage you to read Joëlle's story and enjoy the wisdom that flows from this intelligent woman. It is freeing for every individual to find their identity and understand their purpose in God, a purpose that transcends their marital status. Throughout the pages of *The Unexpected Gift*, you will be encouraged to thrive in every sphere and season you find yourself. Well done, Joëlle, for embarking on this journey of bringing hope and life to every reader.

Julia A'Bell
National Leader, Australian Christian Women

It has been my privilege to have known Joëlle for over 20 years. She is a practical and gifted culture changer – a persistent hard worker who is prepared to ask difficult questions whilst working intelligently within community. As a medical practitioner in the area of trauma for 30 years I know that singleness is such a common condition (or season). Joëlle has grappled with this complex subject with intelligence and sensitivity, in the context of history and culture. She has not just done this from theory or intellectualism but from practical application and empathises deeply with those to whom she has written. This book is from the Master's heart.

Dr Rama Spencer
MBBS (University of Queensland, 1989) FRACGP

The Unexpected Gift is a book we wish we had during our single years. The stigma of singleness is so prominent in the church and this take on what a gift singleness is, to God and to ourselves, is not only beautifully refreshing but also needed for so many.

Rebecca and Marissa Karagiorgos
Twice Blessed, Creative Directors, Digital Content Creators, Melbourne Australia

The Unexpected Gift is indeed what is says. This book not only speaks to singles, but gives insight to pastors and those in positions of leadership about how to minister to singles in an inclusive way. Joëlle discusses the struggles and challenges many singles face in life and even in church, but through her own story you will be empowered to have hope and never give up on God. Singles you will discover your true identity is in Christ and not in a wedding dress and that He loves you regardless of your status. This book is a must read if you want to understand your assignment as a single person and walk in joy and confidence on your journey.

Prophetess Betty Ohen Apraku
Senior Pastor of Dominion Centre, London United Kingdom

Joëlle has such a zest for life that people want to be around her and listen to her stories. And with so much life experience, that makes for an interesting journey filled with faith, wisdom and her delightful humour. She speaks and writes with such passion and honesty you will feel refreshed and inspired to step into your own journey with a new outlook: glad that you spent time with her.

Carolyn Donovan
Artist, Writer, Brisbane Australia

Joëlle explores the many dimensions of singleness. Upon reflecting, we can all identify with many of its aspects in our day-to-day lives. Singleness is certainly an unexpected gift and not to be seen as a punishment. It is an opportunity to reflect on our own individual capabilities and development. I have no hesitation in recommending this book to all women in whatever situation of life they find themselves.

Rev Peter Bondole and Claire Bondole
New Covenant Miracle Centre, Melbourne Australia

DEDICATION

À Ma Mère

Maman, Marie-Claire Ngalula. My héroïne and voice of reason, this is for you. You declared grace and hope over this project, I will continue building on your legacy. Thank you for who you are and all you have done for us on this side of eternity. I love you and miss you so much.

Twasakidila Mamu!

CONTENTS

Sealed With a Bow	xv
To You	xvii
To the Pastors	xxiii
Part I Single Out	**1**
1 Joëlle	4
2 Divinely Chosen	14
A Woman's Longing	15
Identity Theft	17
Defining Singleness	18
God's Perspective on Singleness	19
An Exemplary Life	24
Tegan	29
3 The Stigma of Singleness	34
'Singlism' and 'Matrimania'	36
What About the Church?	40
What is a Victim Mentality?	47
Part II Two Become One	**53**
Koko	55
4 A Desire to Marry	59
Desiring Marriage	60
The Delay	64
Where are All the Brothers At?	67
Loneliness vs. Singleness	71
Tick-Tock Biological Clock	78
Charlene	85
5 Colouring Your World	90
In the Meantime	91
Live in the Moment	100
Don't be an Island	104
Ditch the List	108
Kim	113
6 Single & Single Again	118
Content Singles	120

Settled	120
Abide in Christ	124
Single Again	131
Highly Favoured	132
My Redeemer Lives	137

Part III Herstory — 145

Lizzy	147
7 Looking Back	151
Women in the Bible	152
Surrogacy	154
The Nameless Girl	156
Heroic Women	157
Judaism, Jesus and Paul	159
Women in Africa	164
Before Colonialisation	166
Warrior Women	168
The Value of Women	169
Colonialisation	170
Resilience	174
Women in the West	174
Before the Industrial Revolution	175
British Queens	177
The Fight for Equality	178
Where to From Here?	183

Part IV Reclaiming Our Identity — 189

Kelly	191
8 Identity Theft	196
We are Loved	199
We are Family	204
What's in a Name?	208
Role vs. Purpose	213
Poised for Greatness	217
Koda-Jo	225
9 Let's Talk About Sex	230
What does God Say about Sex?	233
The Case for Purity	237
Science, Culture and Purity	241
Sexual Chemistry	243
Same-Sex Orientation	251
Connection, Vulnerability & Motive	254
U-turn and Restoration	258

Part V The Unexpected Gift — 265

Ebony — 267
10 Is Singleness a Gift — 273
Singleness is a Gift! — 277
Shifting our Mindset — 279
Learning to Trust — 283
Thank You — 285
The Power of Worship — 286
A Posture of Reverence — 288
Esther — 289
Elizabeth — 294
Grandma Anna — 297
My Cup Overflows — 298
Letting God Define Us — 298
Abundant Freedom — 301

Part VI Eternity — 305

11 Now and Forever — 306
The Kingdom of God — 308
Good News — 310
Kingdom Freedom — 313
Kingdom Perspective — 318
His Rockin' Church — 322
A Party in Heaven — 327
Don't Miss Out! — 335
Let Out Your Roar! — 337

Last Thought! — 343

Appendix A — 347
Summary of 2018 Singles Survey — 347
Summary of 2010 Singles Survey — 349

Thank You — 350

FOREWORD

Joëlle is someone who from the moment you meet her is full of life and joy with an authentic heart for everyone she encounters. To know Joëlle is to know someone who is devoted, loyal and invests her heart and soul in what she believes. She is greatly treasured by all who know her and is such a blessing to our LIFE community. We admire her courage and as you will discover through the pages of this book, she is captivated with a deep passion for everyone – for you – to know nothing less than God's absolute best.

Throughout this book you will see into Joëlle's life. I know many will relate to the very present challenges singleness can bring, including the tensions, the misunderstanding and isolation that comes from today's culture which embraces the narrative that if you're single, someone is missing and something is wrong. Despite where you stand right now, whether long time single, recently single, starting to consider relationships or in a season you thought you had graduated from; your singleness must not be a place of grief and disappointment. It should rather be a gift to be received and embraced. We cannot be limited by our current circumstances or the narrative of others.

Can we implore you to 'go there', as you read through the chapters and as your own journey is brought into the spotlight?

FOREWORD

Allow Joëlle's wisdom and life experience to shape your next step. Let the promises spoken, not just be for someone else, but for you as well. Let them renew how you see this journey then determine to rise up, reset your vision and know your best day is not some day in the future, but today.

For friends, family, church leaders and pastors reading this who, like us, are no longer single; would you embrace this book with a heart to understand in depth a season that is different to your own? Let's widen our perspective and make it a focus to champion those we love and support. Let's change what needs to change in our sphere, so we can increase the support and encouragement for those walking this journey.

We also want to commend Joëlle firstly for the decades that she has lived out the contents of this book and also for the years of research and hard work in bringing this project to life. As you read this, may you receive great insight and clarity, find healing and a very real knowing that you are seen and are someone of incredible significance right where you are today.

Well enough from us; jump in with great expectation because we know you will be so refreshed and restored by all this book has to offer.

With love

Craig and Nadia Clark, Lead Pastors, LIFE, Melbourne

SEALED WITH A BOW

TO YOU

It was one of those beautiful winter mornings in Queensland, Australia. Warm sunlight beamed through the window as 10 of my girlfriends and two of my younger sisters gathered to help me launch my YouTube channel. They giggled and laughed as they settled on the couch in my sister Marie's beautiful living room. Our camera man Joel smiled, nodded, and readied his equipment while we sipped coffee and shared about our lives.

The focus of the morning was on the value of singleness. I asked my guests the question: *Do you believe singleness has a stigma in our society?*

The Macquarie Dictionary defines stigma as a mark of disgrace; a stain, as on one's reputation, and as a characteristic mark or sign of defect, degeneration and disease.[1] I was asking my friends if they thought the world considered singleness to be a defect or problem to be fixed before a woman could be happy and complete.

Two friends, sitting on opposite ends of the couch, presented extreme responses to this question. A 48-year-old friend said there

---

1 *Macquarie Dictionary Online* 2020, Macquarie Dictionary Publishers, an imprint of Pan Macmillan Australia Pty Ltd, viewed 20 February 2020, https://www.macquariedictionary.com.au>.

was a huge stigma attached to being single, another 25-year-old girlfriend said there was none. Why two opposing views?

Was it because my 48-year-old, not-yet-married girlfriend, had lived longer and experienced many critical remarks and questions regarding her status as a single woman? Had she felt the expectations of those around who wanted to 'fix' her up with a partner? Or did her journey as a female minister make her feel as if she was expected to work more because that's what you do when you are single and married to church work? Perhaps she was a statistic, representative of women who spend too much time with their career and then, by the time they want to find someone, it seems too late. Meanwhile, men of her age are getting on, preferring to date women younger than her.

Was my 25-year-old friend too young to have experienced these problems? Or had those who had gone before and fought to challenge the status quo, lessened the stigma of singleness for younger women?

As I explored this area, and interviewed many singles, I found myself not just investigating the stigma of singleness but asking even deeper questions. There are different kinds of single people – how do their needs differ? Does a young woman who is looking to find a partner experience singleness differently from an older woman whose biological clock is nearing midnight? In what way does a woman who is single, because she has lost her partner to death or divorce, see the world differently from a woman who has never wanted to be married?

I thought further and realised that every one of us – every human being – will experience singleness at some stage of our lives. Even if we marry young, it is rare that both spouses will die together. Singleness is part of the human condition, so it is vital that we understand how to navigate such times with grace and power.

As I wrote these thoughts down, the vision for this book coalesced. What if I could write a work where Christian singles could learn what it means to not just exist, but thrive in God's kingdom? What if all Christian women could live powerful, confident lives full of hope and purpose, irrespective of their marital status?

And so, over several years, this book began to take form. I realised this topic was huge, so I decided to limit my discussion to Christian women. That way I could speak from my lived experience as well as from the qualitative research I undertook.

But I haven't just shared my experience. I have intertwined within the pages of this book, stories of women, both young and mature, who have bravely shared their experiences of a God who meets us where we are. They are an example of how God weaves our stories into his, all the while reminding us that we are loved and that we matter.

This book is also influenced by my background. I am both African – I was born in the Democratic Republic of the Congo (DRC) – and Australian. I love to embrace my African heritage but also this land, which has been my home for much of my life. As we journey onward, you will find that this dual heritage influences both the content (look out for the section on the history of African women) and the way I've structured this book. Whereas Western thinking tends to be linear, Africans often think more cyclically, building concept on concept, each time giving greater detail to the picture. So, while you will still find a good deal of Western logic here, you may find it helpful to think of the early pages of this book as an overview – like the sketch an artist makes before she fills in the detail of her painting. Each time through she adds more features and colour. I hope that by the time you reach the end of this discussion, the picture will be complete, and you can grasp the fullness of what it means to thrive as a single Christian.

The other thing I must say is that I write from the perspective of the Christian faith. I believe that the Bible is God's inspired and inerrant love-letter to the world, so that will colour my words. I believe that if we can align ourselves with God's view – the ultimate voice on our singleness – we can live with strength and hope.

So, please join me as I talk about how divinely chosen and complete we are in God's eyes. Explore with me the stigma that's been applied to single women historically and today. Walk with me through the challenges we face as singles when we desire marriage, groan with the pain of being single again and deal with questions of sexuality. Discern with me the amazing truth about our identity and discover that singleness is an unexpected gift from our good, good God – an opportunity not to be wasted.

Finally, rejoice with me as we contemplate eternity. The Bible begins with marriage and ends with marriage! Ladies, the church is Christ's bride and one day we will get to wear a dress-that-ends-all-dresses. How amazing is that? I can't wait to party in heaven!

My hope is as you read, you will be encouraged, empowered and challenged by the living God, so that you can thrive as a single Christian woman. Our God in heaven *sees* us and *knows* us, never holding out on us. He doesn't see us as broken or incomplete in our singleness. On the contrary, he is holding onto us and propelling us towards a life filled with meaning and significance. Be encouraged that you are a beautiful daughter of the King, and that the Spirit of Christ lives in you. Learn how to walk in him and be all you are meant to be. Revel in your singleness – a beautiful, unexpected gift – wrapped up and tied with a bow!

TO THE PASTORS

Pastors and leaders, we have a key role in helping the single people in our churches thrive. We live in a world where social boundaries are loosening and issues of identity and gender fluidity are constantly in the headlines. We have a mandate to help our people navigate these changes by offering God's perspective on such issues – including that of singleness. What we once knew as the traditional nuclear family is being continually redefined.

According to the Australian Bureau of Statistics, the crude rate of marriage (number of marriages each year per 1,000 persons) has dropped from 5.9 in 1998 to 4.8 in 2018.[2] While marriage actually increased by 5.5% from 2017 to 2018. Statistics show this was due to same-sex marriage. It is interesting that since 1998, the divorce rate has dropped slightly, but there were still over 49,000 divorces granted in Australia in 2018.[3]

---

2   *Marriages and Divorces, Australia, 2018* 2019, Australian Bureau of Statistics, viewed 20 February 2020, <https://www.abs.gov.au/statistics/people/people-and-communities/marriages-and-divorces-australia/latest-release>.

3   *Marriages and Divorces, Australia 2018* <https://www.abs.gov.au/statistics/people/people-and-communities/marriages-and-divorces-australia/latest-release>.

People are marrying later, and more and more people are living alone. The Australian Institute of Family Studies states that one person households are on the rise in Australia. Between 1986 and 2016 single person households increased from 19% to 24% of the total households in Australia, while family households decreased.[4]

These statistics tell me that, as pastors and leaders, we need to accept that demographics are changing and act accordingly. We need to change the way we do things. It's not enough to say we are a family church and support the people who are married with children, when just under one quarter of all households around us contain single people. Our churches are full of single people and they need to be heard.

In 2010, I conducted a survey where I asked over a hundred single women what they felt about issues of singleness and their place in the church. In 2018, I undertook additional research that focused on singles' needs (both men and women) and the way they engage socially inside and outside of the church. The findings of these surveys are threaded throughout the book, but you can find a summary in Appendix A. The discoveries I made in 2018 inspired the birth of the ministry *Thesp_ceBetwn*, an events-based movement, focused on engaging and growing Christian singles.

Singles are facing diverse challenges including limited opportunity to find partners. This has implications for family

---

4   *Population and households 2018*, Australian Institute of Family Studies, *Population and households*, viewed 20 February 2020, https://aifs.gov.au/facts-and-figures/population-and-households>.

and for the elderly who can easily find themselves living alone and isolated from support structures. Couple this with the fluidity of relationships in the modern transgender society and singles, including Christian singles, can become confused about issues of family and sexuality.

These challenges provide a timely opportunity for church communities to engage in new ways of speaking the gospel into this changing world. I long for churches to show a fresh understanding of the value of singleness. As pastors and leaders, we need to debunk the myth that marriage is for everyone, while addressing the stigma and attitudes that are sometimes projected towards singles.

Some long-term singles have problems with their self-image and may feel as if they don't quite fit. At other times our humour, if overdone, can make singles feel out of place. We also need to be careful not to push singles toward people who might not be right for them, just because we'd like them to have a partner.

> *"Some long-term singles have problems with their self-image and may feel as if they don't quite fit."*

In reality, our role is to help empower singles to live a whole and fulfilling life, so they can find contentment and purpose and not feel 'less than' their married counterparts. My belief is that singleness is a gift to be embraced, not a state to be avoided, hence the title of this book: *The Unexpected Gift*.

I hope this book can help empower singles in your church. I'd love it to be the foundation of group discussion to stimulate deep thinking around the issues of singleness among your people. It would be wonderful if everyone, including singles, could feel empowered and released to be all they can be in our communities and to know they belong, irrespective of colour, gender or marital status.

If I may, I'd like to make some suggestions that could help singles be integrated into our communities. These come not just from my experience but from the accounts of the many singles I interviewed. It's not an exhaustive list but I hope it helps to get the discussion started.

- At times singles might feel uncomfortable initiating conversations about their status. It might help them engage if we can start the conversation.
- Keep encouraging the families in our communities to include singles socially.
- While it is good to encourage those who want to marry, let's try to minister with a clear awareness that marriage isn't for everyone.
- Unsolicited advice can sometimes shut the door to a great conversation.
- Normalise teaching about the value of singleness. Cover singles with hope and dignity when teaching from the pulpit and in our small groups.
- Consider inviting visiting speakers who model singleness well.

We all need encouragement and Christian singles are no exception. It's not that we are not doing these things already – we are – but there is more work to be done. I hope as you read

TO THE PASTORS

these pages you will be inspired to raise up the singles in your congregations and enable them to be all they can be in Christ.

Let's keep doing community well!

Joëlle Kabamba – Pastor

SINGLED OUT

"I was a timid girl and I struggled with low self-esteem. I was bullied in both my primary and high school years, starting in the DRC and continuing in Australia."

1

JOËLLE

Welcome! I'm excited that we are going on this journey together. In this first chapter of the book I'd like to tell you about myself and how I came to be here, writing a book on singleness.

I was born in the Democratic Republic of the Congo into a large family – I'm one of 13 children. My Dad, André, and a couple of his colleagues, were jailed for political reasons. They wanted to reform their university. This eventually led to us moving to Zambia to take refuge. After two years there, my dear pregnant mum, Marie-Claire, along with Dad, myself, three brothers and eight sisters were finally accepted as refugees to Australia.

With such a large family, almost a tribe, we always stood out. This began right on arrival day at the airport. I think people thought the whole of Africa had just arrived.

When I was a very young girl, my little heart felt overwhelmed when my parents mentioned we would move to Australia. I wasn't sure I wanted to move to an unknown place. I recall feeling lost when news came that we would indeed live in Australia. I was perfectly comfortable where I lived and how life was. I didn't want things to change.

There and then I prayed a vague prayer: 'If you are a God out there and can hear me, if you look after me and my family in our new country, I promise to serve you all the days of my life'. That prayer did not come out of a relationship with God. We went to a Catholic church on the weekends, but I saw church attendance as no more than a ticket to heaven back then. I don't think I understood what I was doing, except that God was the last – and only – resource I had to cling to at the time. Who would have thought I would have been living out that prayer throughout my entire life?

I was a timid girl and I struggled with low self-esteem. I was bullied in both my primary and high school years, starting in the DRC and continuing in Australia. Despite making a few friends, I hated school. There were few students with a dark complexion in those days in Australia. At high school I had little confidence to speak English and I faced ignorant comments from peers that crushed my spirit and reminded me that I did not fit in. I looked and sounded too different. Comments about me looking ugly sunk in and I started believing them. I often cried myself to sleep, praying and asking God why he made me so different.

My last three years in high school ripped me apart. I felt lost. And it wasn't just about being black. Friends seemed to have already worked out their careers and when and who they would marry. Even how many children they would have. They seemed to have their lives all sorted and this made me nervous. I felt I had some idea in terms of career but not about who I would marry. I had no clue and did not even think it should be on my radar. It was too far-fetched.

How the heck does anyone in high school know who they will marry, especially if they did not even have boyfriends? I have no issue with having a dream, but looking back, I see there was something else going on with me. I was afraid of marriage.

Now, after many years, I know that the fear stemmed from what I saw marriage to be. I looked around for inspiration, but I was mostly surrounded by couples whose marriages did not excite me. I did not envy married life, and at times that included what I saw in the people closest to me. I would often think that if that is marriage then I do not want anything to do with it.

> "I lay on my bed one Saturday afternoon, thinking about my future. Although I had no idea what I wanted to do career wise, I knew I still wanted my life to mean something."

But the fear also stemmed from my naivety. I became a follower of Christ in my last year of high school. A month before I was to finish school, I lay on my bed one Saturday afternoon, thinking about my future. Although I had no idea what I wanted to do career-wise, I knew I still wanted my life to mean something. As I considered this, a warm presence filled the room and I felt God speak into my heart. 'If you want a significant life, you have to become my friend.' I was a mess. Tears streamed down my face and I fell on my knees and said that I would follow him. When I got up, my life shifted. My whole countenance changed. I began to memorise scriptures like Psalm 139:14. I was fearfully and wonderfully made. Another verse that inspired me was in Jeremiah. God told me he had plans for me – plans to give me hope and a future.[1] *But I had no desire for those plans to involve marriage.*

I desperately wanted to serve God. I did not think I should pursue marriage because I thought it would distract me from my singular focus on God. I continued with this mindset over several years – I saw no need for marriage in my life.

As a young adult I developed a sanguine personality and was always out for fun. I easily made friends, both male and female. Over the years, when guys showed interest I simply overlooked their attention and was happy to be just friends. Most of these guys became frustrated with me because I would change the subject or would try to match them with my girlfriends instead. I kept doing this over and over, unaware that this was due to my fear of marriage.

It was not until one of our church youth camps, where I was a leader, that the Holy Spirit confronted this fear. One morning session, a guest speaker shared on fears and how to address them. At the end of the message, the pastor encouraged us to identify areas of fear in our lives. I then heard a whisper in my ear: 'You have a fear of marriage'.

I turned to respond to whoever had said that. 'No, I don't!' The whole back row of people looked straight at me, surprised at my talking to myself. I felt awkward when I realised that no one had said anything. God had spoken in an audible way.

---

1   Jeremiah 29:11

This was the first time God revealed to me that I had a fear of marriage. Until then I had not been aware that this fear existed in me. A couple of my close girlfriends often wondered why every time the conversations would turn to guys, I would either change the subject or turn the focus to another girl in the room. The camp encounter began a whole new journey for me where God began to bring healing in this area.

After the camp, I noticed that God began placing couples around my life whose marriages were not perfect, but who were demonstrating grace and genuine love in their relationship. He was showing me that marriage can be exemplary when done right, and I learned to appreciate marriage from the example of these couples. Many were in ministry. God was showing me that ministry does not take away from marriage but can add to it. Ministry and marriage can work well and be done well. Over the years I have grown to understand this truth even more.

> "Back then, women in ministry were not as freely accepted as they are today."

I am grateful to have been influenced by parents who taught us to always go after the best, no matter how others may see us. So, growing in confidence in who and whose I was, in the late 1990s my calling into ministry began. I felt compelled to serve God wherever he placed me in the community. I did not stay stationary, nor did I ignore what I had to offer. I let those around me know I had something to say, regardless of any resistance I faced.

However, even though I felt my voice was relevant, it was being largely unheard. One issue was that women's voices, at that time of male-dominated ministry, were rare. The role of women was uncertain; and they were not given much of a platform. Female mentors to support those, who like me were starting the journey, were few and far between. Women were not often encouraged or provided with opportunities to excel.

I did the best with what I could at the time, bridging the gap by building relationships with other young women who were also pioneering in ministry. In those days, I worked in schools as a high school chaplain and youth minister, so I found others like me to do life with and glean wisdom from.

In the winter of 2004, Youth Alive (Queensland, Australia) sent several teams to minister in Japan (Tokyo and Kyoto) for two weeks. A youth pastor friend of mine and I were to look after one of the teams. When it came time for me to speak at one of the local churches, the local pastor did not hide his emotion on finding out it was me, a woman, preaching next. He nearly fell off his chair and asked again in bewilderment if what he heard was correct. My pastor friend Paul (Slim) smiled and reassured him that it was the case, while I stood there as if I was invisible. But worse for the local pastor – he then had to interpret my message. What a double dose of difficulty.

Some might say, 'But that's Japan; what else can one expect?' Well, I beg to differ. This also resembled some of the attitudes I experienced in Australia, although thankfully we have come a long way since 2004. Praise God.

Back then, women in ministry were not as freely accepted as they are today. They were not common in church leadership unless, for instance, the woman was already married to a minister. But this young, black and female 'me' in a sea of white faces, was pressing on to answer God's call on my life. I didn't know of any other young African-Australian girls in ministry back then. I was encountering many challenges and much resistance, both as an African-Australian and as a woman. I won't pretend it was easy. There was much resistance from those who wanted to remind me that I did not fit, with comments like, 'You are a girl and young, so you need the covering of a man or the church to preach'.[2] The word 'covering' was used consistently in those days and most times it was taken out of context. It became a profane vulgarity to me, when focused on women called to speak at church.

From my years of school bullying, I knew how to identify subtly offensive comments and refused to dance to their drumbeat. I realised I was not the one with the problem, no matter how often some wanted to remind me that I did not fit into their circle. On one occasion a couple said they would never give me an opportunity to speak even if they knew I was gifted and called. Wow! Sometimes comments like that really hurt. At other times, I let them pass and kept on with what I had to do at the time.

By the time I was ministering I had already settled on who I was, whose I was in Christ, and what my position in him was. I was not defined by how people saw me. Instead of playing that game, I used my differences to be all I could be in God.

---

2   A Mickelsen 2001, *Q&A: Does a Woman Need a Male Covering Over Her Ministry?*, CBE International, viewed 25 October 2020, <https://www.cbeinternational.org/resource/article/mutuality-blog-magazine/qa-does-woman-need-male-covering-over-her-ministry>.

The struggle was real. It seemed that in some circles my female, dark complexion and single status, did not fit some people's criteria for service and ministry. It was all too astounding to absorb. At the same time, I was becoming acquainted with the subtle Australian way of dismissing someone when not wanting to include them. I wished people would just speak their mind. The unsettling sense that I wasn't welcome became so normal that it stirred me further to keep my heart sweet and not shy away from these challenges and the call before me.

As time went on, I learned simply to focus on those who wanted me as part of the team rather than the others who did not. It started to make sense to me that the story God had carved in my life was defining me for the better. I was learning that my unique differences were an advantage. They were my strengths, not stumbling blocks or something to retreat from.

> *"As a single minister, I have served in many areas and under many great leaders, and I am thankful for the many open doors I've had to serve, not only in this great nation, but also abroad."*

Here I was, carving my way to minister amongst a very white community. I was comfortable to be all God was calling me to be. Unlike my high school days, I was to focus on who I was called to be and to not be distracted by disruptive issues that would only kill my passion. Through it all I was not seeking accolades or a special position in the church, but rather to simply function, using what was in my hand to serve God and people.

My singleness is another area that has, on occasion, caused me to be overlooked in ministry. This has happened both in church life and in other workplaces. At times I have been disqualified for a role or task because of my status as a single person. Often the role was handed to someone ill-equipped instead. Now on top of being sidelined because of my gender, youth and colour, there was the stigma of my singleness. I will share more on this particular part of my journey later in this book. This is one of the reasons I chose to write on this subject – so that others who want to walk the road I've walked will be encouraged to keep going.

Be that as it may, I know that I am who I am as a result of lessons I've learned through my life's journey. I wouldn't want it any other way. It has made me the strong woman I am today, and God's grace and kindness has never fallen short. He always works things out for good.[3]

As a single minister, I have served in many areas and under many great leaders, and I am thankful for the many open doors I've had to serve, not only in this great nation, but also abroad. I live from a place of gratitude.

As a woman of faith, I have learned to understand and welcome the curve balls of life. Without them my character wouldn't grow to its capacity. So, I embrace life in its fullness and strive for the best, so as to not miss out on any great opportunities and lessons in life. I have learned to journey with strength and lead with confidence, grace and dignity from a thankful heart. I have also learned to take a look at myself and laugh sometimes, because life is for living and

---

3   Romans 8:28

JOËLLE

you cannot take things so seriously. Forgive along the way and let things go – and don't take yourself too seriously. Why not try it?

2

DIVINELY CHOSEN

Friends, there are paradigm shifts occurring within Christian singles' groups, calling for new messages on how to thrive as single people in our community.

Paradigm shifts. A paradigm shift occurs when we change the framework through which we view a situation.[1] Over the centuries, single people, particularly single women, have often been viewed as 'lesser' than their married counterparts. There are many reasons for this, and I'll talk about these in more detail later. However, I'd like to present you with a different paradigm – one that says we are called and chosen by the living God. You and I were always destined to have a value and purpose beyond our marital status. We are meant to be limited only by the goodness of God our father and his purposes for us.

How does that resonate with you? Perhaps your reason for picking up this book is that you relate to the word 'single'. Perhaps you are single and desire marriage at some stage in life, or have found yourself single again, or are widowed. Or

---

[1] Macquarie Dictionary 2020, www.macquariedictionary.com.au, viewed 5 March, 2020, https://www.macquariedictionary.com.au/features/word/search/?search_word_type=Dictionary&word=paradigm+shifts>.

maybe you are happy to stay single for the rest of your life. Perhaps you are simply curious to know what I have written because you personally know me and want to support me. If so, you are awesome, thank you, but I feel you will be challenged too. Even if you are happy to be single, there will be some timely reminders and encouragements here to live an even deeper, richer and more purposeful single life. You will also find some gems to support your single girlfriends who may face different challenges. Whichever group you fit in, I know as you read, this content will help you make changes for the better.

In all that I write, my deep desire is that every one of us would know that we are not an afterthought. We are not the leftovers who have missed out on the abundance of life. Instead, we are divinely chosen women of power who have the living God on our side. Wow! How about that?

> *'To the Ancients, Friendship seemed the happiest and most fully human of all loves; the crown of life and the school of virtue.'*

A Woman's Longing

Have you ever stopped and considered what your deepest desires are? Are you like my school friends who wanted a certain job when they left school and to be married by a certain time? Could it be that the wanting of these things is a symptom of an even deeper desire?

I have reflected on this in my life and talked to many other women and girls. In the process I've come to understand that as God's treasured daughters we experience three major longings:

- A desire to have true intimacy – *to feel love*
- A desire to belong in an authentic community – *to have an adventure alongside others* and
- A desire to live a far greater life – *to have a purpose that matters.*

> *"In this complex world, the key to a great life as a single person involves aligning ourselves with the view of our maker."*

These longings all come from our master and designer, who has made us for love, his kingdom and for eternity. I believe that no matter what else happens in our lives, these are the things that will give us true satisfaction. And as they come from God, each of us can have them in our own way.

I trust in the giver of life, God himself. And when it's all said and done, when I reach the end of my life, it will not be about whether I was single or married but whether I lived my life to honour him. It is not about our status as single or married people. It's all about Jesus in us, living out his love in our world today. But to live like this we need to know who we are and understand what singleness is and how God sees us. We must know that we are complete in ourselves. We need to stop our identity from being stolen.

Identity Theft

Have you heard that someone is trying to steal your identity? I don't mean the kind of identity theft that happens online where you click on a link and spyware is downloaded onto your computer, or a 'Nigerian prince' asks for your bank details. No – I mean a kind of identity theft that comes with a different kind of download.

Later in this book you will find a whole chapter devoted to this issue, but I wanted to mention it here as it is fundamental to the framework through which we can understand the truth of our lives. If the devil, the father of lies, can download untruths into our hearts, he can cause us to believe we are powerless or disqualified from God's grace and goodness. We crawl away and hide as believers, losing our confidence instead of prevailing against the gates of hell. Single women, often already marginalised, are very susceptible to this tactic. We believe lies that we are unwanted, ugly and incomplete; and therefore don't live our lives as we should – as strong, beautiful daughters of the King.

> *"These longings all come from our master and designer, who has made us for love, his kingdom and for eternity."*

We feel at sea in the shifting waves of the modern age, our worth and identity reduced to our relationship status or our sexual preferences, our unworthiness worn on our sleeve as people lacking and not 'chosen'. How can we combat this?

The good news is that there is a way of protecting ourselves. Just as we can shield our computers with anti-virus and anti-spyware programs, we can shield ourselves with the truth of God's living word. In this complex world, the key to a great life as a single person involves aligning ourselves with the view of our maker. In that light, let's look at what singleness really is.

Defining Singleness

It was only recently that I was struck by a word which I think epitomises singleness perfectly. When I opened up conversations with friends and acquaintances on this matter, I asked each guest to find a word that best described what the word 'single' meant to them. Without hesitation, my good friend and amazing teacher, Michael Knight, boldly stated: *'Single: Indivisible, which means not divisible; not separated into parts; incapable of being divided (but it can be added to).'*

> *'Single: Indivisible, which means not divisible; not separated into parts; incapable of being divided (but it can be added to)'.*

Sometimes we use words without thinking what they mean. The voices in the world, the church and in our head clamour away, telling us that to be single is to be incomplete – to be lonely and lacking – to be empty of all that we need to be happy. The truth is that the word 'single' has many meanings but this one, *indivisible*, is my favourite. It means that we are the opposite of lacking. We are complete; whole in ourselves. Undivided.

Yes, singleness is the quality or state of being separate from others. But single people are also distinct, unique, and complete.

Single people can have singleness of purpose and singleness of heart – which is the opposite of double mindedness and complication. Single people can experience aloneness, but this does not necessarily mean loneliness – unless your understanding of this state has been misconstrued. Defining the word 'single' to mean that a person cannot be separated into parts – and is complete and fully purposed as they are – makes my heart sing. It confirms that the more entrenched understanding that single people are lacking and need another to make them complete, is only a distorted myth projected by society.

You couldn't find a better term to define singleness than *indivisible*. What an amazing and beautiful word. But what does God's word, the Bible, say on this matter? Does it back up this definition of singleness?

> *"Both men and women bear God's likeness, and if you like, his completeness."*

God's Perspective on Singleness

The Word of God should always be our point of reference in settling important matters. King David says in the Psalms, 'Taste and see that the Lord is good.'[2] God is always intentional in his goodness to us. He created us in his image, whole, complete and with purpose. In him we find not only our worth but peace of heart and fulfilment in life now and ever after.

One of my favourite verses in the scriptures is Genesis 1:27. 'So God created mankind in his own image, in the image of God he

---

2   Psalm 34:8

created them; male and female he created them.' This verse makes it clear that both male and female are made in God's image. A woman is not a lesser reflection of a man. Both men and women bear God's likeness, and if you like, his completeness.

But what are we to make of Genesis 2:18? 'It is not good for the man to be alone. I will make a helper suitable for him.' It's clear that God gave Adam, Eve, as a mate and that this was the first ever marriage. It was a wonderful solution to Adam's loneliness and meant that the human race could be born. But some people use this verse to indicate that singleness is a bad thing and that marriage is good. Is this the best and only interpretation of this verse?

> *"If the devil, the father of lies, can download untruths into our hearts, he can cause us to believe we are powerless or disqualified from God's grace and goodness."*

To begin with, Adam had no other human beings to relate to. He had dogs and cats and lions and maybe even the occasional hippopotamus, but he didn't have another person to commune with. He had no one who thought like him and talked like him – and that was bad. I take this to mean that one of our fundamental needs as people is other human beings. The core truth of this verse is that we don't live well isolated. Even though Adam had the perfect relationship with God, and was completely free of sin, he still needed another living, breathing human being to relate to. Whether we are married or single we need to do community well to be physically, mentally and emotionally well.

In his book, *The Four Loves*, C.S. Lewis says, 'To the Ancients, Friendship seemed the happiest and most fully human of all loves; the crown of life and the school of virtue.' The modern world, in comparison, ignores it.[3] Lewis is right – and he wrote that in 1960. Nearly everything we hear in the visual and written media today is about sexual love. But we suffer when we ignore the blessing of deep friendship.

> *"In saying this Jesus is affirming singleness – not only as an expression of our circumstances but as a choice we can make."*

Do you remember the television show, *Friends?* You can still see episodes on reruns. This show wasn't just successful because it was funny and had good looking actors, but because it hit a nerve in the psyche of single people. We do life better when we do life with others. I'm convinced that God's statement about Adam's aloneness was not just about having a sexual partner but about finding true companionship.

Jeremy Erickson, in his article, *What Does Genesis 2:18 Really Teach?*[4] compares Genesis 2:18 with Matthew 19. When a Pharisee challenged Jesus about divorce, Jesus argued from Genesis 1-3: that that which God joined together shouldn't be torn apart. The disciples, floored by this hard teaching, said it was better

---

3   CS Lewis 1960, *The Four Loves*, 1st ed., Gutenberg.ca, Project Gutenberg, viewed 5 March 2020, <htt=ps://gutenberg.ca/ebooks/lewiscs-fourloves/lewiscs-fourloves-00-h.html>.

4   J Erickson 2013, *What Does Genesis 2:18 Really Teach?* Spiritual friendship: Musings on God, Sexuality, Relationships, viewed 5 March 2020, <https://spiritualfriendship.org/2013/07/16/what-does-genesis-218-really-teach/>.

not to get married. Jesus didn't contradict them. In fact, he said that for some people it can be better to be unmarried. Here Jesus not only says that some circumstances will make people live the single life but that others will choose this life for the sake of God's kingdom. In saying this Jesus is affirming singleness – not only as an expression of our circumstances but as a choice we can make. Not only that, but because it's the choice *he* made. For isn't Jesus the ultimate example of one who laid down his life for the sake of his purpose?

The Apostle Paul echoes this idea in his first letter to the Corinthians. Like Jesus, Paul was single. He must have been married once to be considered a rabbi and a Pharisee, but it is clear that he wasn't married when he began his ministry. In chapter 7 he says this:

> *'I wish that all of you were as I am. But each of you has your own gift from God; one has this gift, another has that. Now to the unmarried and the widows I say: It is good for them to stay unmarried, as I do. But if they cannot control themselves, they should marry, for it is better to marry than to burn with passion.'*[5]

Here Paul introduces an idea that is central to this book – the idea that singleness is a gift. I want to look at this in much greater detail later – you may be surprised by some of the things I say about this. I believe understanding this concept is key to living with power as single people – it is part of the book's title

---

5   1 Corinthians 7:7-9

after all – but I will unpack this a lot more later. For now, I want to say three things:

- Paul isn't saying that everyone is meant to be single. A lot of the chapter discusses issues of marriage. I believe in marriage – I just don't think it's the whole story.
- Paul is pointing to the freedom that single people have to be all that they can be for God.
- Paul is elevating singleness as something good – a gift to be embraced – not something to be ashamed of.

'We don't have to feel lesser as single people because the great Apostle Paul says singleness is a good thing. We don't need to disqualify ourselves from life and ministry, or believe we are somehow rejected because we are not married. Singleness is a noble thing, filled with possibility.'

Was Apostle Paul lacking in the life he lived for God? Jesus was single. Does this mean that he was lacking, lonely, or somehow lesser than his married friends? Or was he complete in himself, whole, undivided?

If the one who made us was complete in his singleness, are we not then complete when we are made in his image and his Spirit lives in us?

When we wear singleness well, it has the opportunity to cultivate and spur great things in our lives. We mustn't see singleness as a burden to bear and allow outside voices to define this in us.

But it's not scripture alone that can help us do this. Sometimes we have to see the single life lived in order to see how rich it can be. Of all the people I've known I think the life of my mother exemplifies what it means to live a divinely single life. Let me tell you her story.

> *"She lived every day as a vessel of good work,*
> *breathing Christ's hope and love to*
> *those around her."*

An Exemplary Life

My mother's life is a great reminder that God never promised us a rosy journey. She showed me hard times can be navigated through God's providence, as we embrace both sunshine and rainfall in our lives.

9 May 1945 – 11 July 2015

When you look at my dear late mother's tombstone, the tiny dash between the year she was born and when she was restored to glory can be easily overlooked. Yet it represents so much. That dash is the sum of her whole life. My mother at 70 years old poured life and passion into every person she interacted with. My mother birthed thirteen children, and in her younger years was a primary school teacher, businesswoman and designer of clothes. She was a lover of God and lover of people, which was seen in her generous words and deeds. She was remarkably passionate about God's kingdom, never missing her 4 am prayer appointments every morning.

She was larger-than-life: open, humble, generous and always extending love to others with grace and humility. She lived every day as a vessel of good work, breathing Christ's hope and love to those around her. My mother pressed on with strength and passion even in her later years. She always had great capacity even though she lived half of her life as a single mother. Her love for others meant that she included them, even when this meant taking trips to other parts of the world to extend her generosity and love of God for the benefit of humanity. She travelled more than some of her own children.

> *"Of all the people I've known I think the life of my mother exemplifies what it means to live a divinely single life."*

The dash on her tombstone says to me that she is a general of heaven, who was readily welcomed into glory, because she lived her life knowing full well who deserved her attention most.

And so, as I ponder her exemplary life, I wonder have I, have we as singles, understood how rich and strong our lives can be? Are we standing complete and undivided? Have we embraced our identity in God – the knowledge of who we are as single people – or are we allowing the theft of our purpose and sense of self? Are our eyes on Jesus first and foremost as we live life to the full like my mother? Have we embraced the truth that we are divinely chosen?

What will the dash on your tombstone mean? I will leave you to ponder that thought as we explore in greater detail some of the issues we face as single people. Before we can overcome challenges, we must recognise what they are.

Let us now delve deeper into the stigma that surrounds singleness.

> *"She lived every day as a vessel of good work, breathing Christ's hope and love to those around her. The dash on her tombstone says to me that she is a general of heaven, who was readily welcomed into glory, because she lived her life knowing full well who deserved her attention most.".*

TEGAN

This was, by far, one of the most important days of my life. I took a deep breath as I walked with care up the wooden steps of the quaint suburban chapel. My white dress trailed behind me as I gripped the perfectly arranged flowers with both hands. As I waited with my dad and two younger sisters for our cue to enter, waves of emotion gushed with every glance and tear-filled smile. The anticipation and excitement built as family, friends, and the expectant groom waited for the arrival of his bride—my beautiful sister Marly.

I was 28, the eldest in my family and very much single. That day was a standout moment. Not just because my beautiful sister got married, but because it was the day my imagined 'worst possible situation' became a reality. Both of my younger sisters were married and starting families before me.

I was the last one standing.

I grew up in a small 'blink and you'll miss it' country town in Victoria called Cudgee, but I was 11 years old when my parents gave their lives to Jesus and followed God's call. They sold everything and we all moved to Fort Worth, Texas, where my Dad went to Bible College. Through an amazing turn of events, after a year of study Dad was offered a ministry position in Brisbane. My hopes of returning to our country life didn't eventuate as I was enrolled in a Christian school and started life as a now thirteen-year-old in the city. Not far into my teenage years I decided to follow in my parents' footsteps and begin a personal relationship with my heavenly Father.

I started to plan my future and convinced myself that finding a guy, getting married and having kids was the ultimate goal. I spent countless lunch breaks sitting on the port racks with my four closest friends discussing our dreams of getting married and having kids. Yes, we sometimes discussed university, and at a push our career aspirations. But the popular subject was our dreams of having a family. We spoke of marriage as if it was all that mattered.

I attended a great church and made some amazing friends in the years after school. Boys and marriage were still a popular topic for conversation, prayer points and private journaling. The night of my twenty-first birthday party was a moment of clarity. I was in tears and feeling devastated as I got ready for what should've been a carefree and happy night. I couldn't believe that I was 21 and single. I remember thinking, and even telling my mum, that there must be something wrong with me. I had dated a boy I liked for a time when I was 19, but two years on I was feeling hopeless.

Being the melodramatic person that I am, I'm sure phrases like 'My life is over' and 'I'm going to be alone forever' were thrown around. But behind the drama was a genuine fear for my future and my ability to find a guy who wanted to be with me.

I started to find some direction in life in my early to mid-twenties. I completed a bachelor's degree, took steps in developing my career and travelled the world. During this time, many of my friends found partners, married and started to have kids. I felt like the real-life Katherine Heigl from the 2008 romantic comedy, 27 Dresses. The saying 'always the bridesmaid, never the bride' carried a bit of a sting, but as I experienced life and grew closer to God, I began to realise that I was single because I hadn't found the real deal. So being a happy, single bridesmaid was a much better option than being married to someone I didn't love. I didn't mind now being 'Aunty Teegs' to many special little people.

I didn't let go of the dream, but I started to let go of the fear of the dream not coming to pass and the stereotype of what a Christian girl in her late twenties needed to look like. I wanted the crazy, head-over-heels kind of love – or nothing at all. The promise of eternity through salvation in Jesus was everything I needed: marriage, kids, houses and jobs were just a bonus. I found freedom in taking my focus off marriage and finding that purpose was all around me. It was wonderfully distracting. Of course, there were still times when I was lonely and questioned the desire for marriage that I felt God had put in my heart as a teenager.

Most days I held tight to God and all the good that he had in store for my life, rather than putting conditions on what I thought a 'good life' looked like. There were still days where the fear of being alone or not being good enough would creep back. But there were other days where I felt a sense of peace about my situation.

Yet it wasn't uncommon for me to be defending myself or justifying my relationship status to others. I loved my extended church family and friends, but sometimes it felt like some of them couldn't see past my singleness and almost seemed to be grieving my singleness *without permission. Some friends who were in the same singles' boat as me, proved to be a blessed ally. Like Angie.*

I met Angie through friends at church but the first time we spoke properly was when we were bridesmaids together – how ironic! We had something in common: our singleness and the number of friends getting married. We became long-time housemates, and ten years later, we're the closest of friends and perfect travel companions.

Angie and I taught each other to be honest in the good and the not-so-good days. Being transparent with each other, rather than denying our feelings, meant we could let things go, and then remind one another how good our lives were. We also encouraged each other to keep dating!

My friendship with Angie has shown me that the loneliness that can come from singleness is avoidable. When we're in a community that encourages us, it's hard to be fearful and doubt. I believe that's why God sent me Angie. We would spend hours talking about our futures – and marriage wasn't the only thing that mattered. Just like Daniel in the Bible, we believed that God would deliver us, but if not, he was still good.

But back to Marly and Ben. Their wedding day was perfect. I remember how much fun their reception was as I danced with Angie and her new guy Tim (her future husband). Of course, I wanted to find everlasting love and feel the butterflies, but I was happy and had some big dreams of my own. I had just finished up a role working with the Queensland Premier and was running for a local representative role.

Two days later, I was greeting people on the door at church when I met Mark, who asked me to lunch the next day, and then to marry him a year later. God certainly did deliver.

3

THE STIGMA OF SINGLENESS

I remember a day when one of my much-loved brothers looked at me and asked, 'What are you doing with your life?'

His tone and body language said it all. I knew what he was really asking:

'Why are you still not married?'

To me, his words implied I was wasting my life being single. While I didn't believe this to be true, it caught me by surprise. How often are we made to feel that 'we are not there yet' or that we have failed if we have not found the right person to marry? How often do well-meaning people sideline us with misplaced comments – disqualifying us from fullness of life just because we don't have a partner?

In the last chapter I spoke of the identity theft that can happen when we start believing things about ourselves that aren't true. If our self-worth is already fragile, and words from others feed into the misbelief that we are not complete unless we marry, the devil can do his work. We can lose sight of who we are and feel disempowered. He can feed into our frustration and sow in us the insidious idea that we are missing life's fullness because we are single. Even if our sense of self is strong, unwise words can still unsettle us and rob us of our peace for a time.

Words, words, words. They're so powerful, aren't they? My research has shown me that not just words, but actions, can make single people feel marginalised in many walks of life.

I'd like to accomplish two things by writing this chapter. If you have felt sidelined in any way as a single person, I want to validate your pain. You are not imagining that the world sometimes feels built for couples. But I'd also like to encourage us *all* to work together to make our faith communities shine as safe places for single people. There are some wonderful churches that do everything they can to integrate single people within their communities. But some are better at this than others. And even when we are doing well, we can always find ways to do things better. That's a rule for everything in life.

To do community well we need to understand one another. Only then will we be able to build each other up as our loving God intended.

Are you with me? Great! Let's look first at the stigma of singleness in the wider world.

> *"To do community well we need to understand one another. Only then will we be able to build each other up as our loving God intended."*

'Singlism' and 'Matrimania'

Now in her sixties, renowned research psychologist and commentator on singleness, Dr Bella DePaulo, doesn't have any desire to be married – she loves being single.[1] However, over the years she has seen many instances of prejudice against both herself and other single people. This, along with her research, led DePaulo to coin two words to describe this bias. 'Singlism' – the 'stereotyping, stigmatising, marginalising and discrimination' of people who are single, and 'matrimania' – which is the 'over-the-top hyping of marriage, weddings and couplings.'[2]

DePaulo once commented on a magazine article which said that people from Finland have a high level of equality and very little poverty.[3] DePaulo argued in her comment that one person households had extremely high levels of poverty in Finland. Yet every single person who replied to DePaulo's comment dismissed her words, saying those statistics probably referred to students or old people. In reality DePaulo was right, the statistics showed that just over 26% of 35 to 64-year-olds in one-person-households

---

1   B DePaulo 2020, *About Bella DePaulo*, Bella DePaulo, viewed 27 April 2020, <http://www.belladepaulo.com/about-bella-depaulo/>.

2   B DePaulo 2018a, *Singlism and Matrimania*, Bella DePaulo, viewed 27 April 2020, <http://www.belladepaulo.com/2018/11/singlism-and-matrimania/>.

3   B DePaulo 2013a, *Celebrations of Finland's Success Leave One Big Group Behind*, Psychology Today, viewed 1 May 2020, <https://www.psychologytoday.com/us/blog/living-single/201307/celebrations-finland-s-success-leave-one-big-group-behind>.

were poor or at risk of being poor. Households with couples in this age group did not have the same problem.[4]

The point is that *all* the people who replied to DePaulo tried to deny the discrimination or explain it away. Why?

> *"DePaulo agrees that sometimes people are uncomfortable with words like discrimination and marginalisation when they are applied to singleness."*

DePaulo suggests two reasons. The first is that people fear they won't be believed – and even be judged – if they say they've been discriminated against. The second is that most of us are invested in our worldviews and ideologies and feel uncomfortable when they are challenged.[5] In another article, DePaulo writes of a reader's response to a piece she wrote on singleness for *Time Magazine*. The reader commented: 'as long as women bounce around kidding themselves that life is full when alone, they are putting their hedonistic, selfish desires ahead of what's best for children and society.'[6]

---

4   B DePaulo 2013b, *Denial of Discrimination: What Motivates It?*, Psychology Today, viewed 27 April 2020, <https://www.psychologytoday.com/us/blog/living-single/201307/denial-discrimination-what-motivates-it>.

5   DePaulo 2013b.

6   B DePaulo 2011, *Why People Cling to Mythologies about Marriage and Coupling: Consider This*, Psychology Today, viewed 24 April 2020, <https://www.psychologytoday.com/us/blog/living-single/201102/why-people-cling-mythologies-about-marriage-and-coupling-consider>.

Wow. Listen to the anger here. This man didn't know DePaulo. Why was he so upset that single people could be happy? Why did he feel so threatened?

DePaulo says that the key to understanding this is 'system justification', a psychological term about the need to defend the status quo.[7] People want to believe things are okay the way they are. Life has predictable rules: there is a right way and a wrong way that should always be followed. Predictability brings security. To say change is needed makes people feel less safe – and when people feel fear they lash out.

> *"Singles are expected to work longer hours, find it harder to get effective health care, and single women are more prone to sexual harassment than married women."*

But the subliminal desire to keep things the way they are has real-world effects beyond the harsh words of DePaulo's readers. While the injustice against single people isn't on the same level as racism or sexual exploitation of women, many single people are given an unfair deal in day-to-day life that can have serious social, physical and financial consequences.

In a group of studies, DePaulo and her colleagues investigated the bias single people experienced while trying to rent a property. When everything else was equal, the results overwhelmingly

---

7   DePaulo 2011. For more on the system justification theory see: JT Jost & MR Banaji, 1994, The role of stereotyping in system justification and the production of false consciousness. *British Journal of Social Psychology*, vol 33, no. 1, pp.1–27.

showed that a married couple was preferred as the tenant – the only reason given for this choice was that they were married.[8] In a further study, participants were asked to consider a landlord who was given the option of two different people who were interested in a property. In each example, a person from a group that experienced social discrimination, offered to pay more than a person from a recognised social majority. Each time the landlord went with the person from the social majority: a man over a woman, a Caucasian person over an African-American person, a straight person over a homosexual, a thin person over an obese person, a young person over an elderly person and a married couple over a single person. Of all the discriminatory decisions, which do you think was considered the most legitimate by the study participants? Yes, you've guessed it. In each case the participants called out the landlord's choice as discrimination – except for the case of the married couple versus the single person.[9, 10]

DePaulo says that because of laws in the United States that favour married people, housing, health and taxes could cost a single woman a million dollars more over her working life

---

[8] B DePaulo 2010a, *Housing Discrimination Against People Who Are Single: 4 Studies*, Psychology Today, viewed 1 May 2020, <https://www.psychologytoday.com/us/blog/living-single/201010/housing-discrimination-against-people-who-are-single-4-studies>.

[9] B DePaulo 2010b, *What Singlism? An Experimental Study of Obliviousness to Discrimination Against Singles*, Psychology Today, viewed 1 May 2020, <https://www.psychologytoday.com/us/blog/living-single/201010/what-singlism-experimental-study-obliviousness-discrimination-against>.

[10] J Gross, 2015, *The price of being single*, ideas.ted.com, viewed 1 May 2020, <https://ideas.ted.com/the-price-of-being-single/>.

compared with her married counterpart.[11] A similar problem is seen in the workplace. In a study of male identical twins, the twin that was married was paid an average of 26% more than his single brother.[12] By the time single people reach retirement age, a disproportionate number will end up in poverty.[13]

Singlism also steals time and recreation, with singles expected to work longer hours or cover weekends and vacation time for their married counterparts.[14]

Do these problems surprise you – or do they reflect your experience or the experiences of those you love? Being single in this world can at times be a challenge to navigate.

But what about the church? How do Christian communities fare on the subject of the stigma of singleness?

> *"Part of the problem is that many Christians marry young and have no experience of long-term singleness – it's hard to truly understand something we don't know."*

What About the Church?

An engagement was recently announced at my local church. After the service a young female friend of the couple pulled me

---

[11] B DePaulo 2018b, *Singlism: How Serious Is It, Really?*, Psychology Today, viewed 1 May 2020, <https://www.psychologytoday.com/au/blog/living-single/201809/singlism-how-serious-is-it-really>. /

[12] DePaulo 2018b.

[13] DePaulo 2018b.

[14] DePaulo 2018b.

aside. I could see something was on her mind and after some discussion, her vulnerability showed through: 'What about me? Why are there no prayers for singles too, so I can find someone?'

She went on. 'We hear prayers being made for couples to fall pregnant and for marriages to be mended, but who is praying for us, the singles?'

Now my church is a loving, supportive community but it's not perfect. No faith community is. I know that as pastors and leaders we want the best for our people, but sometime single people can feel their voice is lost within the busyness of church life. They can also experience frustration as they relate to their married friends.

In one of the studies I mentioned earlier, I collated results from 100 single Christian women, aged 18 to 50 years, who lived in Queensland, Australia.[15] The categories surveyed included: never married, separated, divorced and widowed. Most said they felt some bias from their married friends regarding their singleness and said they could be criticised by their friends if a man asked them out on a date and they didn't invest time exploring the relationship. Divorced singles indicated their married friends sometimes felt insecure around them, fearing that their now-single-again friends may want to spend too much time with them.

I've been part of church life for most of my life and I love belonging to a community of believers. The church is God's

---

15 Appendix A.

beautiful bride and I'm grateful for all the support that's been heaped upon me as I've been equipped and released into ministry. My leaders are super-awesome people and have given me, and many others, opportunities to minister irrespective of our marital status or gender. I also want to affirm that my leaders and those in many Christian communities are doing their best to care for their congregation and would never deliberately ignore or marginalise any minority group within their congregation. Having said this, even in loving Christian circles single people can sometimes feel hurt. Not deliberately, but because of a subconscious bias that says marriage is 'better'.

Part of the problem is that many Christians marry young and have no experience of long-term singleness – it's hard to truly understand something we don't know. Demographics are changing now, but many people I know who are currently in leadership were married in their twenties.

We all have a profound need to feel as if we matter and belong, and singles are no exception. It was obvious from my research that Christian singles want to feel as if they are as significant to their church as married people.[16] I think most churches identify themselves as 'family churches' because they want to make everyone in their church community feel welcome and part of God's universal family. However, when programs and preaching focus on strengthening marriages, building up children's ministry and celebrating Friday night youth meetings, some singles can feel sidelined – as if they don't really fit into this family.

---

16 See Appendix A

As I've pondered this subject and surveyed many single Christians, I've discovered several repeating themes. Have you experienced any of the following problems?

1. People sometimes make comments that lead you to feel as if there is something wrong with you because you are still without a partner.

In her story at the beginning of this chapter, Tegan shares how she needed to shake off the stereotype of what a Christian girl in her late twenties was supposed to look like. In her world, the good life equated to marriage. This was magnified by the fears and questions of others that meant that she often had to defend and justify her relationship status.

2. You sometimes feel rejected when you are excluded from certain social settings or from discussions on children and married life, because people think you are naïve (don't talk about sex – she's single) or have no interest in children. This is a big one.

A senior colleague once recounted the story of a friend who had been in a recent break-up. Prior to the break-up he'd had a great social life, doing many things together with other couples. But as soon as the break-up happened, invitations to dinners and other social settings dried up. Then one of his mates told the man that he was not being invited because they were sparing him the pain of turning up alone. They had decided not to invite him because they thought he might feel awkward being the only one in the group without a partner. He was furious that they did not allow him to choose for himself. They put his status as a single person before their relationship with him as a valued friend.

I have many female friends who have found themselves excluded socially after a break-up because the other women in their circle feared the newly single friend might disrupt their marriages. This type of story has been shared with me again and again as I've researched this topic. We need to stop doing this to one another.

3. You have been excluded from ministry you've trained for because you don't have the 'life experience' to deal with certain issues or the 'covering' of a husband.

> *"These classic one-liners might get us to laugh for a moment, but they can often feel like character assassinations."*

As you read through the stories placed between the chapters of this book you will come across the testimony of a pastor called Kelly. At one stage there were people in her church who wanted to disqualify her from ministry because she didn't have 'the covering' of a man. When she ministered in the Ukraine, Kelly discovered that a single woman was not esteemed in that country and that her ministry was looked down upon because she was a single female with no children.

4. You sometimes feel as if you are not taken seriously. This is a tricky one as we are all up for a good laugh. I love opportunities that let me have fun and connect with people and I know many pastors and leaders do, too. Even female pastors can

be masters of the 'dad joke'. However, sometimes we can feel uncomfortable if the laughter is at our expense. Check out this common scenario: The pastor speaks: 'Fred is visiting from another campus to speak today... And oh, by the way he is single. Whoever is single, raise your hand today. Well, this is your lucky day, ladies!' Everyone laughs. But to the speaker and the single women in the congregation it can feel 'old'. They've heard the joke many times and it still makes them feel as if they are not being taken seriously and are yet to arrive in life. We laugh it off, but it still stings sometimes.

If you are a pastor or a leader and reading this, I'm not saying we shouldn't joke around. We have the ability to create an atmosphere where people can engage through humour – which is great; can we just be aware that this can sometimes be an issue?

5. You have been offered unsolicited advice that is meant to encourage but in practice has the opposite effect.

> *"As a single, how often have you heard lines like these?*
> *Why are you still single?*
> *You're married to the church.*
> *Don't worry. It will happen.*
> *Your biological clock is not going to wait for you to keep fussing.*
> *You should meet this guy. He's the one for you.*
> *You have been left on the shelf.*
> *All the good men are gone.*
> *What a waste!"*

These classic one-liners might get us to laugh for a moment, but they can often feel like character assassinations. Another I have often heard is:

> "How can a gorgeous girl like you be still single?'"

Um, wait ... Is that implying that the not-so-gorgeous girls *should* remain single? I'd be a rich girl if I collected money every time I heard that statement.

All of these comments may be well-meaning, but if you hear them again and again, they can hurt. If they are said to a woman who is settled in her heart about her singleness, they might make her feel as if she has made the wrong choice – that she shouldn't be happy with her single status. If they are said to a woman who yearns to marry and have children, she might feel as if she has failed or that there is something wrong with her – that she is not whole as she is.

In the next chapters, I'll talk in more detail about some of the individual challenges many of us face as single women, but the point here is that even when people are trying to be kind, they can say and do things that make us feel we haven't really made it unless we are married.

But you know, having said all this, I would have found it very hard to survive singleness and still have a strong faith, without the community of believers loving me and cheering me on. We won't always get it right, but we all have a part to play in the church growing and building itself up in love.[17] We need to look out for one another and be sensitive to each other's needs. But when challenging things happen, we also need to forgive one another and not develop a victim mentality.

Victim Mentality?

A victim mentality is a deep inner belief that says the world is against you. It means you internalise the negative actions of others and create a world view that can also lead you to negative actions. The stereotyping and stigma that singles can feel, reinforced by others' attitudes and words, has propelled many of us to feel as if we need 'fixing'. I know from my own experience that there are times the singleness situation can bring me down. You take the negative words and actions of others on board and act out of that, taking matters into your own hands.

> *"Those who leave, forever wrestle with the love-call of our Saviour in their spirit. A call that whispers, 'Return to me my beautiful one'."*

The struggle is real. When we hear comments like, 'Hurry up and get married because there are no good men left,' over and over in multiple contexts we can start to believe that we have missed out on life. This is magnified if we feel excluded because of our marital status. We might feel like we don't fit in or that God has let us down. This is a serious issue. The sense of victimhood can make some feel lost, bitter, and confused about their faith. Some may choose to give up and walk away.

---

17   Ephesians 4:16

Have you ever felt like that? That you may as well treat your own pain by removing yourself from a difficult space, choosing to find like-minded people outside of church? Have you thought about finding a marriage partner out there where there are a lot more available men? Have you ever *done* this?

I know of single and otherwise marginalised people who have acted out of their hurt and left church because they felt they didn't fit. The problem is that while leaving may feel good for a moment, it doesn't bring lasting peace. Those who leave, forever wrestle with the love-call of our Saviour in their spirit. A call that whispers, 'Return to me my beautiful one'.

Even if you've never thought of giving up – if you have been around the church for a while – you will know people who have done exactly this.

How do we help one another? How do we stop our friends from giving up? How do we stop giving up ourselves?

I believe that we all – whether we are married, single, young, or not so young – need to work together to build authentic communities of faith where no one feels left out and everyone is valued. This responsibility of building that community falls upon us all.

Let me unpack this a bit more. I hope that my words haven't triggered painful memories or made you relive awkward situations, but if they have, I want you to know that your pain is valid. It can be hard to combat stereotypes or deal with subtle or not-so-subtle slights. But there are some things we can do to make things better. Here are some suggestions that might help:

- Decide not to be a victim. Own your hurt, validate it, but choose to rise above it.
- Share how you feel with another person – but choose that person wisely. Make sure it's someone who will genuinely listen and not judge. If it's another single, then don't choose someone with a negative mindset. Talk to someone who understands what you are going through but has hope in their heart. Someone who will help you look upwards rather than down. Bitterness grows well in the fertile ground of complaints.
- Extend grace to the people who upset you. Know that other Christians do care, even though they say and do inappropriate things sometimes. We all say and do dumb things and can hurt those we love. God forgives us, so it's important to extend the same grace to others and forgive them too.[18]
- Don't be afraid to speak up if something is bothering you. It's highly likely that the offending person or group has no idea their words or actions are hurting you. Don't wallow in silence – say something. That way you can be an agent of peace rather than a victim of strife.
- Commit yourself to a good faith community and look out for singles groups in your area. It's important to have a place where we can belong. While belonging can make us vulnerable, it's also the way of love. If something goes wrong, don't just leave without trying to make things better.

---

18 Luke 6:37

Stand with your brothers and sisters in Christ and be family to one another.
- And always, always, always keep trusting in Jesus Christ. Don't turn your heart away from him – because he will never turn away from you.

As one who is single and who is also a pastor, I long for the ideal of a community where we can all be ourselves and be accepted without bias for who we are – with all people set free to be who God made us to be. But there is still more work to do, not just in Australia but in the rest of the world.

Only recently an African colleague told me about one of his clients from a northern African community. In this community girls are normally given in marriage at age 12 – usually to a man twice their age. The girl married unusually late at 15 years old. When she had her first child, she was scolded by her family because she had wasted three years where she could have had more children. I know, right? That horrifies us in the West because we know that a 12-year-old should be trying to find her way in school and figuring out adolescence – not having babies or thinking about how to breastfeed their first child. The girl was experiencing the weight of the stigma of her previous singleness at 15!

We may not have had that situation here but we do have a subtle undercurrent in our society that flows against the gospel of Jesus – where all are welcomed before the throne of grace.[19] You could certainly add 'married or single' to Paul's declaration

---

19   Hebrews 4:16

in Galatians 3:28 and following, that all are one in Christ Jesus.[20] But living out that reality is easier said than done. We have to work together to defeat every bias we face – including that of the stigma of singleness. It may not happen overnight – but together we can make a difference.

---

20   Galatians 3:28-4:7

TWO BECOME ONE

KOKO[1]

Not everything 'turns out' the way you think it will… but we'll get back to that soon. Here are some things that have definitely turned out for me: I have a challenging and rewarding career that I love; I've had the time and space to travel and experience other cultures; I have plenty of moments when I'm savouring great food with people I adore, soaking in a moment; I'm excited about so many aspects of my future, including branching into new enterprises in the coming years; and I love God, who I know to be real, loving and intentional about my life.

That picture is completely true, it's just not complete. You see, I have seasons when loneliness is pretty damn pronounced, or when I wonder what's wrong and why I'm single. Or when I toy with wedging myself even deeper into work as if that might fill the gap. One season, I'll be putting myself out there, taking on new work challenges, travelling and expanding my worldview, volunteering and doing further study. The next season I'm staying at home – a lot – with my favourite takeaway and a stream of TV shows to take my mind off how I should tackle the next chapter of a life that I didn't see coming.

---

1   Name has been changed.

I've had to make some decisions on my own that I never expected to have to make while single, like buying a house. Apartment for one? Family home? Hedge my bets with a mid-size home? Then where? Close to family? Close to places where I might meet more people? It was tough and really emotional along the way. I kept second guessing myself because I was trying to predict what is absolutely impossible to predict: what my life might look like in a few years' time. Yet, I've had to make other decisions on my own that were so much easier. Independence comes with its own brand of magic if you make the most of it.

The undercurrent of it all for me is faith, but even then, it's not straightforward. I'm often thinking about what it means to be single as a Christian. I consider my boundaries, what I forego, and whether they are still realistic or 'fair' the older I get. After all, we don't get to switch off our sexuality. And then there are hopes and promises… and all those scriptures about God giving us the desires of our heart. Well, it turns out there are more women in the world than men, so if every woman wanted a soul mate, it ain't happening!

Singleness as a Christian has demanded that my worldview get a lot broader. For example, I believe in the Word of God, so a scripture about God giving me the desires of my heart is something I choose to believe. One of my desires is to marry and share life and love with someone and there is a real possibility that won't happen. I decided many years ago that my understanding of that scripture needed to get far less like a bumper sticker of 'perfect joy' and much more like a two-way with God. I don't have to give up something I long for, but I do need to be open to finding more and new desires.

Fortunately, while 'that clock' is ticking against me, time is also my best friend. Time has helped me learn to value myself so much more. I still have to regularly shut down the stream of self-talk that suggests I'm faulty and that's why I'm single, but seriously, peculiar people are in love all over the world! I'm learning not to let my singleness rob me of my confidence or sense of value, or even desirability. I'm not faulty. I'm just single and, while I am, I have this gift of learning about myself more deeply.

I've seen amazing love stories but also cautionary tales out of my age group. If I do get the opportunity to partner with someone for life, my eyes are wide open, and hopefully that means I'll be a better wife and have fairer expectations of my partner too. If I don't have that opportunity, I've also seen how love can fulfil in many other ways than romance.

In this season I have extraordinary freedom and flexibility. That includes being able to pour myself more easily into helping others because I have the 'extra' time. And I give myself every chance to make each season count and make plans for the next season, with nothing holding me back.

Every year or so, I take time out for a few days away from home, family and friends to reflect on my life and plan the next season. I look at what's changed for the better or worse, map out where I want to be in a few years' time and really challenge myself on what I need to do to get there. I also look at the progress I've made. The main thing is, I keep pushing forward in life.

I have also found the value of trusted friends, behind the scenes who support and encourage me and know my story. If it wasn't for being *wisely transparent, one friend would never have known to talk with me about getting my eggs frozen. I would never have thought about doing that. I was fortunate to be able to afford this so I could keep my options for having children open just that bit longer.*

I have learned that every choice is an opportunity and singleness, however long it lasts, can help you make the kind of choices that give you an ever-richer life. I aim to embrace my singleness in each season and hold my hope that I'll find my person one day. My story is still playing out.

4

A DESIRE TO MARRY

Have you ever seen this? A large moth flies into a nearby spiderweb and the poor insect struggles against the sticky filaments. The spider edges towards the insect – and the moth panics. It flaps and wriggles until it breaks free, heading for the light and leaving the spider to mend its web and start again. Phew!

Does it ever seem to you that when you are single you can get caught in a web of challenges? These challenges are as numerous as there are different kinds of women in the world. Women of every race, shape, colour, creed and age can find themselves journeying through life alone: a kaleidoscope of different women from different cultures in different circumstances, all with different needs. How can a book like this deal with all the challenges Christian singles experience? Can it help free us from the sticky web that limits us?

No one book can speak into every situation, but in the next three chapters I'd like to look at some of our deepest desires as single women – and how we can overcome the challenges and discover the joy in our circumstances.

Do you relate to any of these categories? You are:
- Young, single and haven't found a partner yet – but you yearn to marry
- Single for a long, long time and you are wondering if marriage will ever happen for you, or if it will happen too late to have children. Yet you long for both
- Content to stay single – or you would like to be content
- Single again and want to rise above the pain and grief.

I hope that, as you read on, you will find insights to help you navigate these challenges. There is much to be enjoyed in our amazing world. Let's learn how to break free and soar high as women of God.

Let's start by looking at single women at different stages of life, who *desire marriage*.

Desiring Marriage

From the ancient lines of Shakespeare's *Romeo and Juliet* to modern day movies where love conquers all, rhythmic themes resound proclaiming the importance of falling in love. How many books, how many films have romance at the centre? What about some of my favourites: *Titanic, Brown Sugar, The Best Man* or *Bridget Jones's Diary?* Or more recently, *Just right, Nappily Ever After, P.S. I Love You*. And then there are the songs: *No One, Crazy in Love, I Will Always Love You, All of Me, One Love…* I could fill pages and pages with the names of love songs past and present. Ain't love great?

Yet sometimes we let the desire for love tie us up in knots. In the last chapter I talked about the things people say to us when we haven't yet found love. If we yearn for that life partner, we can almost agree with the person who says we should try harder to find someone. But deep down we know the right person hasn't come along and we have tried as hard as we know how to find them. And then we wrestle with the cringing feeling that says we are not sufficient as we are. This can go around and around in our heads – taking energy that we could otherwise spend on enjoying life.

Another seemingly opposite knot can entangle us. Have you read 1 Corinthians 7:1-9? In this chapter the Apostle Paul seems to say it's better to be, and stay, single. Singleness is a gift and marriage is a concession for those who burn with desire. Is this right? Am I being less spiritual if I desire marriage? Am I letting Jesus down? Some people think this, and it has led whole denominations to declare that their priests must be celibate.

There is so much in this chapter that we can address, and we'll dive into it further, but for now, consider that Paul wrote these words in the context of his call. The church was being established and his singleness let him focus wholeheartedly on his call as an apostle. He wanted others to be as free as he was to outwork their calling.

> *"We are wired for desire because it is a reflection of the all-consuming love God has for us. Marriage is a good desire that was knitted into our DNA."*

Both Jesus and Paul were called to be single for the sake of the gospel. It's true that sometimes God calls us to lay down our desires for his kingdom. But I don't think Paul is saying it's wrong to want to marry. Marriage is a good desire that was knitted into our DNA when God formed us in our mother's womb.[1] If you desire to find someone you love and marry them, you desire a good thing.

The need for love is one of the deepest human desires. I mentioned in the last chapter that C.S. Lewis thought friendship was one of the most important loves, but he wrote about some other types too:[2]

- *Storge* – Affectionate love that seeps through the substance of life.
- *Philia* – The love between friends.
- *Agape* – The highest form of love. The unconditional love shown when God the Father gave his son to die on the cross for us – and
- *Eros* – Romantic love and passion.

Some say *Eros* is a less important love because passion can be fleeting. Lewis agrees that there is a danger in following blindly after feelings of passion, but he also says true romantic love leaps over our selfhood and puts another person at the centre of our being. We love someone as we love ourselves, wholly and completely. It's no accident that the Bible again and again likens God's relationship with his people to the bond between husband and wife.[3]

---

1 Psalm 139:13-14

2 CS Lewis 1960, *The Four Loves*, 1st ed., Gutenberg.ca, Project Gutenberg, viewed 5 March 2020, <https://gutenberg.ca/ebooks/lewiscs-fourloves/lewiscs-fourloves-00-h.html>.

3 Lewis 1960

> *"And I love how women today have so many opportunities to fulfil their potential in all walks of life."*

I believe that God has built the longing for *Eros* into each of us. Our DNA isn't just wired this way, so we'll desire to find a mate. We are wired for desire because it is a reflection of the all-consuming love God has for us. The yearning to be loved and be pursued arises from our deep-seated need we all have for the Eros love from our creator himself.

I can't guarantee any of us will marry in this life. But there is a bridegroom who has given everything to rescue us and make us his own. There will be a day when he will return to make the collective church his bride. The ultimate marriage where all of our yearnings will be satisfied. Let's talk more about this in a later chapter but for now know that if you long for the fire of love, you long for something holy.

> *"I can't guarantee any of us will marry in this life. But there is a bridegroom who has given everything to rescue us and make us his own."*

Should marriage be your desire, then own it. Embrace it. Don't hide it or feel you need to make excuses for it. God made us to love and to be loved. Our maker intended us to have real human connection. The Bible says, 'God is love.'[4] He designed us for relationship and connection with him and each other, whether that's within marriage or friendship/mateship or any

---

4   1 John 4:8

other relationship. Would you like this? Then hold onto it and celebrate it. I can only spur you on. Stand your ground. Don't hold back if others hold a different view to you. Seek God. Talk to him about this. Tell him what you want and why. Open your heart to him and ask him for a suitable mate. But at the same time know that marriage might not happen in your timing – or it might not happen at all. And you are not less worthy if it doesn't!

The Delay

What? Have I poured ice-water on the conversation? I've been affirming your desire to marry and telling you to pursue that desire, but then I say it might be delayed or not happen. Really?

Yes. Really. We live in a fallen world where many things don't happen the way we think they should. The delay in finding love is a genuine struggle for many precious women. There are all kinds of factors involved: the choices we make, the choices others make and the hard things that come about because we live in a world in which sin dwells. There are many things in life that we desire but don't get – or the getting is delayed – and a marriage partner can be one of those.

We call out to God and ask him *why*. Sometimes we hear his whisper in our hearts and sometimes we don't – but we must remember we are only seeing things from our perspective. What may look like a delay to us may look very different from God's point of view. He knows the end from the beginning, and he loves us. Faith is trusting in God's character even if we can't see what he is doing.[5]

If you don't want to be married this won't depress you but extended singleness is a problem more and more women are facing. Some time ago I read an article in the *Sydney Morning Herald* that said, 'The 30s are worrying years for high-achieving women who long for marriage and children as they face their rapidly closing reproductive window surrounded by men who see no rush to settle down.' The writer goes onto say that the number of partnerless women in their 30s has almost doubled since 1986.[6]

The 2014 Pew Report looked at cohorts of people who were 25 to 34-years-old in 2010 and stated that by the year 2030 one quarter of these people were likely to remain unmarried.[7] It also said that while some people will marry for the first time after the age of 54, statistics show that it is unlikely. In the United States only about 7 per 1000 first-time marriages involve people over 55 years.[8] If you are in this age group and you want to get married for the first time, this isn't great news.

---

5   Hebrews 11:1

6   B Arndt 2012, *Why women lose the dating game*, The Sydney Morning Herald, viewed 19 May 2020, <https://www.smh.com.au/lifestyle/why-women-lose-the-dating-game-20120421-1xdn0.html>.

7   W Wang & K Parker 2014 *Record Share of Americans Have Never Married*, Pew Research Centre's Social & Demographic Trends Project, viewed 19 May 2020, <https://www.pewsocialtrends.org/2014/09/24/record-share-of-americans-have-never-married/#will-todays-never-married-adults-eventually-marry>.

8   Wang & Parker 2014.

I can see why the delay occurs. In the twenty-first century, women can access study and career opportunities that were significantly limited 50 years ago. I'll talk more later about how some of those hard-won freedoms have come about, but I love how women today have so many opportunities to fulfil their potential in all walks of life. But that freedom may come at the cost of forming relationships.[9] Economic challenges also feed into this situation. The cost of living in some circumstances presses in on people to either work multiple jobs or expand their learning, hoping to secure a higher income. Although the desire to find a life partner might be there, the diversion of our attention and energy in these areas can mean that we don't meet and date potential partners.

But what of Christian women? Surely men in the church are more focused on marriage than playing-the-field in the wilds of the world. On first glance this would be true. But there is one question many Christian women who desire marriage have been asking:

Where are all the men? Hey, brothers?

> *"The 30s are worrying years for high-achieving women who long for marriage and children as they face their rapidly closing reproductive window surrounded by men who see no rush to settle down."*

---

9   Wang & Parker 2014.

Where are All the Brothers At?

Where are the brothers? The reality is that social circumstances and church demographics mean that Christian women often find it hard to meet Christian men.

In the survey I mentioned earlier, many Christian women said there were a lack of available men in their church.[10] They said that they wanted to be planted in God's house and engage in their faith community – it was very important for spiritual growth – but that they were surrounded by many more women than men. Overall there were less men than women in church and the ones that were there were in their 20s or early 30s. Single men between 35 and 50 years were especially rare in church communities. Men in this age group were often already married, engaged or dating someone. The result is that many women over 35 find it hard to find men within their churches, to just be friends with, let alone form a relationship which might lead to marriage. Although we may find male friends in other contexts, my survey was focused on men within the church. Some of the women said they received many more compliments from men outside church than from Christian men. This resulted in disappointment, angst and anxiety for some of the women.

Shouldn't it be easier than this? Where are the brothers? Are they rejecting the community or Jesus? The truth is the few Christian men I've met at church in recent years, who are around my age group, have not stayed long. I've seen a trend where some of these guys with 'potential' are not staying grounded in one place.

---

10   See Appendix A.

I asked some male friends about this and they said that Christian guys exist – not that I doubted this – but you don't always find them in church. They are doing life outside for various reasons. This may include not being able to make meaningful male friendships within our communities.

I discussed this topic with my married older brother, Christian. Amongst many other things, Christian is an entrepreneur, civil engineer and personal trainer of many years, so he mixes with a lot of different types of people. Through his professional experiences and research, he said that, unlike Christian women, men like building strong, genuine relationships with others in a variety of settings. They will go to the gym, spend their weekend with their sports teams of preference and build strong lifelong relationships there. They can go to church, but if they don't build strong relationships there, they will look for this outside of faith communities.

We women tend to place a lot of emphasis on church life and activities. Most of our strong relationships with friends come from within our own church – or other associated churches – especially if we are involved in ministry. We tend to invest our energy into maintaining these relationships rather than making new friendships. It often feels easier to stay within our comfort zones – and enjoy the circle of our existing friendships.

> *"Surely men in the church are more focused on marriage than playing-the-field in the wilds of the world."*

Of course, this is a generalisation. Some sisters are brilliant at extending themselves in building and nurturing new relationships. And there are guys who prefer their own small friendship circle and have no desire to make new ones.

So, what do we do? How do single Christian women connect with like-minded brothers nowadays? How do we find 'brothers' and potential partners? Go out into the world and look for them?

Yes – but it can be difficult. I talked about this with a few girlfriends over brunch. They said that many single Christian women are unsure if they should go beyond their churches to find potential partners, for fear of not finding a man who shares the same faith values as they do. It's a valid concern. Just because a man says he is a 'Christian' does not always mean his theology and understanding of faith is the same as ours. We live in a society where our individual beliefs can differ vastly – much more so than in previous decades. Many of my girlfriends have dated guys who don't see faith the way they do. When you want to keep walking with God, yet desire to marry, the struggle is real.

Ladies, if we want to marry, it's good to look for ways to grow and engage with Christian men and connect with others. If you like photography, join a photography club. If you have a dog, take it to dog training. Don't just do this because you want to find a man but do it so you can be a well-rounded person and take our Lord outside of our churches to the community. That way there is no pressure and if you meet a good Christian guy, it's a bonus.

I can't emphasise enough how important it is to be open to what God might do and not have an agenda. We can often have a one-track mind, setting our desire on that one person, while overlooking other men. We can dismiss people who might be very good for us just because they are different from what we expect. However, if we shift our focus and engage with people without an agenda, we can get to know them without boxing them into our expectations. If we want more than friendship, it can get obvious and awkward. Be yourself and be a friend – and you might be surprised by what happens.

> *"'Recreational dating', all with the careless aim of having the thrills now without commitment."*

Another way to meet people is by internet dating. Some say they prefer the old-fashioned way of meeting someone: they prefer everyday interactions rather than online sites. But others have tried online dating. I have to say I've tried this and ended up more disappointed than when I started, especially as the aim of many men is to have casual encounters. We are living in an age of casual sex and, as my nephew Trezor puts it well, 'recreational dating', all with the careless aim of having the thrills now without commitment. Recreational daters are not interested in getting to know a person or taking the time to commit to something worthwhile. Having said this, some Christian women have found life partners with similar values through internet dating. Pray about it, go in with open eyes and an open mind. Even if you don't meet a marriage partner you might make some excellent male friends. As with all dating, be careful not to put yourself in any dangerous situations. Be wise and seek counsel from those you trust and respect, so they can walk the journey with you.

> *"How do single Christian women connect with like-minded brothers nowadays?"*

So, we've talked about how marriage is a good desire and about the unfortunate lack of men in our churches. However, we all know that's not the only challenge we can face as singles. Has loneliness ever been part of that equation?

Loneliness vs. Singleness

Loneliness is a problem that nearly all single people experience at some stage or another. It's not just an issue for a particular personality type. One way or another, everyone has gone through this experience – or will do so at some stage of their lives. So, if it's the way you feel at the moment, don't despair, you have plenty of 'company'. Seriously, I've felt like this and I know how terrible loneliness can be. I bet most of you reading this have felt that way too. But sometimes loneliness is misunderstood. Have you ever stopped to think what loneliness is and what it's not?

> *"Loneliness is not a synonym for singleness."*

Loneliness is not a synonym for singleness. Of course it isn't, you say, but in the minds of many, singleness and loneliness can be confused. It's one reason why well-meaning people keep insisting we find a man – any man! If we don't have someone, people think we must be lonely.

Singleness is about being complete in yourself. We are undivided in both our own self and the things we give attention to. Single people can sometimes be alone, but aloneness doesn't always equate to loneliness.

People associate loneliness with lack of company, but it's much more than that. It's a state of mind characterised by deep sadness and feelings of isolation. Sometimes loneliness happens because you miss someone in particular. Other times it happens because you long for someone – anyone – to connect with in a deep way. Loneliness is never a positive emotion. It can occur at any age and it can even happen when you are in a sizeable group of people. If it becomes chronic it sits below the surface of your life and eats at you, like the spider I mentioned in the introduction to this chapter. How can we escape this snare?

The first thing we need to understand is that loneliness isn't just a problem for single people – it is a problem for much of the Western world. The incredible Mother Teresa, who dedicated her life to caring for the poorest among us, challenged the West to esteem the poor and give them dignity. She has often been quoted as saying that the West has a different kind of poverty – that of loneliness and spirituality.[11]

> *"Singleness is about being complete in yourself. We are undivided in both our own self and the things we give attention to."*

---

[11] L Vardey 1995, Mother Teresa: A Simple Path. New York: Random House; 1995.

Cigna, a US global health services company, provided an extensive analysis of the root cause and impact of loneliness.[12] They surveyed over 20,000 people, 18 years and older, on the impact of loneliness and isolation. The results were telling. Nearly half of those surveyed admitted feeling alone (46%) and left out (47%). One in four felt as though people rarely understood them. Two in five felt isolated and thought their relationships had little meaning. One in five said they had no one they could talk to and they rarely felt close to anyone. Americans who lived with others were less likely to be lonely compared to people living alone – unless they were parents and guardians living with children. But the killer was the group of people aged 18 to 22. The young adults known as Gen Z were the loneliest of all. Almost half of those surveyed said they were lonely – and had the worst health. On the other hand, adults 72 years and upwards were the least lonely and said they had good health.

These figures show that loneliness is not a single person's problem. Any of us can get caught by this affliction. We don't have to be alone to be lonely. We can suffer this way when we are surrounded by multiple people, are in a relationship, or even when we have a family.

Loneliness is a soul issue where people feel isolated from meaningful connection with other human beings. It can make you feel out of place and misunderstood. The craving for connection has led to modern social inventions like the internet

---

12   CIGNA 2018, *The state of loneliness in America*, www.cigna.com, Cigna Corporation, viewed 21 May 2020, <https://www.cigna.com/assets/docs/newsroom/loneliness-survey-2018-fact-sheet.pdf>.

and social media, but that can sometimes further isolate us as we substitute face-to-face interaction for an online chat. In the Cigna survey, social media use alone did not predict loneliness, but they noted that younger people who used a lot of social media were lonelier than older people who didn't.[13] Reading social cues are becoming more of a challenge as people lose the art of engaging with one another and being present with each other. We may then feel less comfortable face-to-face when it's exactly that kind of organic community we need to cultivate. This isolation can lead into devastating seasons where we make bad decisions and do self-destructive things.

> *"The first thing we need to understand is that loneliness isn't just a problem for single people – it is a problem for much of the Western world."*

It's like we've got this long, long list of characteristics we want to find in a husband, then we whittle it down to three main points. We wait and wait until we say, 'Just give me a man and forget about the list, I want my loneliness to go!' If we do more than say this – if we act on these feelings – we can get into trouble.

A few years ago, one of the worst seasons of my life happened when I fell into grave loneliness. I had just moved to Melbourne, leaving behind over 28 years of living within a strong network of friends and family in Brisbane. Within just six months of this move, my dear mother passed away. You've read what a significant place she played in my life. I was grieving and the

---

13 CIGNA 2018

process of finding friends in a new city was slow. My work didn't help. I had a full life and I was travelling a lot, so it was hard to connect with people. Loneliness and grief churned inside me, like a monster craving to be fed. My need to numb the emptiness pushed me to find ways of filling the void. This led me to make some of the worst decisions of my life. I'm sure many of you have your own stories of regret. But please hear me: there is always another way. I wish I had given myself more time to better process my feelings of grief and isolation. Unfortunately, I failed and learned the hard way.

> *"Two in five felt isolated and thought their relationships had little meaning."*

At the time, I was settling into a new local church, which I have now come to love. But back then I struggled to connect with others and didn't like who I was becoming. Something needed to shift. I had to try and be vulnerable.

Author Bréne Brown says that vulnerability is a two-sided coin. On one side there is love, belonging and joy and on the other shame, scarcity, fear, anxiety and uncertainty. If we want to move from one side to the other, we need to be brave enough to step up and seek to change.[14]

Loneliness is a powerful weapon that can destroy our personhood, and the enemy loves to use it against us. In isolation we stop growing. We become less vulnerable and teachable and develop

---

14 99u 2013, *Brené Brown: Why your critics aren't the ones who count*, YouTube, viewed 21 May 2020, <https://www.youtube.com/watch?v=8-JXOnFOXQk>.

the victim mentality I spoke of earlier. We can then further isolate ourselves from others and make our situation even worse.

We are daughters of a loving Heavenly Father – made in his image. As Father, Son and Spirit, he is relational to his core. Like our God we are wired with an imperative to connect with him and others. One of the keys to unlocking the loneliness that bound me was to admit it first to myself and then to another. I made myself vulnerable so I could find a solution to struggles and find a way forward. Once something is brought into the light, darkness can't affect it.

Find your community, then go to work at it. Forgive when you are wronged but don't give up trying to find faith-filled people you can connect with. It's God's desire for you to be in Christian community – it's even a command – not because of some arbitrary rule but because God knows we need other people to thrive.[15]

> *"Loneliness is a soul issue where people feel isolated from meaningful connection with other human beings."*

Another key is to realise that as Christians, there will be times when we don't fit into the world. Expectations can be a killer and we need to accept that we are in the world but not of it.[16] We are made for heaven, not here. The writer of Hebrews likens believers to 'foreigners and strangers on the earth' who

---

15 Hebrews 10:24-25

16 John 17:16

are 'longing for a better country—a heavenly one'.[17] That's our destination and that is the place where one day we will truly belong. If we expect to always fit in here on Earth, we will be disappointed. It is important to train ourselves to desire heavenly things or we will feel forever frustrated in our search for fulfilment.

To do this it is vital to lean on God – our ever-present help in time of need.[18] We can bring our feelings of loneliness to him. He understands. He cares. How lonely was Jesus in the garden of Gethsemane before he was taken prisoner and crucified? One of his followers had betrayed him and the others had fallen asleep, leaving him to face his darkest time alone. He sweated drops of blood in his anguish.[19] Note that he also lived the life of a single man, so he knows how it feels when you just want someone to hug you.

> *"Social cues are becoming more of a challenge as people lose the art of engaging with one another and being present with each other."*

Not only does he know how you feel, he has sent the Holy Spirit to live in us so we can live with power and hope and experience his love. We are not orphans, abandoned to the hard things of life. We are pilgrims on a journey, and he's promised to be with us every step of the way.

---

17 Hebrews 11:13-16
18 Hebrews 4: 15-16
19 Matthew 26:36-46

The only other thing I'll say about loneliness is that it helps to do the practical things of life.[20] It gets worse if you don't look after yourself. Self-care is paramount. Get a suitable amount of sleep, eat well and do regular exercise. Anything that lifts your mood and increases your wellness will help defeat negative feelings. Perhaps do some of these things with new friends. That will help beat your sense of isolation. Extra points if you pray together too.

Wow. Are you still reading? Loneliness is a major issue, but there is another challenge that tests many single Christian women. The unremitting ticking of our biological clock.

> *"Loneliness is a powerful weapon that can destroy our personhood, and the enemy loves to use it against us."*

Tick-Tock Biological Clock

One of the greatest fears many women have – especially when we reach our late 30s or head into our 40s and beyond – is the fear that we might not have children. Childbearing is a God-given desire and women are intricately designed for giving birth to children and nurturing them. It is a natural desire and nothing to be ashamed of, but the ticking of the biological clock can lead to panic. The lack of available men and the social dynamics that drive women to engage in study or work longer hours can decrease our opportunities to find a marriage partner. For a while we can go on our way, doing life as we can, but then one day a terrible thought strikes us: *What if I never have children?*

---

[20] CIGNA 2018

I remember the first time this happened to me. One afternoon in 2014, after I had moved to Melbourne, I can remember laying on my bed thinking about the issues that come with settling in a new city. Then it struck me hard. A wave of emotion welled up: *What if I never give birth?*

It was the first time I had given the possibility of childlessness a thought. Up until then, it was not a concern, nor did I see any need to let my thoughts go there. I was just full-on with living life. Maybe it was brought on by the move and the loneliness I mentioned but it was a shock. Fear gripped me. I might not be able to have a little precious person who would look like me to nurture, love and hold and call me 'maman'. I sat with the thought for a while as waves of sadness washed over me. I had to accept that this could be a reality. But at the same time, I didn't want it to consume me. I talked to God about it. A sense of peace enveloped me even amidst the wash of emotions. Only God knew what would happen.

> *"What if I never give birth?*
> *I had to accept that this could be a reality."*

It was a very sobering moment, but also a much-needed tap on the shoulder. Until that time, I hadn't thought too much on this, but now it hit home. New emotions were surfacing and even though I had fears, God was ministering to me. Some of you might not believe me, but the sense of peace was significant. I found myself saying: 'You hold my life, so whatever you have for me will be great!'

I don't mean to make light of your grief in this area. We can love and trust God but sometimes the peace is hard to hold onto. There are women who from the moment they hit puberty long to be mothers. It's a wonderful dream encouraged by others around us. When it doesn't happen – or looks like it won't happen – it can cut deep. It can erode our sense of purpose and how we see ourselves. *Who am I if I can't be a mother?* It can also build on the sense of stigma I talked about in the previous chapter – when women feel that they have failed and are not 'enough', because they haven't married and had children.

The question is, how do we face it? How do we move beyond this grief if having children is something we deeply desire?

> *"Childbearing is a God-given desire and women are intricately designed for giving birth to children and nurturing them."*

One of the most important ways is to allow God to reframe our thinking. The desire to procreate is wired into our biology but physical birth is not the only way to be a mother. Isaiah 54:1 says:

> *'Sing, barren woman,*
> *you who never bore a child;*
> *burst into song, shout for joy,*
> *you who were never in labour;*
> *because more are the children of the desolate woman*
> *than of her who has a husband,'*
> *says the Lord.*

> *"The desire to procreate is wired into our biology but physical birth is not the only way to be a mother."*

What? The women with no husband had more children than one who does. How can that be? While Isaiah was referring to the redemption of Israel here, we can take this beautiful truth and apply it to our lives. I mentioned in the last section that a lot of younger people are lonely. How many in our churches need our mother-hearts to reach out and love them?

In my work as both a youth pastor and school chaplain I have seen many situations where young people needed a role model. They needed someone to nurture them – to be like a mother or an aunty to them. I gave myself to that role and saw young people overcome obstacles and flourish. One example still warms my heart when I think of it.

> *"If we have maternal instincts that are not being met, there is a world out there waiting for our embrace – fragile hearts longing for love and care. It could be children."*

Some time ago, I worked as a case manager for refugees and asylum seekers. When I first met with four young men, two were always at odds with each other. I felt like a mother to them as I listened and learned about the horrendous journey they had experienced. I tried for some time to encourage them and bring them together as a group. Years later I bumped into the same group of young men at a town festival. They were now sharing a home together and had called themselves the 'band of brothers'. They had come together and now considered each other to be practically family. It warmed me inside that my mother-heart had made a difference.

Ladies, it doesn't matter if you are in your early 20s or your biological clock has hit midnight and your ovaries have said 'enough'. If we have maternal instincts that are not being met, there is a world out there waiting for our embrace – fragile hearts longing for love and care. It could be children. It could be teenagers. It could be young adults. People need to be loved and nurtured. We have an awesome opportunity to make Isaiah 54:1 our reality. We mustn't miss this in our grief. Let's expand our minds to this fresh way of thinking and acting. If we do, we will feel deep satisfaction.

> *"Not all dreams have to be dashed.*
> *This truth is that God's presence*
> *and power is always with us."*

There are other things we can do: practical actions that may suit some more than others. As singles today we have options that can increase our chance of having a family. Not all dreams have to be dashed. Some, like Koko, are planning for their future marriage. She shares in her beautiful story that someone suggested she freeze her eggs. She had the financial means to take advantage of modern medicine so that if she married late, she might still be able to have children. I think this is a great idea, because she was planning for marriage in the first place. If she stopped ovulating by that time, she still had a chance to have a baby with her husband.

Some singles are considering adopting or fostering children, other women are choosing to have children on their own. However, I would encourage us to pause for a moment and not just simply accept what is becoming more socially acceptable just so we can fill a void or meet a deep longing we have for a child.

I do believe we will continue to see more of these shifts take place in our society. As people find alternative ways to create family there will be both challenges and opportunities. My hope is we don't sideline those who embrace creative alternatives when it comes to motherhood, but I also hope that we will continue to see the importance of family and the role of both a mother and a father in rearing a child.

My greatest hope is that whatever our situation, we don't let the desire for children rob us of our joy now. I once sat with a girlfriend who has cried many times over this issue. She is now in her mid-50s and fears living – and dying – alone. I try and encourage her to know there is hope and peace in giving this part of our heart wholly to God. And there is an entire world out there waiting for her love. She doesn't need to be alone.

This truth is that God's presence and power is always with us. He understands the web of challenges that can snare us as we navigate the single life – and he loves us. I've talked here about some ways we can navigate the issues that arise when marriage is delayed. One area I haven't said much about is sex. Yes, the elephant in the room isn't forgotten. It's very relevant so I've given it a chapter all on its own, later in the book. But for now, I want to look deeper into ways we can colour our world during these 'delays'. Let's look at more ways to live a fulfilled single life.

CHARLENE

Hi there, my name is Charlene. My passions include design, people, music, organisation and a good cup of tea. My most treasured passion is God and I love embracing life with him.

I have certainly wrestled with being single. Let's go back to my teenage years. This was the beginning of this 'hello other sex' light bulb. Although the crushes I had did not turn into boyfriends, and I never dabbled in the party scene, in hindsight this was a blessing in disguise.

I was 15 when I went along to a youth group with my twin sister. This was the beginning of my 'me and God' journey and a pivotal milestone in my life. I met Jesus and saw clearly for the first time that there was more to God than attending church on a Sunday with my family. The last couple of years of high school were tough with moving out of home at 16. But I leaned on and trusted in God, and boy, am I glad I had him! This trust is a life principle that we don't ever stop learning to practise.

Finding myself in a beautiful church family was a blessing and well, the 'I want a boyfriend' thing went to a whole new level... 'You're telling me there are nice boys out there who love God, play guitar and sing?' Cue journey to finding this perfect Christian boy. It's okay to laugh out loud. I am. On a serious note, I was also *pursuing God, discovering my purpose in life and working out who he made me to be.*

I was 18 when I finished school and started to work, and I couldn't believe I still hadn't found anyone. I'd had many crushes up until this point and many bold conversations with these Christian boys. It makes me cringe and laugh as I reminisce on how often I would straight out ask a guy if we had something, or not. The way I saw it was I didn't want to put myself through more emotional turmoil than I needed to. Makes sense right? Although 98% of the time the answer was a clear no, it gave me clarity, freedom, a few tears (okay a lot of tears) and a returning to God with my heart's desires, trusting him… God really did have my path.

The common theme I have found in choosing to do life with God, means choosing to let him into every part. I don't know why some people meet their significant others at a certain age and others don't, or why some people find their life passion early on and others start one degree only to switch to something different halfway through. That's my story. I studied nursing for two and a half years, until some health struggles forced me to take some much needed 'time out'. This ultimately taught me that change is okay. I remember reading Jeremiah, chapter 29 and it challenged and encouraged me to keep living and keep going. God is in every season.

Around this time friends were getting engaged left, right and centre. They were all meeting those Christian guys who played guitar and sang, and I wondered if I'd be the last one standing. This was one of the toughest bumps in the 'singleness roller-coaster' I had experienced and making it through this was a personal victory. I became stronger – and when the lonely thoughts and feelings came, I was able to get back up by embracing God and focusing on Him.

The following year I went on to study interior design, which included a stint overseas in Leeds, United Kingdom. I told a guy I was dating at the time, that as much as I was enjoying getting to know him, I would go if I was accepted into the course. And I am glad I did because that relationship didn't last long.

The year of exchange was such a crazy-amazing time. I learnt so much about myself, and it was the first time I experienced a dream coming to pass. I discovered a love for architecture and old buildings, and I made friendships that are still strong today. I'm so glad I took this time out and navigated it independently. Something came alive in me during that year and it strengthened my relationship with God immensely. There was no 'boyfriend' in my life and yet God gave me great joys. Finding a life partner and getting married isn't the be all and end all to my life. I do however, have a responsibility to steward the places, people and things that God puts in my hands. Everything God adds to my life outside of me is a gift: friends, family, my job and perhaps one day, Lord willing, a life partner.

When I finished my degree, I moved to Melbourne to work as an Interior Designer. It was a wonderful time of progressing in my career and doing life in community with a beautiful church family. In my second year there I began dating someone at the same time as four of my closest girlfriends were dating guys. My relationship was short-lived and left me heartbroken, and they all got engaged. That was tough, however I decided to be happy for them. I intentionally made the decision to choose joy over self-pity. One day it will happen for me and I want my friends to be rejoicing for me. I can happily report that I had the best time at all of those weddings. It was a beautiful thing to witness my friends marry wonderful men and oh, those dance floors were fun!

The post-break-up journeys for me included a very important lesson in learning to enjoy my own company. I was feeling down one Friday night, and I remember calling my sister and telling her. I'd finished work and had nowhere to go. My housemates all had partners. My sister said, 'Don't look at it as a negative thing. Do whatever you feel like doing.' So, that's what I did. Whether it was having a bath, watching a movie, or playing music, I had a pocket of time where I had this freedom to choose. Soon a favourite joy became making myself a nice meal and eating it by candlelight. I would picture Jesus sitting with me as I enjoyed the meal. If it was not for cultivating these beautiful times during those 'lower' seasons, I would not have discovered what I really enjoy – things that I continue to this day.

I think it is important not to single ourselves out (excuse the pun) for being single. My pastor once said to me, "Don't lose your confidence. It's more attractive than looks." Everything else shines in a person when they are confident. We need to be confident in who we are and work on us.

I continue to learn that new and better perspectives are discovered, not just on the mountaintop, but in the valley: on our knees and in our room, with tears rolling down our cheeks and our hearts poured out to God. It's always going to be us and him as we navigate new jobs, face challenges, move cities, make new friends or go on *wonderful adventures. He has so much good in store for us and wants to journey with us daily. And maybe one day, I will be partnered with another wonderful human he has made. Regardless, I have learned that it is important to keep living, keep discovering and keep moving forward with my hand in God's hand. This really is the best place to be. And I hope to be a continual, tangible influence wherever my unique path may lead.*

5

COLOURING YOUR WORLD

I love colour. Colourful food, colourful clothes and colourful people. I adore the fresh hues of spring and the vibrant shades of summer as flowers and trees dazzle with their blossom. When I get time, I paint with bright, abstract colour. Colour adds verve, colour brings joy, colour brings life. I love colour! But what about us? What does it mean for our lives to have colour?

As single people we can sometimes be trapped by both the stigma and the delays mentioned in the previous chapters, into a monochrome existence where the hope of light and life is focused on finding a life-partner. We go about our days yearning for something we don't have right now – waiting for things to change so that we can have the lives we want. We may not realise we are doing this – it can be a subconscious thing – but deep down we feel that life will be better when we find someone. If we are not careful, our lives can reflect shades of grey instead of radiating light.

In the same way, if we are settled in our heart that we don't want to marry, the more colour our lives have the better. Our married friends may look at us with jealous eyes and say, 'I'll have what she's having!'[1]

> *"We go about our days yearning for something we don't have right now – waiting for things to change so that we can have the lives we want."*

So, if you feel caught in the space between singleness and marriage, or if the picture of your life needs a more vivid hue, then come with me. I'd like this chapter to build on some of the thoughts we pondered in Chapter 4. There are no wasted days in the hands of God, he grows us as we make the most of our time and connect with the right community. Let's grab our brushes and paint and do the art of life together. Let's create a picture of what it's like to make life meaningful *now*. Let's colour our worlds.[2]

In the Meantime

I've mentioned my maman many times in this book; and I make no apology for that. She was a remarkable woman of God and I still miss her. In Chapter 2, I referred to the small dash on her

---

[1] B Houston 1998, *I'll have what she's having*, Hillsong Australia, Castle Hill, New South Wales. This may be a line from the well-known romantic comedy, 'When Harry Met Sally,' but it is also the title of this excellent book by Pastor Bobby Houston, which focuses on empowering women.

[2] I'd like to make a shout out here to Hillsong Australia and their annual Colour conference, which encourages women to find ways to meet the needs of others here and around the globe – a great way to colour your world. https://hillsong.com/colour/

gravestone that symbolised the period from the beginning to the end of her life.

9 May 1945 – 11 July 2015

She accomplished so much in those years and rode through many challenges. Life wasn't perfect but she never let that stop her from bringing delight into the lives of others, wherever she went, including her children.

A dash like this is often seen on a gravestone or written in a book to denote the dates a particular person lived. However, I sometimes feel that with us singles it can refer to a time when we do not feel alive. Instead of symbolising our life from birth to glory, this dash can denote the period of waiting until we find the right man to marry.

> *"Doing your own thing in your own strength can have consequences!"*

You have probably heard the term 'in the meantime'. We say things like, 'I'd like to go to the shops, but they're not open yet. I'll wash the car in the meantime.' The meantime is the place of waiting – where you do other things while you wait for the right time to do what you want to do. For singles, the meantime can refer to the period from when we begin to deeply desire a husband, to the time the right man comes along. With me so far?

Two problems can occur in the 'meantime'. The first is that we may place such an emphasis on the holy grail of marriage that we stop living to the full.

The second is that *the meantime*, can become a *mean*-time, with the emphasis on the word *mean*.

Let's look at the second problem first. When something doesn't happen in our timeframe, we can begin to see God as a miserly being who has let us down rather than a good father who understands all things, and whose timing is perfect. Dumping our desires for bucketloads of bitterness, we become closed to the possibilities God has for us. We lose our vision for our lives and sometimes even our faith.

> *"Instead of symbolising our life from birth to glory, this dash can denote the period of waiting until we find the right man to marry."*

Alternatively, we can take things into our own hands – like Sarah and Abraham. When they didn't have the children God had promised, in their timing, Sarah told Abraham to take her servant, Hagar, as a surrogate mother for their children.[3] You can read about this in greater detail in Part III when I talk about the history of women in the Bible. Hagar bore Ishmael but when Sarah had her own child, Isaac, Hagar and Ishmael were banished from Abraham's household.[4] God looked after them and made Ishmael into a great nation too – his descendants becoming progenitors of Northern Arab nations – nations that later became Islamic and warred against the

---

3 Genesis 16
4 Genesis 17:17-27, 21:8-20

Hebrew people.⁵ Doing your own thing in your own strength can have consequences!

In Habakkuk 2:3 the Lord talks about a vision coming to pass at the *appointed time*. The prophet, realising that God is in control in a time of great difficulty, pens these famous lines:

> *Though the fig tree does not bud*
> *and there are no grapes on the vines,*
> *though the olive crop fails*
> *and the fields produce no food,*
> *though there are no sheep in the pen*
> *and no cattle in the stalls,*
> *yet I will rejoice in the Lord,*
> *I will be joyful in God my Saviour.*⁶

It's this attitude, of rejoicing in the Lord no matter what, that allows our lives to have colour amidst the delays.

If your desire is for a husband and you haven't found him yet. Don't lose the vision. Don't let a bitter mindset creep in and take your joy. I'm not saying you should be striving every day with every thought towards it, but don't lose the possibility that it could still happen. God can do amazing things. He once told a friend of mine that she would marry one day – and it happened 18 years later. That's a long wait, but God had to do things in her life and in the man's life to make them ready for

---

5 *What does the Bible say about Muslims / Islam? | Bibleinfo.com* 2019, Bibleinfo.com, viewed 29 May 2020, <https://www.bibleinfo.com/en/questions/what-does-bible-say-about-muslims-islam>.

6 Habakkuk 3:17-18

each other. However, he may want you to wait for a completely different reason.

I love God and believe that everything he gives me has a purpose – even my singleness. In Isaiah 55, God says:

> *'For my thoughts are not your thoughts,*
> *neither are your ways my ways,'*
> *declares the Lord.*
> *'As the heavens are higher than the earth,*
> *so are my ways higher than your ways*
> *and my thoughts than your thoughts.'*[7]

And in Jeremiah 29:

> *'For I know the plans I have for you,' declares the Lord,*
> *'plans to prosper you and not to harm you, plans to give you*
> *a hope and a future.'*[8]

Wow! When you take these two verses together, we see that God has great plans for us, but the way he thinks, and acts, can be very different from the way we think and act. This is true for all of life – not just singleness – but it definitely applies to our topic here.

If I had my way, I would have found a fine man and had children but that hasn't happened. If God is good, and I know he is, then I know he has a special purpose for me right now.

---

7   Isaiah 55:8-9
8   Jeremiah 29:11

If I spend my life brooding about my singleness, I might miss that purpose and joy that comes from being in the right place at the right time, doing his will. I might miss the chance to live life to the full right now.

> *"I love God and believe that everything he gives me has a purpose – even my singleness."*

I've always found times of waiting to be stepping stones to maturity. God wants us to learn something or grow in a particular way. If we didn't have periods of waiting, we could easily become like spoiled children, always wanting more. Our loving father in heaven knows what is good for us. Sometimes he does have marriage for us in the future but we're not ready. 'Ha!' you say. 'I'm more than ready.' Maybe, maybe not. Marriage can be tough. It has some advantages, but my married friends assure me that marriage has its own set of challenges. I don't know how many times I've heard married friends say, 'I wish I'd really appreciated my freedom as a single,' or 'once you have kids, overseas travel is off the cards,' or 'his snoring is driving me mad.' Sometimes there are deeper issues to deal with. When two people marry, they bring their woundedness as well as their strengths to the kitchen table, the living room and even to the bedroom.

> *"We see that God has great plans for us, but the way he thinks, and acts, can be very different from the way we think and act."*

Are your ready for the tough things? Are you ready to serve the other person? Are you good at resolving conflict and compromising? Are you happy to give up some freedoms so you can love and honour one person for the rest of your life?

A married friend once said that we can spend so much energy on finding the 'right person' that we forget to focus on learning to *be* the right person. The more confident we are in ourselves and the happier our outlook on life – and the wiser we are – the better prepared we will be for the challenges of marriage if and when they come. If we focus on being the best person we can be, we can live lives full of colour and delight. We will be happier as we are and be better able to discern if a particular man is good for us, or fits with God's plan for our lives. Our confidence will also make us more attractive to the opposite sex.

> *"When two people marry, they bring their woundedness as well as their strengths to the kitchen table, the living room and even to the bedroom."*

But it could be there is another reason this so-called delay is taking place. It may not be to ready you for marriage one day. None of us know what will happen. That makes it even more important to live life for today, not some imaginary tomorrow.

Are you giving yourself permission to live to the full or are you in waiting mode, or worse still, the *mean*-time mode? Are you limiting your life by your single status in a way that diffuses your value and purpose? Are you assuming that you can only shine when you have a partner? Is the meantime for you a point of waiting, of holding your breath, a pause in fulfilment or accomplishment? Or is it a time where you say I'm not limited by anyone or anything other than God's will?

Have you ever found yourself saying, 'Someday when I get married, I will...?'

Say you have a heart to preach God's word, but the only women you know who are doing this are pastor's wives or the wives of those in leadership. The waiting mindset says that you should wait until finding that certain someone before you fulfil your dream. Ho-hum. The colour-your-world mindset says go for it. Seek out and talk to other women who are doing this. Find out how they got there. Go to Bible college, study God's word. Let God refine the dream – and he will do it. There will be a day when you find yourself proclaiming God's word and your heart will be filled with the wonder of God's grace and goodness. As you go, God might give you the other part of the dream – a husband to stand beside in ministry – or he may give you a different dream. There are plenty of significant women preachers in the world whose husbands aren't pastors. And there are others who are single and loving it.[9]

I'm not saying that we should seek a platform ministry. I'm saying that it's important to find the dream that God has planted in *your* heart and *go for it*. Just because it is delayed doesn't mean it won't happen. Let's not apply a fast food mentality to life. It could be that you are a nurse and you really

---

9   Two brilliant women preachers who embody positive singleness are Lisa Harper and Nancy Alcorn. You can find them both on Instagram: https://www.instagram.com/lisadharper/ and https://www.instagram.com/nancyalcorn/.

want to be a chef. The desire has nagged at you forever and you feel as if God is nudging you in that direction. You have always been a foodie and you'd love to do that full-time – maybe in business one day with a suitably talented husband. Again, don't wait. Take up a cooking course, invite friends around to taste test, refine your style, let God lead. Follow your heart and amazing things can happen.

> *"Are you giving yourself permission to live to the full or are you in waiting mode, or worse still, the mean-time mode. Life isn't just to be tolerated, it's to be lived."*

Have you read Charlene's story? If you haven't, it's right before this chapter. Two aspects of her life bring light to this topic. The first is she adapted her plans when 'life' led her to leave her nursing degree. This adaptation led her to find her true passion – interior design – and even travel overseas to study. She put her purpose and fulfilment ahead of a relationship that was never going to work. The other thing was that she didn't mope around when her housemates went out with their boyfriends on Friday nights. Instead, she discovered things she loved doing. That's what I mean. Life isn't just to be tolerated, it's to be lived.

It is good to have goals – including romantic ones. Have you said this? 'Some day, when I get married, I will go to that top restaurant on the hill and have a romantic dinner for two.' Part of that particular desire has to wait for that special someone. You can go to the restaurant by yourself or with friends, but the romantic part has to wait. You may want to keep that one particular restaurant for that special someone – that's okay – but there is nothing to stop you going other places with incredible food and a spectacular view, with some friends. If you like fine dining, make a date with a group of guys and gals and go to a different restaurant once every quarter. Buy one of those books of entertainment vouchers between you; and have fun. Be intentional about living life – don't give up on your dream – but don't sit at home waiting, either.

> *"But in the meantime, colour your world,*
> *keep a soft heart towards God and give b*
> *itterness and despair a kick out the door!"*

Which version of you would you find most attractive? The key is to trust God and not rush his work in you. Wait for the appointed time. Every season needs to mature before you can move to the next one. You may well want to find a partner. If so don't give up the desire. But in the meantime, colour your world, keep a soft heart towards God and give bitterness and despair a kick out the door!

Live in the Moment

One of things that has helped me to flourish as a single person is learning to live in the 'moment'. Some people might use the word 'mindfulness' but I've chosen not to do this as others might associate the word with non-Christian world views. But I believe there is a deep truth centred in the idea of taking time to live in the moments God gives us – rather than being driven by the tyranny of busyness.

It is important to live life fully today rather than waiting for our romantic lives to flourish. If we set our minds on pining for an unmade future our lives will be dull and colourless. Tomorrow isn't ours yet. Memories created in the moments make us rich in so many ways. Especially when we include God and others in those moments.

Let's consider two very different bible verses that speak into this space: Ephesians 5:15-16 and Matthew 11:28-30: 'Be very careful, then, how you live—not as unwise but as wise, making the most of every opportunity, because the days are evil.'[10]

And…'Come to me, all you who are weary and burdened, and I will give you rest. Take my yoke upon you and learn from me, for I am gentle and humble in heart, and you will find rest for your souls. For my yoke is easy and my burden is light.'[11]

One verse is saying we are meant to make the most of every opportunity. The other is telling us to rest. Is the Bible contradicting itself?

The answer is *no*, of course. Resting in Jesus is part of making the most of every moment.

Let me explain. When we read that we need to make the most of our time we can sometimes feel a push to get busy. Another translation says we live in desperate times. Hey, there is a world to be loved and saved and we need to get on and do it – that's

---

10   Ephesians 5:15-16
11   Matthew 11:28-30

true. But not in the frazzled kind of way that the world imposes on us.

It's almost as if busyness is today's badge of honour. Like it's the currency of the 21st century. If you are not 'busy', you are not measuring up to society's expectations. It happens in every space including our churches too. Serving God in ministry is really important, but it can be easy to use this as a means of gaining approval if we are not doing it from a place of centredness in Jesus. Are we doing things because God wants us to, or are we doing them because it feels self-important to be busy and we like spiritual pats on the back?

> *"Resting in Jesus is part of making the most of every moment."*

If it's the latter, we will burn out pretty quickly. You can see I'm not a fan of the word 'busy.' I prefer the word 'intentional.'[12] If we are to live a full and satisfying life as a Christian single, where our existence is full of colour and vitality, I think it's important to throw aside busyness for busyness' sake and live intentional lives for Jesus. Part of living intentionally involves recognising the rhythms of life and walking with Jesus, being settled in the moment. Taking time to 'be still' and know Jesus is God.[13] Life works best when we follow the maker's instructions – when we let our Lord be in control of our lives in the small moments as well as the large.

---

[12] My pastors, Craig and Nadia Clark, always use this word 'intentional'. Every meeting or conversation they have is 'intentional' and has a purpose in their life and ministry.

[13] Psalm 46:10

I'm talking about intimacy with Jesus here. Realigning our body, mind and spirit with his ways so that we live life out of a place of quietness and power.

> *"When we live like this it takes away the desperation to fast forward our lives to attain some future ideal, like marriage."*

Failure to do this was part of the reason I fell into the trouble I talked about in the previous chapter. Working long hours and travelling a lot stopped me from forming new, authentic relationships which were essential for my wellbeing. Making the most of our days means spending time *being*, as well as *doing*. It includes time spent building relationships with others as well as growing in intimacy with Jesus. If we do this then we can have a solid foundation for living life and serving God. Our singleness should not be an excuse to cocoon ourselves from everyone different to us.

> *"Our singleness should not be an excuse to cocoon ourselves from everyone different to us."*

When we live like this it takes away the desperation to fast forward our lives to attain some future ideal, like marriage. Now is good. Now is important. Now is the moment where Jesus gives us every breath. Now is the place of joy – even when we are caught up in the mundane activities of life – because Jesus is with us in those moments.

Don't be an Island

'No man is an island entire of itself.' Christian poet John Donne penned the famous line in 1624 and the truth is still valid today.[14] We are not islands, self-sufficient and needing no one. Human beings are interconnected with each other and with God. We don't function well alone. If we are to colour our worlds as single people, it's important to live life surrounded by good people.

I touched on this in the last chapter when I said that Christian women should try, in a safe way, to find friends of both sexes, and to have some interests outside of the church. I'd like to unpack that a bit more.

As we've already seen, community is at the heart of who God is. He is three in one and he made us to thrive together in unity, like he does. That means that one of the key goals of the devil, the enemy of God, is to sabotage and hinder the relationships of believers. He loves to isolate, destroy and place fear in people so that they stay away from certain relationships after they have been hurt. He creates anxiety – preventing people from opening up their world to others – building barriers to making friendships and growing genuine relationships. If we're not careful these barriers may hold us back, increasing our loneliness and limiting our ability to thrive as whole women of God.

Our singleness should not be an excuse to cocoon ourselves from everyone different to us. We can at times be caught in our own

---

14　Biography.com 2014, *John Donne Biography*, Biography.com, viewed 27 May 2020, <https://www.biography.com/writer/john-donne>.

bubble, believing for a spouse yet feeling uncomfortable talking to people who are not normally part of our circle – including men. If we stay away from our brothers in Christ and don't have them as part of our lives, we can seem weird and out of touch. This will only make them avoid us. Not a good thing if you are wanting to find a life-partner!

> *"If the Messiah chose friends to be with him, how much more do we need to build good relationships – with God and with others."*

I am often amazed at the number of women who say they want to meet someone, yet they spend their weekends with their girlfriends only. When an opportunity presents where they could meet or talk to someone of the opposite sex, they make themselves unavailable or speak little or not at all. They then take things to the extreme when asked for a coffee, taking it as if they have just been proposed to. Why? Because they feel self-conscious like the metaphorical fish out of water – flapping on the shore and gasping for air – completely at odds with their environment.

Ladies, the great news is that we can get better and better at relationships. All we need to do is practice. When the new person comes to church, why not step away from your usual group and say, 'Hi!' Maybe give the other person an opportunity to talk about themselves. I don't just mean men here. I mean people who are not normally part of your circle. Maybe they are from a different ethnic group or a different age group. Get practice talking to people who can challenge you to see life through a different lens. Be relatable without being weird. It can feel awkward at first but then it is wonderful.

Live large and be inclusive but kill the agendas, especially when you talk to a man you like. Guys can smell agendas a mile off. Be real, be genuine, be a friend – without trying too hard. And avoid diving in too deep too soon. My married friends assure me friendship is at the foundation of every good marriage.

If you get hurt or disappointed, try and forgive and move on. Be the kind of girl who grieves then bounces back. This is so important. Relationships can be hard to navigate. Some thrive and others don't. That's okay. Each friendship is a new adventure so have fun and throw bitterness and fear out the window.'

I was once in a relationship that I thought had ended well, until I was challenged a few months later when I read something about the way people handle break-ups. It was important to remember that the person you are breaking up with is God's son or daughter. Even if we are upset with them, they should be treated with honour and respect, irrespective of what went wrong. They are still part of God's family. That's a pretty hard truth to digest when that person brought hurt to your life.

As I reflected on this, I realised I needed to treat my ex like a family brother, with love and dignity, even if I'd felt hurt when the relationship ended. I was moved to write him an email and ask for forgiveness – letting him know he was forgiven – again. I'd done this before, but I wanted to reassure him. My heart was open and accepting of him as a son in God's kingdom. I did this because I did not want to be a prisoner of this pain in my future. Nor did I want him to assume that I was still living with resentment towards him.

If we are to have good relationships, one of the best examples is our Lord. In Mark 12:4, we read that Christ chose the twelve apostles *to be with him.* That is the key. The Messiah chose 12 to be with him, to be his friends and companions, before he sent them out to do ministry. Friendship before agenda – although saving the world is a pretty good agenda! If the Messiah chose friends to be with him, how much more do we need to build good relationships – with God and with others – as we live life and do the things God calls us to do?

> *"If the Messiah chose friends to be with him, how much more do we need to build good relationships?"*

Note that while the disciples were male, Jesus had many female friends – like Mary and Martha. He praised Mary for choosing to sit at his feet and learn, like his disciples.[15] That was radical in Jesus' day – he treated those women like family. Did you know that in Psalm 68:6 it says God sets the lonely in families? See those around you as part of your family and treat one another well. Take the focus off yourself and your needs and give another your attention. Don't be an island, be a sister, and you will feel as if you fit. There is nothing that brings more colour to your life than feeling like you *belong*.

---

15   Luke 10:38-42

Ditch the List

A few years ago, there was some teaching around that said Christian singles should create a list of the characteristics they wanted to find in a partner. While praying specifically has some merit, when your list goes beyond wanting your man to love Jesus, love worship and have a good relationship with his mother, one can build expectations that are hard for any man to meet.

> *"Dignity, grace, and a great sense of life will give us a certain mystique."*

As females, let's be real and not make a soap opera out of our relationships. Creating a list of what you are looking for in 'Mr Right' can sometimes build expectations that are unrealistic. We can end up out of touch and disappointed. And let's face it, sometimes we are way too dramatic in those disappointments. I'm not saying have no expectations but do be flexible. If you have in your head that you want a guy with the body of Chris Hemsworth and the spirituality of the Pope, you might find it hard to find someone. Yes, I'm exaggerating, but you know what I mean. Work on being friendly rather than checking every man you meet against some list that describes the perfect male. And be yourself. If you are always trying to change yourself to attract a certain man, you can lose sight of who you are. A girl who is trying too hard isn't relaxed. Focus on being the right woman – godly, friendly, fun – rather than obsessing about finding the right man. And be confident – confidence is always attractive.

The greatest drawcard a woman can have is a genuine sense of self. Dignity, grace, and a great sense of life will give us a certain mystique. Even better if we are kind and have a sense of humour. Being able to laugh at ourselves and not take ourselves too seriously will always win us friends around the dinner table.

But I understand it's not always easy to find this confidence. Our backgrounds influence who we are. If we've had the kind of home life where we've been told we'd never achieve anything, we can take that on as our identity. In the schoolyard, if we are too gawky, too small, too tall, too fat, too poor, too pale, too black, too anything – and other kids say we are ugly – it can be hard to throw that off as we get older. It's as if insults are written with permanent marker on the insides of our eyelids, constantly reminding us of our failures.

How do we overcome this? The good news is that we can. I've previously shared my story about how hard I found it to fit in at school. I was timid – I wouldn't speak in a room with more than three people. On many occasions I went to bed crying because I believed what people were saying about me was true: that I was ugly, black and no good at all. I questioned why God had made me that way and I walked with my head down, looking at the ground.

But one day God spoke to me. 'Lift up your head and look around you.' In my spirit he seemed to say there was a much bigger perspective here – so much to see. When I looked down all I had was my lap. But if I lifted my head, I could see his creation. I could look at things differently. That perspective changed me forever.

I stopped looking for people to give me permission to be me. I started to like myself as I began to meditate on the scripture. I discovered who I really was: fearfully and wonderfully made, the beloved daughter of the king.[16] God's word was the truth, not the word of some bitchy group of girls in Year 11.

Ladies, if we are looking downwards because of the lies people have put on us, that's all we will ever see. But if we lift our gaze not only will we see things from a wider perspective, we will see ourselves as we really are – beautiful women of God, placed in this world to bring his love and grace to others. If we choose to believe what the scriptures say, we can stand in confidence before others – no longer believing we are 'less than'. We can look the world – and other people – in the eye, standing strong in God. I keep this truth foremost in professional space, my church work and within all of my relationships; and it has made a remarkable difference.

> *"Lift your head and know that you are worth liking.*
> *I stopped looking for people to give me*
> *permission to be me."*

Please try this. Choose to lift up your head. Go to God's word and see who you are. Look at yourself in the mirror and give yourself permission to be *you*. Choose to like yourself. And if confidence doesn't stick at first, keep believing until it does. In Romans, Paul says that we should be transformed by 'the

---

16 Psalm 139:14

renewing of our minds'.[17] Sometimes it can take a while to erase the old lies, but as you keep going you will discover the new you.

Be confident. Make friends. Don't judge yourself by other's actions or their perceptions of you. When that man you like smiles at you, know you are worth liking. When that man you like doesn't smile at you, smile at him and move on. Lift your head and know that you are worth liking. You are a brilliant, amazing woman of God. Stand tall!

Wow! We've come a long way as we've learned to colour our worlds. I hope the paint or the chalk dust or the crayons are everywhere: in your hair, on your face, on your hands, and on your clothes, as you've dived into this chapter with me. We haven't just been drawing on paper, we've been splashing colour all over our lives. That can get messy. Sometimes we get it right and other times we don't. But we keep going, heads high, drawing close to others and to our God, birthing beauty as we go.

The more we can cultivate this life of colour, the better off we will be. And if one day we do marry, what a fortunate man he'll be!

---

17   Romans 12:2

KIM

As a young girl, the words I thought would describe my life were family, wife, children, happily married and contented. I could never have imagined back then that my life would also be described by terms like death, grief, sorrow, heartbreak and widow.

When Darren and I met, it was like a scene from the movie 'An Officer and a Gentleman': the young handsome RAAFie from Melbourne carries away the heart of the girl born and bred in Ipswich, Queensland. I was 20 and he was 21 when we got married and immediately moved to Darwin to begin our life together.

Not long after the birth of Sharni, our second child, Darren began to sense a call to ministry. He left the RAAF and we moved back to Ipswich so he could go to Bible college and, later, take on an executive pastor role in a large Assemblies of God (AOG) church nearby. After 10 years we felt God's call to go back to Darwin where Darren took on a role as a senior pastor.

We had four children by then and quickly settled into a wonderful routine. We made new friends and worked hard at building into the spiritual life of our church. I went back to university to finish my Bachelor of Commerce degree – majoring in accounting – which I had started part-time when all the kids were at school. I had always enjoyed working with numbers, so it seemed the natural thing for me to study. Little did I know then, but it would soon be vital that I could earn enough income to support myself and the family.

On a warm Friday night, in October 2005, I was waiting at work for my husband Darren to pick me up so we could get a head start on moving some things to our new house. It was next to our Darwin church and closer to the city than our current home in Palmerston. As darkness descended, I started to worry. Darren was not always the most punctual person, and I knew he had been travelling back and forth between our old house and the city. So being a bit late was understandable. Still… something was wrong.

Panic set in and tears started to flow. On the fourth or fifth attempt to call his mobile, a policeman answered. All he said was there had been an accident and I needed to get to the hospital.

You read about these things happening to other people. They don't happen to families like ours. Not ones who are living for God, following his plan and purposes for their lives, doing as he asked. But it was happening, and I soon found myself at the hospital with our oldest daughter, being ushered into a small room next to the Emergency Department. There I was told that the owner of a red Holden Commodore had been involved in a serious car accident and had died on the way to the hospital.

My beautiful, brave girl, just 20, wouldn't let her mum identify her father's body by herself. She came with me to see her dad lying on a cold trolley, looking even colder as the life and spirit that was once our Darren, my life partner, her loving daddy, was now long gone.

Our world was shattered.

Darren was just 43 when he died. I was 41.

Everything became a blur as we lived the next few days, weeks and months in a teary-eyed state of disbelief. I was thrust into the life of being a widow and single mother to our four children. How could we survive without him? How could my boys, then 15 and 12, enter manhood without their dad? How could my girls not have their daddy to walk them down the aisle when they got married? How could I keep on living without my partner, my soul mate and my life? How would our church keep going without their beloved leader and mentor?

But we did survive, and our most loving and faithful heavenly Father never left our side. I decided early on, after great advice from a friend in ministry, not to keep going down the 'why' road but to ask the 'what' question instead. What would God have me do now? What can we do that will honour Darren's memory? We may never know the answers to why something happens to us, but we don't have to – we just have to know how to move forward and to keep trusting God no matter what our circumstances may look like.

Journaling was helpful in that first year. I could vent my feelings, be honest with God and let my true self come out. Or to just hide for a while if that was needed. Certain scriptures would also leap off the page and envelop me in his peace and comfort.

Being single again was hard to navigate because my singleness now stemmed from the death of my beloved partner. When Darren died, we had been married for longer than I had been a single woman, so I was well out of practice. People who knew me, and knew what had happened, obviously didn't ask the awkward questions. But as soon as I met someone new, when they found out I had four children, their next question would often be, 'And what does your husband do?'

'Oh, he died in a car accident.' Instant conversation stopper.

At times I felt like an outsider in situations that used to be comfortable and easy for me: a barbecue at a friend's house, church on a Sunday, birthday parties. Having to walk into a room by myself and trying to not have a complete meltdown was sometimes much harder than it looked. I felt like the odd one out.

On top of all this, at the time Darren died, I wasn't a credentialed pastor in my own right, which meant a lot of those connections just disappeared. So alone again, I had to try and remember who I was before I became Mrs Johnson. Before I was a wife and mother.

Psalm 23:3 was one of the verses that captivated me during this time. 'True to your word, you let me catch my breath and send me in the right direction.'[1]

I learned that what has happened to us in the past, or what hasn't happened – the circumstances that we have had no control over; and even the ones that we have brought upon ourselves because of bad

---

1 Psalm 23:3 (MSG)

decisions – none of these things can change God's love for us, or the future he has planned for us. He will let you 'catch your breath'. He will let you recover, and then he will continue to lead you into a new season that will look nothing like you expected or planned for.

It wasn't my choice to be single again, to face all the heartache. But there was nothing I could do to change the situation. My only choice was to continue to trust God through it and believe that he still had a good and perfect plan for me that would indeed bring me hope.² I decided to trust what I had believed all my life was true – even in the darkest of moments – and he has never let me down. Life is truly but a breath, and we need to learn to make the most of the time we have.

---

2   Jeremiah 29:11

6

SINGLE & SINGLE AGAIN

What comes to mind when you think of the word 'contentment'? Is it a beloved dog curled up next to you while you devour a great book? Is it the warmth of a newborn babe snuggling close, as you cradle her to your chest? Is it sitting indoors in the warmth, sipping on a mug of rich hot chocolate, while wintry rain blasts against the window? Is it the bubbling chatter and laughter of friends after you've eaten a great meal together – a meal that you prepared? Or is it the deep satisfaction of finishing a creative project?

> *"I love how there are things that we can do to make the most of our delays."*

I'm sure you can add your own images to the mix. There are many things in life that bring contentment: times when all striving stops and we experience deep satisfaction and rest. Sometimes contentment is just for a moment, and you have to dive back into the challenges of life. Other times it can be more enduring, like when you find an occupation you love doing, or make a new friend. To feel content is to feel a settled happiness with your life as a single. It's a goal we all seek.

Is contentment something people normally associate with singleness? Aren't people always trying to change us? Aren't many of us trying to change our single status?

The past two chapters covered the different types of single people and how singles can add colour to their lives as they wait for a partner, in the space between singleness and marriage. I love how there are things that we can do to make the most of our delays. But is it possible to find true contentment as a Christian single? I believe it is.

In this chapter I'd like us to consider two different groups of singles – the most settled – and often the most unsettled: those who have found contentment in their singleness and those who find themselves single again.

I have many friends who have found a way to flourish after relationships have ended, but for some it may take time to journey through hurt and grief. My hope is that as I look at some of the keys to contentment as a Christian single, my words will encourage you in whatever phase or season you find yourselves in. In the second part of the chapter, I hope to particularly encourage those who are single again.

> *"Contentment is a state of being at peace with ourselves and with God. A place where there is no war within'*

One more thing. Whereas the last chapter had more of an issues-based focus, I'd like us to look here at our beautiful God and how his hand of providence works deep in our lives, to help us live our single lives with confidence. When all else is lost, he is our ever-present help in time of need.[1]

Content Singles

I began this chapter with some images of contentment, but what does a content Christian single look, or feel, like?

In many ways, the single people who are content are those who have learned to apply the truths I shared in the last chapter. They've learned to thrive in the delays by adding colour to their lives and by trusting God's timing. If you said yes to many of the ideas I shared, then you are well on your way to living as a content woman of God.

However, I think contentment is broader than that. I think it's a state of being at peace with ourselves and with God. A place where there is no war within, telling us something is wrong. Notice I said peace, not defeat? Content singles are not those who have given up in defeat, nor are they necessarily those who have decided to stay single forever. No, content singles are those who feel settled in themselves and know that God is in control.

Settled

In Psalm 131, King David writes of his experience of contentment:

---

[1] Psalm 46:1

> *But I have calmed and quieted myself,*
> *I am like a weaned child with its mother;*
> *like a weaned child I am content.*[2]

There was a time in my life where this sense of contentment was substantial. I was in my early to mid-thirties and life was great. I travelled to different parts of the world, serving God and fulfilling his call on my life. There was no war within me; I didn't compare my life with anyone else's. I was right at the centre of his will and it was amazing. Like David I had found my place of rest and purpose in God.

Alas, seasons change, and I've already spoken of some of my struggles. Sometimes the single life doesn't look, or feel, very restful.

> *"Many of us have had opportunities to say yes to a man but we've said no for various reasons. We've known it wasn't right. It can be a lack of chemistry, or the wrong season or place."*

Consider the dating game. Sometimes it drives me crazy. Over the years I have collated stories on dating games. Some are hilarious while others are frustrating beyond belief. The kind of frustration usually depends on what part of the world the men are from. For example, some of my encounters with guys of African descent, even if they were born in the West, were amusing as they were direct and didn't hold back on expressing what they wanted. There was one man who I had

---

2 Psalm 131:2

never met – he only knew me by name – yet he decided to make a proposal on the phone. He chased me hard and even left love songs on my phone. There was another man I met briefly at a funeral. His only contact with me was to say, 'Hello.' Other than that, we never spoke. He asked for my details through mutual family connections and we started a conversation from different states. When he found out I just wanted friendship, he was a gentleman and said he would wait until my emotions caught up with his. Back then I wasn't interested in dating guys, or who knows, it may have come to something, but his approach still makes me smile.

> *"Sometimes the single life doesn't look, or feel, very restful."*

The Australian-Caucasian guys were different. I can attest to this from my experience and the experiences of many of my girlfriends. These men would like a girl for years but never say anything. There were guys I'd be friends with for ages, only for me to find out later that they liked me but did not have the gumption to ask me out or talk about it. Mind you, they would either tell me this after they already had a girlfriend, or I would hear about it from someone else. I know, right. My thoughts are the same. *What the heck?*

While these may be two distinct cultural extremes, many single women feel frustrated by similar behaviours by the men around them. They also feel unsettled when they are accused of being hard to please. It is possible some of you are already thinking, *why didn't you go out with any of these guys?*

Look at it this way. Many of us have had opportunities to say yes to a man but we've said no for various reasons. We've known it wasn't right. It can be a lack of chemistry, or the wrong season or place. They could have different values from us, or our women's intuition might be saying to walk the other way. It is important to follow these leads and not compromise, based on what others around want us to do or because we want to fit in. If there is no peace, then we can't move forward. 'But,' you ask, 'didn't you say in the last chapter that we should 'ditch the list' and be open to what God will do?

The answer is that I did say that, in the context of being friends with men. There's nothing wrong with keeping the door to friendship open if he's a good Christian guy. Be a friend, be open, and, if romance seems possible, move forward with caution. Always listen to wise counsel here. Sometimes other people can see potential issues that you can't. Love can indeed be blind.

> *"If we are to find a settled contentment in any walk of life, not just as a single, it's important to work on deepening our walk with God."*

I believe true contentment will only come when we know ourselves and know our God. We can only have the peace of that weaned child if we put our hope in God and trust in him.

How do we do this? We start by learning to abide in Christ.

Abide in Christ

I think the fast-paced world we live in sometimes makes it hard for us to connect with our own selves, let alone God. We work long hours as our project needs to be done quickly. We have TV dinners because we need to eat and run so we can catch that plane. We eat fast food because we get it ... um... fast. We say hello and goodbye without really engaging, because we are in a rush to get somewhere else. How can we know ourselves and know our God if we never sit still and listen – when from the moment we wake, we dive into social media, getting dopamine kick after dopamine kick with every new 'like' on our profile?[3]

> *"I like to say, 'Talk it over with God.' The best relationships are founded on regular conversation."*

Social media can be a useful way to keep in touch with people. But I hate it when it takes our attention away from important things and robs us of moments where we can be still and know the presence and power of our God.[4]

If we are to find a settled contentment in any walk of life, not just as a single, it's important to work on deepening our walk with God. It's vital to take time to read his Word and to listen to him – to establish an ongoing dialogue with him on the important matters of life.

---

[3] S Weinschenk 2018, *The Dopamine Seeking-Reward Loop*, Psychology Today, viewed 25 May 2020, <https://www.psychologytoday.com/us/blog/brain-wise/201802/the-dopamine-seeking-reward-loop>.

[4] Psalm 46:10

I love that God gets that we like different things. Some might draw close through music; others might choose to go for long walks at sunrise and pour their heart out to God. People who enjoy learning might want to dive into detailed study of the scriptures. Others may like a more devotional method. However we approach him, our beautiful, loving Saviour wants us to draw close and spend time with him. He wants us to abide in him because he knows it makes us strong.

Say you feel unsettled in your singleness. Guys have asked you out, but it's never become a serious relationship. You are frustrated with the lack of men in your church and the nagging voice of loneliness haunts you as you close your eyes to sleep. You don't even know what you should be looking for in a mate because you seem to always make the wrong choices. You feel frazzled around the edges and wonder why God doesn't just fix this for you.

> *"If we clarify our position in God first, it will refocus many of the requests we have about marriage."*

If this is you, he may be inviting you into a deeper dialogue and richer relationship with him. He might want you to come to know him and know yourself better before he gives you a partner.

I like to say, 'Talk it over with God.' The best relationships are founded on regular conversation. It's good if you can spend time with God, regularly focusing on him throughout the week. But sometimes we need to take time out and have a period of extra special focus on talking to him.

You might put a weekend aside. If you can afford it, why not book a hotel room in a nice spot in the hills or near a quiet beach and go away for a weekend with God. Take your Bible along with a journal and pen. Spend time writing in your journal. Did you know there is a companion journal to this book?[5] Get all of your frustrations out on paper, then be still and listen to what God has to say. Read the Bible, go for walks, listen as the wind whispers through the trees; or dig your toes deep into cool, wet sand. And listen. Listen to yourself and listen to God. He loves hearing your voice and he yearns for you to pour out your heart to him. But he also likes space to speak.

I'm sure many of you have done this many times, but if you are yet to do this, I encourage you to give it a try. It can help us all to regularly take time out and silence our strivings, so we can better hear God's whispers in our heart.

Be sure not to just ask him about marriage, seek answers to the big questions first. Questions like: *How should I be attributing each of my days towards the destiny I have been called to fulfil?* That's not just big – it's a *huge* question – so it may help to get your journal, pen and Bible and break this down into smaller, yet still significant, requests:
- Who am I in your eyes, Lord?
- What are you calling me to be and do?
- How should I be using my days for you?
- What should my life focus be today?

---

5   JMA Kabamba 2020, *The Unexpected Gift Journal*, Space Between Publications, Melbourne, Australia.

Once you have reflected on these questions and have a sense of what God is saying, perhaps start asking these questions specifically about marriage:

- Am I meant to marry one day?
- Is it the right time for me?
- What should I be looking for in a partner?
- How prepared am I to serve this person?
- Why haven't I found someone yet?

Note the order of the questions. If we clarify our position in God first, it will refocus many of the requests we have about marriage. I have learned over many years that there is no point fighting God. He knows what's best for us – and his timing is always perfect.

As we give God space to speak, we might get an immediate answer, or we might just get a sense that he has heard us. The deep answers may come in the weeks that follow as we walk with him, but make sure and write down the things you think he is saying. Let it be an ongoing dialogue with him. Listen to yourself too.

Be really honest here. Are you willing to ask yourself why you want a partner? Is it because you have a deep longing to share your life with another? Or because all your friends are getting married and you feel left out? If it's the latter, then maybe it's not the time to be praying for a husband. It might be that God has something for you right now which will satisfy you even more than marriage would.

Each one of us has a destiny and purpose in God and we will only be truly content if we are fulfilling that purpose. The person we choose to marry will have a bearing on our entire life. It will colour everything we are and everything we do.

Maybe we want someone because we are lonely? Is this the right reason to dive into a relationship? It could be that God is wanting to work on us more before we marry. Neediness can be a relationship killer. Or maybe we want to serve God on the mission field and the guy we like is racially prejudiced. Or we are a vet nurse who owns five cats and the man we are dating hates animals. It's never going to work!

Ladies, this step is important, yet we easily forget it and react without questioning our core motivations. Know yourself, know your God, and walk with him. Align yourself with his purpose for your life. No one else can say whether it is right for you to be married or stay single. Keep talking it over with God until you get a sense of what is right for you. When you do, as I said in the last chapter, go for it. Don't be ashamed of wanting someone. Equally don't be ashamed if you want to stay single.

Walk with God and settle these things in your heart with him and you will have a greater sense of self-assurance. You won't be sidelined whenever someone says you are being too fussy or discriminates against you as a single. You will know who you are and what you want. That's part of the confidence I spoke of in the last chapter and it is one of the keys to contentment.

The other key is trust. I'll talk about this more later, but for now let me say that we don't have to discard our dreams to be content, we just have to trust them to God. Let's rest in God's hands knowing that whatever he gives us in *this moment*, is good. Not tomorrow, not next week, not next year. Now.

I know many of you reading this book will have come to the place of choosing to follow Jesus Christ, but how much do you trust him with everything that is important to you? Are you trusting him to give you the right job, the right amount of money, the right relationships, at the right time? Are you believing he will give you all that you need to live and flourish as his beloved child?

> *"The person we choose to marry will have a bearing on our entire life. It will colour everything we are and everything we do."*

If we are not trusting him, what does that say about our faith? Sometimes it's easy to say we believe in him but then live as if we don't. If we live like that, peace will be hard to find.

The Apostle Paul told the church in Philippi that he had 'learned the secret of being content in every situation'.[6] He was speaking about material needs here, but isn't our requirement for love and companionship as important as any material need? Are we trusting God to meet those needs? I think those who are truly content to be single understand this truth. They don't kill their dream, but they run lightly with it, resting in a God who knows them intimately. They know that no matter what,

---

6   Philippians 4:12-13

he will never abandon them, because he gave his life for them. And they live their life for him. Wow!

There may be those reading this who say, 'I'm nowhere near that level of trust yet'. If that's you, that's okay. We're all on a journey and God the Holy Spirit, will 'lead us into all truth'.[7] That's part of who he is and how he partners with us in our lives. We can learn trust by exercising more trust each day.

> *"How can those who are in the midst of trauma find their way to the place of peace and hope?"*

But there are those who will read this and go, 'Yes! I know that place of rest. I know that peace.' If that's you, then please be there for your sisters. Encourage them to know themselves and to know their God, trusting in him more and more each day.

But what of the other group of singles I mentioned earlier? The ones who have loved and lost?

Even as I write this, I know that there will be some who say, 'I understand this, and I was there once. Then I was part of a relationship that I thought was loving, but it went bad.' Or others, like Kim in her poignant story, who are confronted with the stark truth that the one they love has died. How can those who are in the midst of trauma find their way to the place of peace and hope?

---

7   John 16:13

Everyone's experience of pain is different, and I don't claim to have all the answers, but I hope I have words that can help. In that light, please come with me and let's explore together what it means to be single again.

> *"Recovery from the grief of becoming single again can be affected by many things such as poor financial status and the availability of support from family and friends."*

Single Again

When we think of people who are single again, we have to realise that this term covers a wide range of people at different stages of the process. Some of you who are reading this are still reeling from the breakdown of your marriage. Raw hurt is raging inside of you, yet you still have to talk civilly to your ex for the sake of your children. It can happen so suddenly, as Kim shared in her story. Maybe, like Kim, you've lost your beloved husband and friend to an accident or disease, and a tsunami of grief surges inside you as you try and keep a brave face to the world.

> *"Keep talking it over with God until you get a sense of what is right for you."*

It could be that you are a few months on from the devastation and you are picking up the pieces, bit by bit, and rebuilding your life. Maybe you are two years on and have moved on through the stages of grief. Hope is beginning to surge in your heart like new growth after a wildfire.

It could also be that you are experiencing a mix of these things. Life is rarely linear.

Recovery from the grief of becoming single again can be affected by many things such as poor financial status and the availability of support from family and friends. It can also be affected by where we live. If we are isolated from help or live in a war-torn region, recovery could be tough.

As I've mentioned, I've worked over the years with refugees and more recently, asylum seekers.[8] Many have stories that would make you weep. While there is much beauty in the world, there is also much evil, and I've seen the results of this firsthand.

Highly Favoured

In 2006, after many years working in schools as both a chaplain and youth pastor, I boarded a plane to Africa. I was excited to seek God's new direction for my life and to be spending a few months in the continent of my birth. I joined a large team of other Australians in a project called Hope Rwanda: 100 Days of Hope. This project, led by Mark and Darlene Zschech, was designed to bring hope and healing to Rwanda after the genocide in 1994 where over a million people were wiped out.[9]

---

8   In some countries, these terms are synonyms. In Australia, they are different. The Australian Government explains it this way: An *asylum seeker* is someone who is seeking international protection but whose claim for *refugee* status has not yet been determined. In contrast, a refugee is someone who has been recognised under the 1951 Convention relating to the status of *refugees* to be a *refugee*.

9   *History | Hope Global* 2020, HopeGlobal, viewed 13 September 2020, <https://hopeglobal.org/about/history/>.

After a sobering, life changing, two weeks, I headed to Uganda where I spent most of my time while I was in Africa.

> *"Just because you are in a difficult situation, doesn't mean that you are not highly esteemed by God."*

I went there to serve with the Australian missionary couple my local church was supporting at the time. Over the following few months I was asked to run youth seminars and equip both leaders and young people. I was also asked to work with the women in the community.

Up until then they'd had no women's ministry, so it was my responsibility to launch this and to design their first women's conference. I visited women in the community, some who belonged to the church and some who did not. It gave me an opportunity to hear each story. That way I could design a conference tailored to breathe new life and encouragement to the women of that region.

For over two weeks I walked with others through the small laneways and back streets of Uganda as we visited the women in their homes. Their stories showed their remarkable courage in the face of adversity. Many were fighting for their families and raising their children while their husbands were absent. As the two-day conference drew near, I was overwhelmed by God's love for each of the women I met, even though most focused at length on their suffering and hardship.

Many felt forgotten and thought no one saw their pain. I could see how resilient and courageous they were, but they could not.

As they spoke about their husbands abandoning them, some said they thought God had abandoned them. They told us about how defeated they felt, having to wake very early each day to sell goods and find food for their family. I wept for days and felt God speaking to me about the message he wanted to bring to these women at the conference.

I organised small gifts for each woman, including soap, body lotion, lollies and a beautiful yellow rose. We bought basins, washed each other's feet and gave the women pedicures and manicures. The day was filled with so much laughter: these girls had never had so much attention paid to them, nor had they looked after each other in this way.

There were two messages of encouragement that God placed on my heart for these women. The first was that they would be set free to worship God in the words of Moses to Pharaoh, 'Let my people go, so they may worship me...'[10] The second was according to the passage in Luke where the angel visits Mary and tells her she will conceive through the Holy Spirit.[11]

The message I brought to these women is the same as I bring to my sisters today who find themselves waiting, grieving or in complicated situations. Just because you are in a difficult situation, doesn't mean that you are not highly esteemed by God.

---

10   Exodus 7:16
11   Luke 1:26-38

The angel appeared to Mary: 'Greetings, you who are highly favoured, the Lord is with you!'[12] How wonderful to have an angel greet you like that. It's like a kiss from heaven!

The angel went on to say that Mary shouldn't be afraid. This makes me smile. How many times does an angelic being appear to the people in the Bible and say that? Do they forget they look huge, intimidating and scary? But in this case the content of the message was scary too. Mary would conceive and give birth to Jesus, the 'Son of the Most High.'[13]

There was a lot of expectation in Israel at that time. The coming of the Messiah was close and young women were wondering if they would be the one to give birth to the Christ: the one who would lead Israel out of bondage to the Romans. Mary would have known this and would have been hoping that when she married Joseph, she might be the one. Wow. Here was an angel telling her it would be her. Hang on. There was a problem. Mary wasn't married yet. She was a virgin.[14] How could God get it so wrong? Mary was a teenager, a virgin; and while she was betrothed to Joseph she wasn't married yet. In Mary's time, becoming pregnant when you weren't married was a shameful thing, punishable by death. It was the ultimate scandal a young woman could face. At the very least she would be put aside by Joseph and rejected by her community.[15] What could she do? How could she live?

---

12 Luke 1:28
13 Luke 1:29-33
14 Luke 1:34
15 Matthew 1:19-24 Fortunately Joseph listened to an angel sent by God and took Mary as his wife.

It amazes me that she said yes.[16] But God didn't get it wrong. He chose a young woman who was unimportant in the world's eyes to be the mother of the most important man who would ever walk the earth. God didn't choose a queen from a royal family so that his son would be born in a palace. He chose a girl of thirteen or fourteen years old and let his son, the Saviour of the world, be born in a stable because there was no room for him anywhere else. In his wisdom, and providence, he chose a humble girl in the midst of difficulty and called her, 'highly favoured'.

> *"Jesus was moving in the shadows of their daily lives and leading them, guiding them in his providence, esteeming and cherishing each one of them. Most importantly he was telling them he hadn't forgotten them."*

I told the Ugandan women that regardless of how they felt, God had sent *them* a messenger to tell them they were highly favoured. He was using me to remind them that he loved them and wasn't blind to their plight. They may think that because their husbands left and they had to work so long and hard to get enough food for their family, that God had left them, but not so. They were daughters of the King of Kings. Jesus was moving in the shadows of their daily lives and leading them, guiding them in his providence, esteeming and cherishing each one of them. Most importantly he was telling them he hadn't forgotten them.

---

16   Luke 1:38

Isn't that what we all need to know? No matter what our plight, Jesus hasn't forgotten us. We are highly esteemed daughters of the King. We have a Redeemer who is on our case and he longs for us to call on his name. It's not because of our own merit, or hard work. It's because of his mercy. We are his daughters and he is with us. Amen!

There is another Bible story that speaks into the lives of those who are single again – the book of Ruth.

My Redeemer Lives

Have you read Ruth? If you haven't, please do so. It's a rich and wonderful tale. Unlike Mary's story of angelic visitation, Ruth had no such help. All we see is the courage and kindness of a young woman and the providential redemption of her family.

The book opens with the stories of three widows. Famine drove Naomi, her husband Elimelek and her two sons, from Judah to the land of Moab. Elimelek died and her two sons married Moabite girls, Ruth and Orpah. Ten years later, both of Naomi's sons died, leaving all three women husbandless.[17]

When Naomi wanted to return home, Ruth made the choice to go with her. 'Don't urge me to leave you or turn back from you. Where you go, I will go, and where you stay, I will stay. Your people will be my people and your God my God. Where you die, I will die, and there I will be buried.'[18]

---

17 Ruth 1:1-5
18 Ruth 1:16-17

That's what I call loyalty. This is especially profound because it is generally held by Jewish rabbis that Ruth and her sister were daughters of the Moabite king, Eglon.[19] If this is correct, Ruth wasn't just a simple peasant woman. She would have had good prospects for marriage in her homeland – so her sacrifice in staying with Naomi, and following Naomi's God, was huge.

> *"She would have had good prospects for marriage in her homeland – so her sacrifice in staying with Naomi, and following Naomi's God, was huge."*

Ruth was proactive in caring for Naomi and gleaned for grain in the fields of a kind man named Boaz.[20] When Naomi realised Boaz was a close relative and 'guardian-redeemer' – a legal term for a relative who has the obligation to redeem a family member in serious difficulty – she told Ruth to dress in her best and lie at Boaz's feet.[21] Boaz interpreted Ruth's gesture as kindness and agreed to be her guardian-redeemer – and husband – if a closer relative didn't claim the right.[22] The other man gave up the right, and Boaz married Ruth and took on all the property of Elimelek and his sons, maintaining the property in Elimelek's name.[23] Ruth then gave birth to Obed, who gave birth to Jesse,

---

19 T Meir 2009, *Ruth: Midrash and Aggadah*, Jewish Women's Archive, viewed 13 September 2020, <https://jwa.org/encyclopedia/article/ruth-midrash-and-aggadah>.

20 Ruth 2:1-3

21 Leviticus 25:25-55; Ruth 3:1-4

22 Ruth 3:10-13

23 Ruth 4:3-10

who gave birth to David – who became king.[24] Both Ruth and Boaz are later named in the genealogy of Jesus.[25]

Wow, that's redemption. Can you see God's providential hand at work behind the scenes, guiding each of the people here? That's how he works in our lives too: strengthening us, enabling us, empowering us for his purposes – even when we can't see what he's doing.

When I read the book of Ruth it strikes me how much Ruth's story parallels Kim's.

> *"Both women needed to trust God amidst challenges beyond just their grief."*

1. Neither women chose their situation. They didn't want their husbands to die.
2. But when it did happen both women *chose* to focus on God and follow him. For Ruth it was a decision to move beyond her Moabite heritage and identify with Naomi's God. For Kim it was to trust in God and believe he still loved her, and had a purpose for her, no matter what her circumstances.
3. Both stayed in community with those who loved them. Ruth with Naomi and Kim with her children and church family.
4. Both asked 'what?' rather than 'why?' You can see this in Ruth's decision to glean in the fields and to follow Naomi's guidance. Whereas Kim asks questions like, 'What would God have me do now?'

---

24 Ruth 4:17
25 Matthew 1:5

5. Both women needed to trust God amidst challenges beyond just their grief. When Darren died, Kim battled some of the stigma of singleness we talked about earlier. People would ask awkward questions and she felt like an outsider when she went to gatherings by herself. She also felt isolated because she was no longer part of the leadership of her church. For Ruth it would have been leaving her people and her social status. She too was an outsider. She may also have felt scared when she first started gleaning in the fields. Would she be assaulted? And what if Boaz had forced himself on her and disgraced her when she lay at his feet?
6. But both Ruth and Kim experienced God's providence – in powerful ways – as they trusted in him. Boaz married Ruth and took on the lands of Elimelek and his sons. Kim rebuilt her life, supported her kids. She even married again.

When we face challenges, especially difficulties like becoming single again, let's lean into these stories and follow the example of these women to find the courage we need in our dark times. God is our ever-present help. Note that both Ruth and Kim trusted in God *no matter what*. Both had a happy ending, but this isn't always the case. We can't rely on circumstances to make us feel content.

Look at my life. I'd like to find a husband, but it hasn't happened yet. The truth is it may never happen, but that doesn't mean that God isn't good, or that he doesn't love me, or that he doesn't have wonderful plans for me. He adores me, as he does you, and he will work all things to our good as it says in Romans 8:28. But his plans for us may not always be the plans we hope for.

Are we willing to follow Jesus, no matter what happens? This is key in our walk as singles. Sometimes we are tempted to approach God with a what's-in-it-for-me mentality. The idea that if we do all the right things then God will give us good things. But is he only God when he gives us what we are after? If we take this approach, we can lose sight of our faith and who God really is in our lives. We can end up in despair and give up on God when our particular wants don't come through. But life isn't reward-based. Look at Kim, who was serving God with her husband in significant ways when he died.

Lean into God and know that your story is still unfolding. Your *yes* to him has ripple effects in the lives of others, releasing freedom in all kinds of ways. When we are kind to others like Ruth was and walk with God with purpose and strength, like Kim, he can do beautiful things in and through us. God's call extends to others, even when life is tough. Let's be encouraged – stirred by the tenacity of faith of Ruth, Kim and many of the Ugandan women I spoke of. Let's lean into Jesus through the seasons he brings. Be like my maman, who began each day with worship and prayer no matter what challenges she faced. We are called to a life that is more about who we are becoming and less about what we wish to get. How important this is when we realise our life is but a glimpse in the context of eternity.

I'd like to encourage every one of you to know you are prized by the one who matters most. I'd love you to read Isaiah 54. It's the best encouragement ever for single women. Look at verse five and ponder all the different names of God. Each one has something to say about his nature. Our *Maker* is our *husband*,

Lord Almighty, Redeemer, the Holy One of Israel and *God of all the earth.*

How amazing is that? The weight and richness found in just that one verse can settle our hearts. He is on our side! Let's colour our lives in creative ways, leaning into him and sharing our deepest desires. If we follow him in all things, he will always be with us and we will experience his grace and friendship. It doesn't matter what kind of single we are. If we keep him first in our focus, he will give us the strength to meet the challenges each day brings, and we will be like the weaned child King David describes: quiet, still, and content to rest on our maker's breast.[26]

Are you inspired yet? We've been looking at some of the issues single people face and how to walk with strength in God, but in the next chapter I'd like to take a slightly different tack. As I've written about desires, delays, loss, and the stigma that singles sometimes face – as well as the contentment and colour that can fill our lives – it has become obvious that every one of us needs to live out of our *identity* and *purpose* in God. I've mentioned these words a few times, haven't I?

The problem is that this is a struggle for many women. It's as if there is a tide pulling us out to sea, away from our goals, purposes and self-respect.

What is that tide?

---

26 Psalm 131:2

I think it comes from our place in history. How we've been perceived and treated as women throughout the ages. With that in mind, I'd like to look away from singleness for a moment and take a brief tour through history. I'd like us to take a glimpse at the place, purpose and role of women through the ages.

> *"Look at my life. I'd like to find a husband, but it hasn't happened yet. The truth is it may never happen, but that doesn't mean that God isn't good, or that he doesn't love me, or that he doesn't have wonderful plans for me."*

HERSTORY

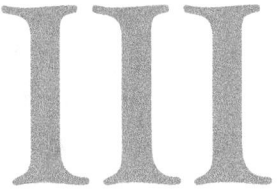

LIZZY

My name is Nyangak Dobol Kuoth, but people call me Lizzy. I was born in Sudan on 15th of August 1991. In 1998, our sole caretaker, our mother, was in a terrible accident and there was no proper medical assistance. I was only six years old when I witnessed my mother bleed to death. As for my father, he had abandoned us when I was a toddler. You can imagine the loneliness I felt as a young girl with no parents to care for me. There was just me, my three brothers and my thoughts.

But then I was separated from my brothers. My grandmother came to mourn my mother's death and decided to raise my 2-year-old brother, Lang. My 4-year-old brother, Rout, and our older brother, Goy, stayed with my mother's older sister. One of my aunties took me in but in 2001 I returned to be with my grandmother. I remember always feeling that I was missing out, especially when I saw kids with their mothers and fathers.

I migrated to Australia in 2005 with my grandmother, my two younger siblings and our cousin as refugees and settled in Melbourne. Like many other South Sudanese people, the civil war forced us to leave our country. We spent some years as refugees in Egypt. The hardship my grandmother suffered, at the age of over 70 years, in order to provide for us was apparent. She worked as a cleaner to provide us with basic requirements such as food and my schooling. Seeing my grandmother work so hard as I was growing up, made me admire her strength but also feel sad.

It was important for me to share with you my background as it has a lot to do with how my life turned out. From a very early age I experienced turmoil and strife including the harsh reality of being on my own and having no one to share my fears and aspirations with. I had to learn to rediscover myself and enjoy my own company. As my grandmother always told me, 'You are your own best friend'. She helped me during those periods when I was seeking the approval of others a little too desperately, putting others first before my own needs. If I put on a miniskirt she'd say, 'my darling granddaughter, you look cute in that but by all means avoid bending over'. My grandmother was a kidder, and she could usually make me laugh. In laughing, I was able to reflect on my decisions and do what best suited me, and in this case, I'd wear clothes according to how I felt as opposed to dressing to impress.

My grandmother also gave me a piece of advice when she caught me worrying too much about boys not liking me. 'An educated woman has a lot more to give,' she told me, and she impressed upon me that a bright intellect, a curious mind, and a passion for learning were priceless commodities. For that reason, I always thought that forcing a young woman into marriage was the worst thing to do. Since men in my culture can have multiple wives or leave you for another woman, I strove to be smart.

To this day, when I am approached by a guy it's second nature for me to point a finger at the side of my head and ask, does he think I need a prince charming to rescue me? Would he add any value to my life? I had my first boyfriend at 16 years old and he dumped me for refusing sex. My grandmother's words stayed with me and I remained single for a while. What I've learned so far is this: if women don't know their worth, they may decide to buy into the societal pressures and expectations that being alone is something a woman should be ashamed of. The fallout of their fear of loneliness is putting aside their needs, hopes and ambitions. I didn't want to be like that.

I realise that the word 'alone' needs to be redefined for it has a negative connotation. I don't presume to be an expert on dating, or all the issues people face. I have however, encountered men and women representing all the age groups and circumstances during my years serving as a community leader and assisting disadvantaged communities. Women sometimes choose – or are forced into – bad relationships and tolerate being treated as sex objects. Others are told that their place is in the kitchen. They stay in a committed relationship with men who are physically and emotionally abusive, because they devalue the power that being on their own can bring them.

Life has those moments when everything seems too hard and you ask yourself, 'Am I going to die alone?' But I've learned to acknowledge that those times pass and that I've got my own back. I owe it to myself to be excited about new opportunities, go on adventures on my own and am not going to waste a minute waiting on someone to knock me off my feet.

I decided a long time ago that I was the captain of my ship. I am a thinker and would do what I saw would fit me well, and this self-assurance helped me with many of my shortcomings with guys. It also helped me to move on, even after a bad break-up. I *have only dated five individuals over the course of my life and was dumped three times. I could look at it from a negative perspective and punish myself for my failures in the dating department or simply appreciate the gift of my ability to be a single, happy woman whose life is in her own hands.*

I tell myself every now and then that I am beautiful and any man who's lucky enough to be in my life will stay – for the rights reasons. I have never sent a rude message to an ex, or spoken ill of them even to myself, because I believe we are all on a journey to discover ourselves. Some learn better through others and some find answers within themselves. No one is completely single; we all carry with us someone we deeply care about, in our thoughts and hearts, so I cherish those moments spent alone.

7

LOOKING BACK

I have a passion for history. I love it. I can spend hours researching events of the past, getting lost in worlds very different from the present day in which I live. I also love how studying the past can give us wisdom that can help us live today. This is certainly true when we look at the role of women.

At the end of the last chapter, I spoke of the tide that can work against women – pulling us away from our goals – reducing our self-respect and sense of purpose. I said that I believed this tide to be linked with how women have been perceived in history. So, in this part, ladies, I'd like us to look at our story. Sometimes to go forward, we have to look backwards. What are the events that have shaped us and made us who we are? How have they pushed us back and limited us? How have women risen to the challenge and overcome these limitations?

This subject is huge and I can't possibly cover it in one small chapter. But have you ever travelled to a big city and taken one of those hop-on-hop-off bus tours? I have. I remember a time when I would take a trip around the world almost every second year. There was much to see, especially in the gorgeous cities of Europe, so I would take a hop-on-hop-off tour. It let me see the main sights, but I could get off the bus and explore when I wanted to see something in more detail. Think of this chapter like one of those tour buses. We'll look at some key issues but stop and dip into more detail when we hit something really interesting and important. Note that I'm also going to limit this topic to the discussion of women in the Bible, the West and Africa because of my dual heritage. Even that is a huge task – but our hop-on-hop-off bus will get us there.

As the Bible has had a profound influence on how many cultures see women, let's start there. Ready to ride? Climb on board! You've got the best seat.

Women in the Bible

I believe God wanted humanity to have what he had in the trinity of Father, Son and Spirit – true community – with man and women working together in perfect loving harmony. But that's not what happened. The role of women in the Bible began well but became fragmented after the fall.

God made Eve by taking a rib out of Adam. She was made from him, for him, to be one with him. What must it have been like for Adam and Eve to behold each other's beauty for the first time, as they stood in their unspoiled Eden? Can you hear Adam's delight when he recognises that his God-given partner is, 'bone of my bones and flesh of my flesh'?[1]

---

1   Genesis 2:23 (a)

Can you imagine God's satisfaction at their joy? The first humans, made in God's image, working together for God's glory. What a magnificent picture.

But something went very wrong. Satan, in the form of a serpent, tempted humanity to want the one thing that they couldn't have: eating from the fruit of the tree of knowledge of good and evil. Satan said they could be like God. The tragedy is that they were already made in God's image. First Eve and then Adam ate the fruit that made them realise they were naked – and want to hide.[2]

> *"The first Biblical surrogacy recorded –
> but that didn't end well."*

They indeed gained knowledge of good and evil. They also lost everything. Adam was cursed with hard toil as he worked the land. Eve was cursed with pain of childbirth – and the dominion of her husband over her.[3]

Equality, harmony and dignity were replaced by strife. In the exchange with God, Adam blamed Eve: 'The woman you put here with me—she gave me some fruit from the tree, and I ate it.'[4] And women have contended with Eve's failure and Adam's buck-passing, ever since.

---

2   Genesis 3:8-10
3   Genesis 3:16-19
4   Genesis 3:12

But what happened after those days? Did Eve's penalty outwork in the lives of Old Testament women?

In the Old Testament as a whole, the greater the status of the woman, the more power they retained, and the less they felt the penalty of Eve's subjugation. The prominent matriarchs of the Torah[5] – Sarah, Rebekah, Leah and Rachel – had a different life experience than the servants and slaves of that time. But at the core was childbearing, the very thing that brought them pain. And they would stop at nothing to get children.

Surrogacy

Let's look at Sarah for example. Sarah, known as Sara, when we first meet her, was the wife of Abram, later to be known as Abraham. God's covenant with Abram was that he would make Abram into a great nation.[6] Yet Sara's childlessness was Abram's great tragedy.[7] God had told him, 'a son who is your own flesh and blood will be your heir' and that Abram's descendants would be so vast in number they would outnumber the stars in the sky.[8] Abram and Sara tried to make this happen by taking Sara's servant Hagar as his concubine – the first Biblical surrogacy recorded – but that didn't end well.[9] Later God told Abram that it was by God's power that Abram's true wife, the old and barren Sara, would have a child.

---

5   The Torah refers to the first five books of the Old Testament: Genesis, Exodus, Leviticus, Numbers and Deuteronomy. Also known in Greek as the Pentateuch.
6   Genesis 12:2
7   Genesis 15:3
8   Genesis 15:4-5
9   Genesis 16

> *"Marriage in these times was so centred on maintaining bloodlines that this kind of close kinship marriage was common."*

You can see God's grace here. He could have let Abraham sire the nation of Israel through a concubine, but instead made Sarah an equal partner with Abraham in the birth of God's people. She wasn't discarded or deemed unimportant. In fact, Sarah had considerable authority. It was Sarah's suggestion that Hagar be used as a surrogate and it was on her insistence that Hagar and her son Ishmael were banished from their household.[10]

What a difficult situation for Hagar. Her plight shows the powerlessness of the servant, but it also shows how God in his grace cared for her. I mentioned earlier how God helped Hagar and made Ishmael into a great nation. Those of us in difficult circumstances today can take heart from that. We can also be encouraged by the story of Sarah and Abraham. Despite trying to take matters into their own hands, God was faithful. They received the answer to God's promise by having their son Isaac in their old age. God is so good. Never rule out what he can do.

Rebekah, wife of Isaac and mother of Jacob and Esau was followed by Rachel and Leah, wives of Jacob, and daughters of Laban.[11] Note that these latter two women are Jacob's first cousins. Marriage in these times was so centred on

---

10 Genesis 21:8-20. If Abram and Sara had trusted in God and not tried to do his work for him Ishmael would not have been born and he and his mother would not have been banished. But God was gracious and helped them, making Ishmael into a great nation.

11 Genesis 24, 27

maintaining bloodlines that this kind of close kinship marriage was common.[12] Not only did cousins marry and female slaves find themselves given as surrogates, but incest took place. An example of this was when Lot's daughters got him drunk and slept with him so they could have children.[13] Similarly, Tamar tricked Judah, her father-in-law, into sleeping with her so great was her drive to have children.[14]

> *"To not have children was to be insignificant and powerless."*

Astle points out that every preeminent figure of the ancestral period of the scriptures, be they man or woman, is renowned because of their parenthood.[15] To not have children was to be insignificant and powerless.

The Nameless Girl

One example of extreme female powerlessness is seen in the story of the daughter of Jephthah. This is one of the saddest stories I've read in the Bible – a young girl has her future ripped away from her because her father makes an impulsive vow.[16] In the midst of battle, Jephthah prays this: *'If you give the Ammonites into my hands, whatever comes out of the door of my*

---

12   C Astle 2019, *Who Were the Matriarchs of the Torah*, Learn Religions, viewed 14 April 2020, <https://www.learnreligions.com/women-of-torah-israel-co-founders-116361>.

13   Genesis 19:30-38

14   Genesis 38

15   Astle 2019

16   Judges 11

house to meet me when I return in triumph from the Ammonites will be the Lord's, and I will sacrifice it as a burnt offering.'[17]

Of course, when he returns home it is Jephthah's beloved daughter who runs out to greet him. A vow is a vow, so she must die, even though human sacrifice was a pagan practice and against Israel's Levitical law.[18] She was allowed just two months to roam the hills with her friends.[19] Her story breaks my heart. She is never named – an indication of how powerless she is. She has no rights, she has no identity of her own, and is seen to be the property of her father. Not only is she sentenced to die, but her great grief is that she will never have children and be able to carry on the family line. Everything that defines her as a woman has been taken from her.

It was hard to be a woman in those times. But not all the stories of Old Testament women revolve around childbearing or patriarchal power. I love how there were women of old who showed strength and did great exploits irrespective of their marital or childbearing status.

> *"She has no rights, she has no identity of her own, and is seen to be the property of her father."*

Heroic Women

Women performed many heroic deeds. Consider Miriam, sister of Moses, who led the song of praise after God parted the Red

---

17   Judges 11:30-31
18   Leviticus 20:1-5
19   Judges 11:37

Sea.[20] Then there was Deborah – a prophet and a judge – who rode into battle with Barak, the general God told her to appoint. Her military decisions led to the deliverance of her people.[21] There was Rahab – the prostitute who hid the Israelite spies in Jericho – and who was named in Jesus' genealogy.[22] And there was Esther, the queen who delivered her people from genocide by risking her life to go before the King without being summoned. This was an act that could have been punished by death but her bravery lead to the overcoming of an enemy plot against her people.[23]

There were many other brave women whose stories are told in the Old Testament, but I don't have time to talk about them all here.[24] One I will mention is the woman from Proverbs 31. She was praised because she was a woman who feared God and this is reflected in how she lived her life.[25] She was a leader in her household, a brilliant businesswoman and a wife who honoured her husband. Verse 10 tells us that to her husband she was worth 'far more than rubies'. Rubies are very valuable and precious stones. If you ever marry, wouldn't it be amazing to hear your husband say that about you?

---

20 Exodus 15:21
21 Judges 4
22 Joshua 2, Matthew 1:5.
23 Esther 4-6
24 I Nowell n.d., *Roles of Women in the Old Testament*, Pontifical Council for the Laity, viewed 9 April 2020, <http://www.laici.va/content/dam/laici/documenti/donna/bibbia/english/roles-women-old-testament.pdf>. This is an excellent short summary of women who made a difference in the Old testament though their heroic actions.
25 Proverbs 31:30(b)

So far on our hop-on-hop-off bus tour through Bible history we've seen that women lost much after the tragedy of the fall and that in the many years that followed, her fate was mixed. Her identity and worth were tied up with a mix of social status and childrearing. Magnificent matriarchs helped build a nation by having children, while slaves, servants and unmarried daughters wept in their powerlessness. Despite this, other women of strength were honoured in the name of God. But what happened as the days of the Old Testament came to a close? How were women faring by the time of Jesus?

> *"Mix this with stories like that of Jephthah's daughter, add a dash of oral tradition, and a tincture of patriarchal power and you have a recipe for pain."*

Judaism, Jesus and Paul
It is fair to say that by New Testament times, the view of women had degraded in Jewish belief and practice.

First century Judaism had several streams of thought, based on both the Bible and on oral tradition. While some of these streams honoured women as mothers, most had a limited view of what women could do outside of the home. Men were seen to have a public role, but women had to remain in private – confined to the sphere of the family. A woman couldn't testify in court or engage in commerce. She was rarely seen outside her home and could only engage in a small trade if she had no other support. If she was on the streets she had to be veiled and couldn't speak with men. She couldn't even do her own shopping unless she went accompanied by a slave. Many women couldn't read and teaching them the Torah was considered foolish by some. They could go to the Temple but had to stay in the Women's Court and couldn't participate in public prayer.[26]

Glasser thinks it's possible that this bias originated from Greek thought,[27] but the glimpse we've had of the Old Testament shows that much of the problem goes back to the blame placed on Eve at the fall. Mix this with stories like that of Jephthah's daughter, add a dash of oral tradition, and a tincture of patriarchal power and you have a recipe for pain. It's no wonder the Jewish prayer book has the infamous line: 'Blessed are You, Hashem our G-d, King of the universe, for not having made me a woman.'[28]

> *"Jesus shattered rabbinical expectations.*
> *He taught women as well as men."*

Many of us would grieve and be confused if this was where the Bible left us, but praise God, Jesus had a different idea. His regard for women was revolutionary.

Jesus shattered rabbinical expectations. He taught women as well as men. He broke tradition when he spoke to a Samaritan woman at a well, teaching her about the Holy Spirit and

---

26 Z Glaser 1988, *Jesus and the Role of Women*. Jews for Jesus, viewed 9 April 2020, <https://jewsforjesus.org/publications/newsletter/newsletter-jun-1988/jesus-and-the-role-of-women/>. This is a good summary of how Judaism perceived the role of women at this time.

27 Glaser 1988.

28 RL Kohn 2017, *Women in Judaism: Who Hast Not Made Me a Woman Part I*, Torah.org, viewed 9 April 2020, <https://torah.org/learning/women-class31>. While the prayer book, or siddur, was finalised in the seventh century, AD., its roots went back to the Torah.

sending her back to her village to tell her people about him. Many believed in him as a result of her preaching.[29]

Jesus associated with women of all kinds of social standing, even prostitutes like Mary Magdalene.[30] After Jesus' resurrection, he charged Mary Magdalene and the other Mary with telling the disciples that he had come back to life. Mary – a woman – was the first preacher after the resurrection. What an honour![31]

When Jesus visited the home of Mary and Martha, not only did he let Mary sit at his feet and be taught like the other disciples, he commended her for choosing the better thing – compared with Martha's extensive meal preparation.[32]

But what about the apostle Paul? Paul is often perceived to have a bias against women. In 1 Timothy 2:11-15 he writes:

A woman should learn in quietness and full submission. I do not permit a woman to teach or to assume authority over a man; she must be quiet. For Adam was formed first, then Eve. And Adam was not the one deceived; it was the woman who was deceived and became a sinner. But women will be saved through childbearing—if they continue in faith, love and holiness with propriety.[33]

---

29   John 4
30   Matthew 28:5-7
31   Matthew 28:10
32   Luke 10:38-42
33   1 Timothy 2:11-15

Paul seems here to be denying a woman's right to lead or teach in church – basing this on Eve's role in the fall – and that childbirth would save her. But is this what he meant?

Good interpretation of the Bible requires a) understanding a verse in the light of other scripture and b) understanding the context into which the words were spoken. In Romans 5 Paul declares that as death came through Adam, life comes through Christ.[34] In essence Jesus is the second Adam who came to undo the curse of the fall. In the book of Acts, women and men prayed together as they waited in the upper room.[35] In Romans 16:3 the Apostle Paul calls women co-labourers in Christ, and in 16:7, he names Junia, a woman, as an apostle. In Galatians he declares women are one in Christ with men because they have the Spirit of Sonship.[36]

> *"While God's word is always true, the interpretation of God's word may not always be correct."*

As far as context goes, the book of 1 Timothy was written by Paul to correct wrong teaching that was springing up in Ephesus. Paul was speaking to a particular situation where prostitutes from the temple cult of Artemis were being saved and becoming part of that church. These women were young Christians and they were teaching wrong things and dressing in the wrong way. Paul told them to be quiet, dress modestly and

---

34 Romans 5:12-20
35 Acts 1:13
36 Galatians 3:28-4:7

learn from others. They were to trust Christ – not Artemis – for help with childbirth.[37]

Paul wasn't discriminating against women at all, nor was he setting rules Christians were meant to live by forever. He was pragmatically speaking into a serious pastoral issue in a young church. Unfortunately, his words have been misinterpreted and used as a means of limiting the role of women in both the church and the world for the last two thousand years.

> *"In Romans 16:3 the Apostle Paul calls women co-labourers in Christ."*
> *"Paul wasn't discriminating against women at all, nor was he setting rules Christians were meant to live by forever."*

Our hop-on-hop-off bus tour of the Bible has shown that having children was an important and cherished role for women in biblical times. This makes sense. Procreation was essential for pioneering a nation and women are unique in their ability to give life to another human being. We are child bearers and nurturers with a God-given desire to give birth and extend humanity. But what about those of us who are single and can't have children?

Like Eve, we are made in God's image. We belong to God. We are his daughters – children of the king – and are not limited

---

37 AJ Young 2007, *Short Answers to Challenging Texts: 1 Timothy 2:11-15*, CBE International, viewed 9 April 2020, <https://www.cbeinternational.org/resources/article/other/short-answers-challenging-texts-1-timothy-211-15>.

by our gender, marital status or the colour of our skin. The teachings of Jesus, Paul and indeed the depiction of the heroic women throughout the scriptures show that women have value and purpose beyond the realm of family and children. There is a big difference between a view that says women have an important, cherished role in society by being a mother, and a view that says the only importance of women is to be married and have children.

> *"There is a big difference between a view that says women have an important, cherished role in society by being a mother, and a view that says the only importance of women is to be married and have children."*

Yet women throughout history have often been limited by a patriarchal understanding of God's word. While God's word is always true, the *interpretation* of God's word may not always be correct. Historically, the Bible has generally been both written and expounded from a male perspective, be they Jew, Greek, Eastern or Western.

This problem has spilled from the church into the world. Male-led authority structures have limited the role of women in many societies, including those that make up the vast and beautiful continent of Africa.

Let's go there now and see what happened.

Women in Africa
And now we arrive at the beautiful continent of Africa – a vast land made up of over fifty countries – many of which have

a complex history where women are concerned. How do we approach this? Can you imagine so many different tribes and ethnic groups, all with their own customs, laws and history? The experience of women is different in each of these places and I can't hope to address then individually. The good news is African women share many things in common. I'd like to look at some of the general principles that apply to most African women and then focus for a while on my homeland – the Democratic Republic of the Congo (DRC) which was formerly part of the Kingdom of Kongo.

"History is always influenced by the one recording it."

Before we start, I must tell you that much of the historical record of African nations prior to colonialisation has been lost. Ours was an oral tradition. In my country, the women would tell stories around the campfire, teaching the young ones about what had gone before. But history is always influenced by the one recording it. The one who is in a position of power writes with a bias toward their opinions or point of view. Where societies are patriarchal, the voice of women can be lost. Where war and conquest have ravaged a land, the voice of the invaded will be quashed.

That is what happened within Africa. Western explorers recorded their own history when they arrived, giving it their interpretation, and over the years many African stories were suppressed or lost. Virtually nothing of what was written has been told through an African woman's eyes. While efforts are being made to recover and write down these stories, I am still relying on oral tradition, passed to me by elders of my people, for some of what I'm going to explain to you.

Let's begin by looking at some of the things common to African women before colonialisation took place.

"Western explorers recorded their own history when they arrived, giving it their interpretation, and over the years many African stories were suppressed or lost."

Before Colonialisation

In many places in Africa, especially in the western regions, women were respected, even revered.[38] She dominated the labour force, agriculture and home to maintain the family as well as its finance, selling wares at the markets.[39] The political area was largely the domain of men but in many tribes the chiefs couldn't make major decisions without consulting the women.[40] Patrilineal groups predominated but there were also matrilineal groups that had women at the centre of kinship and family.[41]

It is generally held that girls married young – at about thirteen years of age – and fertility was prized. Childbearing was of the utmost importance. Polygamy was at the heart of African culture with most men having two to ten wives, although some

---

38 C Coquery-Vidrovitch 1997, African Women: A Modern History (Social Change in Global Perspective), USA, Westview Press, pp.10–13.

39 Coquery-Vidrovitch 1997, pp 30-33.

40 K Sheldon 2017, African Women and early history to the 21st century, Indiana University press, Bloominghton, 32-34.

41 Coquery-Vidrovitch 1997, pp. 9-10.

kings and chiefs had many more.[42] To have many wives and many children was a sign of wealth and fertility. Unlike China where girls had little value, in Africa girls were seen as a source of wealth – a good opportunity for future income.[43]

> *"If his women were rich, a man was rich. Can you hear echoes of the Proverbs 31 woman here?"*

This value fluctuated depending on where she lived. Tswana girls, for example, were abused sexually and physically at initiation, supposedly so she would know the pain of childbirth and develop a subservient attitude.[44] As a wife, she had little control over her affairs and worked hard in the field and in the home. She looked after her children, but she had no authority in her society and was little more than a 'beast of burden' and a slave to her husband.[45] But in many western African regions, even though the man had the final say in the overall production from the land, women often made business decisions and had their own stores of goods. The men liked it this way. If his women were rich, a man was rich. Can you hear echoes of the Proverbs 31 woman here?

Not all women in Africa's history were limited to the home and business realm. Africa has had its share of royal women warriors. Many women of power fought bravely, with grace and dignity, for what they believed in.

---

42 Coquery-Vidrovitch 1997, pp.9-13.
43 Coquery-Vidrovitch 1997, pp 10.
44 Coquery-Vidrovitch 1997, pp12-15.
45 Coquery-Vidrovitch 1997, pp12-15.

Warrior Women

Amanirenas was a Nubian Queen who ruled the wealthy kingdom of Kush from about 40BC to 10BC, taking power after the death of her husband. She was known for her sharp leadership and political skills and for leading the Kushites in many battles against the mighty Roman empire – and winning (27BC – 22BC).[46] There were many others. Hatshepsut of Egypt, Njinga of Matamba, and Amina of Zaria – who sacrificed marriage and motherhood for the sake of leadership – come to mind.[47] All were princesses and rulers within their lands. More recently, Yaa Asantewaa (1840 – 1921) is famous for leading the Ashanti war, known as the War of the Golden Stool, against British colonialism.[48] [49]

"Africa has had its share of royal women warriors. I love how these – and many other – African women stood up and fought for their homelands."

I love how these – and many other – African women stood up and fought for their homelands. We need to remember them and be inspired by them, but we also have to realise they were

---

46 *Amanirenas 2020*, Wikipedia, viewed 4 April 2020, <https://en.wikipedia.org/wiki/Amanirenas>.

47 J Hansen & L McGaw 2004, *African Princess: The Amazing Lives of Africa's Royal Women*, Hyperion, New York, pp. 6-23.

48 J Kabamba 2017, *Joëlle Kabamba - African Heroines Unveiled*, The Collaborative Radio Project, viewed 27 Feb. 2020, <https://soundcloud.com/user-59442898/Joëlle-final>.

49 A Aidoo 1977, 'Asante Queen Mothers in Government and Politics in The Nineteenth Century', *Journal of the Historical Society of Nigeria*, Vol 9, No. 1, pp. 1- 13, viewed April 5, 2020, <www.jstor.org/stable/41857049>.

outliers. The average African woman had no way of exerting this kind of authority. However, she was still very important.

The Value of Women

The best way to explain the regard in which women were held in many African ethnic groups comes from discussions I've had with various Congolese elders.[50]

African people often use symbols to explain their understanding of life. Men are represented by a pyramid symbol while women are represented by a lozenge symbol, which has two pyramids joined at their base, one of which is upside down. You can see these symbols on many African art works and fabric designs. The male pyramid represents 'the day' whereas the lozenge represents both 'the day' and 'the night'. Man's power operates during the day whereas the woman has power both in the day and the night – and also with the living and the dead. In traditional African culture, the spirits of the dead live on and take care of the living. Women are said to have direct contact with the spirits and ancestors and hence they can lead by intuition.[51] So while Africa was a man's world as far as day to day living went, women had power in all realms. Her importance was woven into the full fabric of her society.

Unfortunately, European colonialisation and its patriarchal structures began to break that fabric down.

---

50 Several people have helped me in this regard. These include Dr Clovis Mwamba, Ms Jeanne Ntamounoza, my sister Chantal Kabamba, and my father Dr Andre Kabamba.

51 Dr Clovis Mwamba, word of mouth.

Colonialisation

When Portuguese explorers and missionaries reached the Kingdom of Kongo in the late fifteenth century, they found a rich civilisation containing self-sufficient cities that swarmed with crowds dressed in silk and velvet.[52] There was great order and beauty – mountains covered with houses filled with people living significant lives of commerce and trade. The land was fertile and the earth rich with copper and gold. It was an iron-age community. This meant that the people had the weapons and tools needed to both prosper in trade and defend their land successfully against other nations.[53]

At first some of the outside influence was good. Coquery-Vidrovitch says that the burden on oppressed women such as the Tswana may have been lighter after colonialisation, but she also notes that as we have no record seen through the eyes of the women, it is hard to tell.[54] In the Congo, women were given access to education, albeit at the cost of personal treasure buried on their land. The missionaries also told people about Jesus. Theoretically that should have been a great thing. The African people had a deep spirituality and understood from their own traditions that there was one God. They weren't 'Christian' – they hadn't heard of Jesus yet – but they did believe in one God who was connected to the land and their lives. This background meant that many were open to hearing about this new God and many believed. However, there was a problem. Some of the priests began to teach that black people

---

[52] S Serbin 2018, 'Reines d'Afrique et héroïnes de la diaspora noire' de l'écrivaine et historienne., MeduNeter, Paris, France, pp. 283–297.

[53] Serbin 2018 pp. 283-297.

[54] Coquery-Vidrovitch 1997, p. 15.

wouldn't be in heaven, and the authorities oppressed the people in many ways.⁵⁵ It's likely that there were good men of God who spoke of a true gospel within their tradition, but religion mixed with the politics of power and greed is a recipe for despair. I suspect that this false teaching was a way of dehumanising the people, making them feel lesser and justifying the escalating slave trade to other Europeans.

The patriarchal powers did not like the influence women had in the society – it didn't fit with their patriarchal world view – and they worked to diminish her role in the eyes of the men. Despite this, some women rose up against the colonialists to give spiritual leadership to their people. The most significant of these was Kimpa Vita, known after her conversion and baptism as Dona Beatriçe.⁵⁶

In 1704 an African Saint, Anthony visited Dona Beatriçe in a vision.⁵⁷ Beatriçe was inspired to use Kongo cultural symbolism to create a church that was incarnationally African. She was Saint Anthony incarnate, Christ was born in São Salvador and the church fathers were also African.⁵⁸ She gained a significant following and the Portuguese were scared they would lose their authority. They pressured the ruler of the Kongo, Pedro IV, to have her killed. In 1706 she had a child, while claiming to be a virgin. This gave the Capuchin priests a reason to apprehend her. She was accused of witchcraft and burned at the stake

---

55 Serbin 2018, p. 295.
56 Coquery-Vidrovitch 1997, p. 43.
57 Coquery-Vidrovitch 1997, p. 43.
58 Coquery-Vidrovitch 1997, p. 44.

when she was only 24 years old – becoming known as the Joan of Arc of the Kongo.[59]

> *"The African people had a deep spirituality and understood from their own traditions that there was one God."*

As history progressed and The Kingdom of Kongo was broken up into smaller countries, the persecution against the Congolese people continued. I don't know of any instance of colonialisation by any ethnic group that has not resulted in oppression, death, slavery and rape of both the first nation people, and their land. Of all oppressors, King Leopold II of Belgium, was one of the most evil. He acquired the Congo Free State in 1885 and proceeded to rape the land of its resources. Millions of Congolese died due to exploitation and disease.[60] In 1908, after international intervention by the United Kingdom, the Belgium parliament took over the country from Leopold. Things improved but throughout the 20th and 21st centuries there has been strife upon strife in my homeland through the corruption and injustice that has stemmed from these events. This has happened despite the DRC gaining independence in 1960. The mineral deposits and other natural resources in the DRC are so rich that they could supply the whole of Africa. It is therefore not an accident that the strife, contention and

---

59 Coquery-Vidrovitch 1997, p. 44.

60 *Democratic Republic of the Congo* 2019, Wikipedia, Wikimedia Foundation, viewed 5 April 2020, <https://en.wikipedia.org/wiki/Democratic_Republic_of_the_Congo>.

exploitation experienced by the Congo throughout the centuries, continues to this day.[61]

Women have borne the brunt of the strife. The ravaging of the land and her people in general has been manifest in recent years as rape epidemics of women. Our time is too limited for me to share all the details but the attack of evil on what is now the DRC continues to strike at the women – the fabric of the society. Accounts of pack rape and brutal torture continue to be heard from a country that has been called the rape capital of the world.[62]

I know that there are many other countries with similar history.

Have events, such as these, caused the African woman to lose her confidence? In some places it's been shattered. Centuries of abuse and dehumanisation of the people has created a state where the men do not know how to fight for their women. Today the men abandon many women who are raped because they believe raped women are cursed.

> *"Mary – a woman – was the first preacher after the resurrection. What an honour!"*

---

61 A Kabamba 2010, *Humanitarian Crisis in the Congo*, Acrok Inc, Woodridge, Queensland, pp. 303–308.

62 *Democratic Republic of the Congo* 2019, United Nations Office of the Special Representative of the Secretary-General on Sexual Violence in Conflict, viewed 22 July 2020, <https://www.un.org/sexualviolenceinconflict/countries/democratic-republic-of-the-congo/>.

There are many factors involved in such a diabolical situation, I know that, but it is clear to me that the ravages of colonialisation are living on, long after the ruling parties have left.

Resilience

Yet the African woman is resilient. In the DRC today, women look after women and help them to heal. Others appeal to the United Nations to get justice and medical aid. The African woman has always had to fight, and I believe she rises from this trouble, stronger, rather than weaker. At the end of the day she hasn't lost her place. She is still the foundation on which her society is built – and will continue to be until the Lord returns. Amen!

Did you expect this leg of our bus tour to end the way it did? Can you understand the level of oppression the African woman encountered in the past – and still does in some places? I yearn for the healing of the DRC and other African nations torn by strife. I'll address this further at the end of the chapter, but for now let's take a breather and look at a completely different culture. Let's consider the West.

> *"Yet the African woman is resilient."*

Women in the West

When I set out to look at the history of women in the West, I encountered a problem. While there is not a lot written about the history of women in Africa, there is abundance written about the West. Too much! I kept having to narrow my focus and, in the end, I decided to look mainly at the United Kingdom – otherwise known as Great Britain – but have referenced

Australia and other countries along the way. The British Empire colonised many lands – including Australia and North America – at the height of its power. Its theology, legal systems, and social structures were the womb in which much of modern Western thinking was formed. To further focus our journey, I will look at the role of women before and after a time of great change – the Industrial Revolution.

Before the Industrial Revolution

Prior to the Industrial Revolution, many ordinary women were still carrying out traditional roles, undertaking tasks that women had done since the dark ages. They made and repaired clothing, managed the affairs of the farm, gave birth and took care of the children.[63] A woman was expected to marry young and work hard. In medieval times the most common symbol of the peasant woman was the distaff – a tool often used for spinning flax and wool. Eve is often depicted with a distaff in art of this time, to show her duty to perform manual labour after the fall.[64]

Urban women also worked hard. As well as having children and looking after the family, they often assisted their husbands or fathers in a wide variety of trades and crafts, including running shops and inns.[65]

---

63   History Crunch Writers 2019, *Role of Women in the Industrial Revolution*, History Crunch - History Articles, Summaries, Biographies, Resources and More, viewed 14 April 2020, <https://www.historycrunch.com/role-of-women-in-the-industrial-revolution.html#/>.

64   A Bovey 2015, *The Middle Ages: Women in Medieval Society*, The British Library, The British Library, viewed 14 April 2020, <https://www.bl.uk/the-middle-ages/articles/women-in-medieval-society>.

65   Bovey 2015

> *"The British Empire colonised many lands –*
> *including Australia and North America –*
> *at the height of its power."*

The patriarchy based their view of women on some of the biblical texts that I've already mentioned such as 1 Timothy 2:11-15. In many medieval paintings of the Garden of Eden, the serpent was given a female head, as women were thought to be inferior to men, morally weak and likely to tempt him to sin.[66] Interesting – they never questioned Adam's role in the exchange.

The only woman that held their respect was Mary, the mother of Jesus. They considered her a key means of salvation – a way to approach the inapproachable God. She was sometimes known as 'the second Eve' who had made up for Eve's sins and was the most powerful of all saints – a model of chastity and motherhood.[67]

Even with the reverence of Mary, it was a man's world. As with African women, an unmarried woman stayed within the control of her father: her only other option was to join the church and become a nun. Even among the more privileged classes a woman had little independence. She had to marry the person her family chose for her.[68] However, if she became

---

[66] Bovey 2015
[67] Bovey 2015
[68] Mind you, many men did too!

widowed, and had money and resources, she had considerable independence and legal authority.[69]

Some other women had power. An abbess in the church not only ruled over the women in her convent but in some communities, where there were both men and women, she also had authority over the monks.[70] And then, as with Africa, there were the queens.

British Queens

Consider Queen Isabella of France who married King Edward II of England in 1308 when she was twelve years old.[71] She is famed for overthrowing the reign of Edward II after he scorned her with his love of the scheming Hugh Despenser and took away her lands. Along with her lover, Richard Mortimer, Isabella invaded England in 1326 leading to the forced abdication of Edward II the following year.[72]

> *"It's unfortunate that Elizabeth's rule didn't redefine the role of women of her day."*

And then there was the Catholic Mary Queen of Scots and her Protestant half-sister Elizabeth who became Queen Elizabeth I of England. Elizabeth ruled from 1558 to 1603 and her persecution of Catholics led Mary's husband, Philip II of

---

69 Bovey 2015
70 Bovey 2015
71 E Mason 2019, *Isabella of France: the rebel queen*, HistoryExtra, viewed 16 April 2020, <https://www.historyextra.com/period/medieval/isabella-france-rebel-queen-invasion-england-deposition-husband-edward-ii/>.
72 Mason 2019

Spain, to launch the Spanish Armada to attack England in 1588. Elizabeth made a stirring speech to motivate her troops: *I know I have the body of a weak feeble woman, but I have the heart and stomach of a king.* It worked. England had an unexpected victory over the Spanish, and Britain entered into a prosperous period of expansion under Elizabeth's rule.[73]

It's unfortunate that Elizabeth's rule didn't redefine the role of women of her day. Heisch suggests that Elizabeth I did not rule England as a woman but as an 'honorary male'.[74] She allowed the male dominated systems of government to continue and merely set herself apart as stronger than others of her sex.[75]

The Fight for Equality

A vast number of social changes occurred between the time of Elizabeth I and the Industrial Revolution (1760 – 1840). By the time the Industrial Revolution hit Great Britain, many people were moving from rural areas to urban centres to find work in factories and mines. Pay was low for working class people, especially women, but many women and children entered the workforce, labouring in textile mills and coal mines to help support their family.[76]

---

73   L Worsley 2019, (Foreward) *Women: Our History*, Pengiun Random house, London, p. 108.

74   A Heisch 1980, 'Queen Elizabeth I and the Persistence of Patriarchy', *Feminist Review*, no. 4, pp. 45-56.

75   Heisch 1980 pp. 50-55 While Elizabeth's decision not to marry defied years of pressure from her parliament, her eventual solution was to take on a persona acceptable within the social structures of her day. She took the persona of a nun – on the grandest scale possible – and became The Virgin Queen.

76   History Crunch 2016.

The poor treatment of women led to the birth of the feminist movement, however before women could fight for workplace equality, they had to fight for the right to vote.[77] The suffragettes as they were later called, fought hard for this right, with some politicians supporting the cause and others standing against it – treating the idea with disdain. The movement grew, coming to a head in Britain in the early 1900s. It even had a militant wing which carried out arson attacks and bombings. Between the beginning of the twentieth century and the start of World War I, over a thousand suffragettes were imprisoned for their cause.[78]

> *"Even with the reverence of Mary, it was a man's world. It wasn't until 1918 that women gained the right to vote and become a member of parliament in Britain."*

In general, the suffragettes supported the war effort, embracing roles that had been traditionally undertaken by men. It wasn't until 1918 that women (who met the right age and property ownership requirements) gained the right to vote and become a member of parliament in Britain.[79]

In Australia, women were given the right to vote in South Australia in 1894, making this the first jurisdiction in the world to give women this power.[80] The newly federated Australian

---

77 History Crunch 2016.

78 *Suffragette 2019*, Wikipedia, Wikimedia Foundation, viewed 15 April 2020, <https://en.wikipedia.org/wiki/Suffragette>.

79 Suffragette 2019.

80 Acton, C 2012, 'Women's suffrage | National Museum of Australia', viewed 17 April 2020, <https://www.nma.gov.au/defining-moments/resources/womens-suffrage>

Government gave women the vote in 1902, although this excluded 'aboriginal natives'.[81] In the United States, women gained the right to vote in 1920.[82]

> *"The bias that a woman couldn't give a job her full attention if she had a family remained, and she was excluded from many trades and industries."*

While the right to vote was an incredible breakthrough, the fight for women to be seen as equal to men continued in western countries. There were some victories. In Britain, between the wars, widowed mothers and orphans were given a state pension and the age of marriage for women was raised from 12 to 16. Women also gained gender equality regarding divorce law.[83] However in some industries, women experienced a 'marriage bar' that meant they could not work if they became pregnant or got married. This restriction gradually lifted after 1944 but the bias that a woman couldn't give a job her full attention if she had a family remained, and she was excluded from many trades and industries.[84] She was also paid less than her male counterpart. This began to change in the

---

81 Suffragette 2019. This was the term used in the original legislation. Today the correct term for Australia's first nation people is Aboriginal and Torres Strait Islanders.

82 U.S. National Archives & Records Administration n.d., *19th Amendment to the U.S. Constitution: Women's Right to Vote (1920)*, Ourdocuments.gov.

83 PM Thane 2003, 'What difference did the vote make? Women in public and private life in Britain since 1918*', *Historical Research*, vol. 76, no. 192, pp. 268–285, viewed 17 April 2020, <https://onlinelibrary.wiley.com/doi/pdf/10.1111/1468-2281.00175>.

84 Sisterhood and After Research Team 2013, *Marriage and civil partnership*, The British Library, viewed 17 April 2020, <https://www.bl.uk/sisterhood/articles/marriage-and-civil-partnership>.

1950s when equal pay was legislated for teaching, civil service and local government roles.[85]

The single most important change in women's lives, not just in the Western world but around the globe, happened when women were given easy access to birth control. For much of the Western world this began early in the twentieth century, but it wasn't until the 1960s that birth control became reliable and easily accessible, with the advent of The Pill.[86] The Pill helped families to plan when they had children, and young women to plan their career, but it also contributed to the rise of the sexual revolution.[87]

The career expectations of women were not always fulfilled, however. The increase in divorce in the 1980s and the introduction of the 'long hours culture' made it harder for women – as well as men – to balance family and career.[88] Women still sometimes have to forgo having children to have a chance of reaching the top in business, government or some professions. Paradoxically, I've read research that says women who are childless and single have lesser career prospects than a man with similar qualifications.[89]

I've mentioned improvements in pay for women, but this is still an ongoing battle. In chapter 3, I related DePaulo's findings on unequal pay for single people, but it's obvious that it's a

---

85 Thane 2003.
86 Thane 2003.
87 Thane 2003
88 Thane 2003
89 Thane 2003

problem for all women. The 2020 report by the Australian Government Workplace Gender Equality Agency (WGEA) says that the gender pay gap for full time workers currently favours men by 14%. Men earned on average $253.60 more per week than women.[90] That's a big difference.

> *"Gillard is a great example of how difficult it can be for a woman to succeed in a man's world."*

But it's not just about pay, it's about opportunity and acceptance. Look at the pressure experienced by Australia's first female prime minister, Julia Gillard, who served in this role between 2010 to 2013. Gillard is a great example of how difficult it can be for a woman to succeed in a man's world. In her time as prime minister, she suffered acutely from gender-based smears and stereotyping, her opponents using slogans such as 'Ditch the Witch' to undermine her leadership.[91]

I haven't always liked Gillard's politics, but I do admire her strength and courage in aspiring to the heights of political leadership. It shows that Western society has moved forward and women have gained greater recognition than their forebears. But there is still a long way to go. A lot still needs to happen before the patriarchal bias of the West fades to the

---

90 *Factsheet Series Australia's Gender Pay Gap Statistics* 2020, Workplace Gender Equality Agency, viewed 23 October 2020, <https://www.wgea.gov.au/data/fact-sheets/australias-gender-pay-gap-statistics-2020>.

91 M Gordon 2018, *Julia Gillard: On women*, Pursuit, The University of Melbourne, viewed 17 April 2020, <https://pursuit.unimelb.edu.au/articles/julia-gillard-on-women>.

point where women, be they married or single, are seen to be truly equal to men.

Where to From Here?

Our hop-on-hop-off bus tour has taken us a long way. I'm sorry there was no space to write about other regions and cultures. Maybe this has inspired some of you to write an article or book about women in your culture. If you do, please let me know. I'd love to read it.

> *"Backdrop to the history that has relentlessly tried to diminish us."*

I've given some indication of the complexity, strength and challenges women have faced in her walk so far in history. Patriarchal mindsets, fuelled by a misconstruing of the scriptures, have limited the role of women in many ways. Until recently she has been allotted a restricted place, predominately within the home and family, in both Africa and the West. And in some places, in the aftermath of colonialisation, she has been attacked and tortured, as evil has marched against her.

> *"If women are to rise up and be all they can be – whatever their age, colour or marital status – the past must be acknowledged, owned and dealt with."*

At the beginning of this chapter I said that sometimes we have to look backwards before we can move forwards. If women are to rise up and be all they can be – whatever their age, colour or marital status – the past must be acknowledged, owned and dealt with. I'm not saying we should always be asking 'why?' As

Kim said in her story, our focus should be on the 'what' rather than 'why', but if we ignore the past and try and cover over it, it will fester and become toxic. That's one of the main reasons why we are experiencing racial unrest in the world today. We can't deny it and these systems need to be abolished. We must deal with it.

Today is a new day full of opportunity. In many places fresh, inclusive understanding of the scriptures has given women newfound freedom within our churches. Significant inroads have been made in woman's rights in the West. And the African woman can lift up her head, both in her own land and as a global citizen, knowing that while in some cases she may be bowed down – she is by no means defeated.

A few more words on this… I love how today many African women still excel in business – be it on a subsistence or international scale. And I see many of the diaspora sowing back into their homeland. Can this be a challenge to us all? Can we sow back into our sisters and strengthen them?

It's possible that as you've come along on this bus tour with me, you've had personal experiences with some of the struggles I've mentioned. I stated earlier in this book that I've experienced the intersectionality of bias against my gender, colour and marital status in limiting my access to the pulpit as a young woman. You might have experienced similar issues or maybe you are from a war-torn region and have suffered deep trauma. If something I have said has triggered you in some way, please seek wise counsel and know your sisters stand with you.

I encourage all of us to be looking for ways to build up and strengthen each other – especially other singles. I've focused on women in general in this chapter, but many of the issues I've mentioned are magnified for single people. The unmarried modern woman, for instance, may sometimes be more vulnerable than a married woman, if pay discrimination comes her way at work.

"The unmarried modern woman, for instance, may sometimes be more vulnerable than a married woman, if pay discrimination comes her way at work."

But this applies to all sorts of areas – including the pressure to marry. Marriage and family may be rich, beautiful and very much part of God's plan – but it isn't all a woman is. Wherever we come from, our cultural identity is wrapped up in our history. If we don't measure up to the ideal imposed by our culture, we can feel 'less than'.

I love how Lizzy (in her story) tells us how her grandmother taught her to be smart and become educated. We'd all do well to be like Lizzy and ask ourselves if the guy we are dating adds value to our lives. Does he empower us or merely fulfil a cultural expectation?

My dear father once heard me say something along the lines that singleness is a privilege. His response was 'What? It is not a privilege and it will never be a privilege in Africa. It is all about starting your own family'.

> *"Someone once said, if we don't know our history,*
> *we risk taking on someone else's."*

I explained to him that there are single women, including myself, who desire marriage but are yet to find that guy to settle down with. The privilege is the opportunity to build up other areas of our lives while we can. Marriage is great and brings certain benefits but also takes away some freedoms. He accepted that, reluctantly, but the pressure may still be there. I don't want anyone to feel lesser or to think their background or heritage disqualifies them from being a flourishing Christian single.

How do we move forward?

- Acknowledge the past and the forces that have shaped us – and own these circumstances – then release grace and forgiveness to those whose thoughtlessness condemns them. Note that I said 'them'. If someone holds an unfair bias against you in some way, it is their error, not yours. Someone once said, if we don't know our history, we risk taking on someone else's.
- Be a leader in promoting diversity. We must find ways to accept one another and love one another no matter what our colour, creed or marital status. Is there an area where *you* can promote healing where there has been hurt?
- Understand that no matter what history – or the world – says about us, there is only one person who has the power to define us. Our beautiful Saviour.

Lies and power struggles will always be with us – until Christ returns. Until the Lord puts things right, there will be people who will try to put us down and say that we are lesser than we are. There will always be those who will limit us, manipulate us or hurt us. I've already mentioned that the devil is out to steal our identity. His power and greed serves as the backdrop to the history that has relentlessly tried to diminish us. How does a single woman – any woman – protect herself from this identity theft? In this troubled world how can we rise up and be all our glorious creator made us to be? I'm so glad you asked, because that's the subject of the next chapter.

RECLAIMING OUR IDENTITY

KELLY

At my age, I thought life would be different. In my picture-perfect world, by now I would be happily married with three children in their late teens or early twenties. I would be working as a minister, preaching around Australia and internationally. My husband would be in a well-paying job that meant we were living in our own home and managing a couple of investment properties.

My life doesn't look like this. But is it really less than perfect?

From a young age I was told that I was a 'born teacher' because I was always organising the other children. So naturally I went to university to study primary teaching. During my first few years as a teacher in a Christian school, my life was on track. I was in a profession that allowed my spiritual gifts to work beautifully alongside my natural gift of teaching. I was financially secure, fit and healthy, relationally flourishing, and fully engaged in both my local church's ministry and in ministries beyond. I was even continuing my studies.

Wasn't this how life was supposed to look?

I was meeting and dating different guys and was part of a wonderful circle of friends. As I grew older, many of these friends and my siblings began to marry and have children. But even though

I desperately wanted a life partner, I found myself on the journey of a single woman.

As I moved from the predominantly female profession of teaching to a male-led profession as a pastor, my singleness stood out. I was not invited to 'married' events, and if I went out it was with couples, I always felt like the third wheel. Emotionally, this took its toll on me. Why wasn't I enough?

For many years, I dealt with the internal demon of 'performance'. If I didn't perform well enough in every external area, I worried that people would begin to define me as not good enough. My corresponding negative internal dialogue was compounded by contending with men who believed that scripture taught severe limitations on women in ministry. I often felt 'less than' from kind-hearted but naïve men's off-handed comments about single women in ministry: 'You're married to the church.' When you want to be married and are not, I found this insensitive and cruel.

People even said that because I wasn't married, I didn't have a 'covering' and wasn't qualified for ministry. I saw women who were married to someone popular in ministry getting promoted, seemingly because of their marriage certificate and not their calling. Publicly, men would pronounce equality for all women, but this single Christian woman with a passion to love, serve and minister, felt otherwise.

I felt I had to work better, harder and longer than men – just to be given a look in. Being single, I could easily spend longer at work and found myself in an unhealthy work/life pattern. When I came home, I didn't have a husband to share my hurts and disappointments, joys and successes with. Over time my unprocessed thoughts and emotions were building up. It was then that I discovered the value of surrounding myself with a few trustworthy people who could offer wise counsel while I debriefed.

Through many sessions with counsellors, mentors and friends, I was able to deal with performance and all its attachments, which finally brought my underlying need to perform back into balance.

As a mouthpiece of God and as a teacher, I have had the privilege of sharing God's Word on prominent pulpits and in obscure places, from rooftops in India to kids' camps on the Sunshine Coast, across Australia and internationally. Along the way, my singleness has provided the freedom to serve, and the opportunity to navigate the challenges of other's attitudes.

When on a ministry team to Ukraine in 2004, I sat in a roomful of women as question after question was asked of my married colleague, but I was ignored. I discovered that a woman who was not married and did not have children was not esteemed in that culture.

Later that evening, women were gathering to hear us minister. The men also attended to give them a spiritual covering. We women speakers were not allowed to stand behind the pulpit on the stage and were given a music stand on the floor from which to speak. After sharing directly from scripture, a man came up to me and stated in broken English, 'I will still tell my wife what to do'. Returning to Kiev, I felt rejected and worthless because it seemed that my value had been determined by my gender and marital status. Years of ministry and teaching experience had been rejected because I was a single female.

Yet, only a few days later, as we were on the bus to the airport, the Holy Spirit told me he wanted me to return to the Ukraine to minister again. God made a way for a second trip later that year. Then in February the following year, I moved there to help establish a women's ministry network. I saw first-hand how the Word of God was used to control and reduce women's worth, but I also saw God open people's eyes to see themselves as he saw them. I learned an awful lot about myself and the everlasting faithfulness of God.

Yes, I am a single woman in ministry, but I am no less than anyone else. I know who I am in Christ. He completes me: not my job title, not my marital status, not my bank balance or my street address. In Christ, I am single and absolutely fabulous.

Since going into ministry over 20 years ago, I have seen God do amazing things with me. I graduated from my Master's in Theology, was an Assistant Pastor and then, despite gender challenges, I became Senior Pastor of my church.

When I first was nominated to be Senior Pastor, some people simply refused to come to church because a woman was leading. Others made their theological cases for and against females in ministry. Fortunately, some allowed God to alleviate their fears.

I remember one man coming to the then male Senior Pastor and me with many questions. Rather than rant and rave, he simply held out his Bible and said, 'Show me'. This beautiful attitude allowed us to traverse scripture and equip him with further study materials to answer his questions and alleviate his fears. That man remained part of my board for the entire time I was Senior Pastor.

During my years as Senior Pastor, our church was a lighthouse in our community. We ran a large care organisation providing for our community, body, soul, and spirit. I also pioneered a 'Wholeness Centre' for Christian counselling and prayer ministry and a 'Kids Time Out' program that reached on average 150 community kids fortnightly.

I have not allowed singleness to define me nor limit me. The challenging experiences navigating ministry life as a single woman have all been transformed into amazing tools in the hands of the Holy Spirit, which allows me to minister with grace, love and wisdom.

8

IDENTITY THEFT

> *"The devil's focus on women is often in the area of self-image and our desire for love. The devil is out to steal our identity."*

One of the terms I've mentioned earlier in this book is 'identity theft'. We know our identity can be stolen online. People can steal our email addresses, our passwords and in some cases our credit card details. It's a serious business and people are defrauded of millions of dollars every year by these criminals. Isn't that devastating? Most of us would know at least one person who has been the victim of online or telephone fraud. It's a horrible thing to have happen – especially when the swindlers target the elderly and vulnerable.

Many of us are alert to these criminal acts and know to never give out our bank details or other information online. However, we may be unaware that another type of identity theft is endangering us right now. Someone is trying to steal something even more important than our bank details.

We have an enemy who is trying to steal our identity. If he succeeds, our lives on this earth will be robbed of power and purpose.

The Bible says the devil is prowling around, looking for someone to devour.[1] One of the ways he does this is to download a web of lies onto our hearts and minds – to make us feel as if we don't matter – and disqualify us from our sense of purpose.

His strategy is both big-picture and individual focused. We've seen how the role of women in both Africa and the West has been severely limited throughout history and how the misinterpretation of God's Word has diminished a woman's worth. But we know from Ephesians 6 that our struggle isn't against flesh and blood but against the spiritual forces of evil in the heavenly realms.[2] Similarly, the rape epidemic targeting African women has a human face but is empowered by evil intent. But the enemy fine-tunes his attack on each one of us.

The devil's focus on women is often in the area of self-image and our desire for love. How many times have we compared ourselves to the models on social media platforms? The evil one whispers to us that we're no good unless we have flawless skin or zero cellulite like the person in the image we see. We are lacking and will never measure up. He fails to mention that the image has been airbrushed to remove every blemish and spot of cellulite.

Or maybe the enemy is saying we have failed if we haven't been able to attract – or keep – a mate. We must be ugly, not cool or have a bad personality. Or we are a poor excuse for a woman because we haven't had success in both business *and* family. Or

---

1   1 Peter 5:8
2   Ephesians 6:12

as Kelly shared in her story, we wear ourselves out with striving because of inner whispers that we are not good enough.

Can you see what I mean? We hear the whispers deep within us. It's nasty stuff that pours petrol on the burning coals of our sense of inadequacy. If we believe these lies, our sense of self shrivels up and we die a little more inside each day.

Just as we have to secure the hard drive of our computers online to be safe, we need to secure our minds and hearts if we are to be all that Jesus Christ made us to be. We need to find God's true intent for us – his blueprint for humanity. This means that we need to find our way back to our Lord, establishing – or re-establishing – ourselves in him. He is the basis for our identity. All of humanity finds its breath, its existence, in God, our creator. The only way we can protect our identity and secure a right understanding of who we are, is by learning to see ourselves through the eyes of our designer.

> *"The only way we can protect our identity is by learning to see ourselves through the eyes of our designer."*

As we move forward, I invite you to consider the depth of your identity in Christ. It is the only true guide to who you really are as a single woman. Doing flows out of being. If we can know who we are then it's much easier for us to step into our purpose. Let's begin by looking at one of the most profound truths found in the scriptures. We are loved!

We are Loved

Influential theologian Karl Barth, author of several volumes of systematic theology, was asked in 1962 how he would summarise the most important truth he'd ever learned about God. His reply was to quote the words of a simple song we are taught as children. 'Jesus loves me this I know, for the Bible tells me so.'[3]

How about that? This famous scholar whose works profoundly influenced twentieth century theological thought, says that the most important thing we need to remember is that Jesus Christ loves us.

We've already seen that God is relational at his core. The trinity is the perfect expression of community. God needs community and he knows we do too – we are made in his image.[4] If you remember, I said Christ chose the disciples to be *with* him before he called them to any ministry. That is always how God operates.

I've spoken in past chapters about the different words the Greeks used to describe love: familial or affectionate love (*storge*); friendship *(philia)*; romantic love (*eros*); and spiritual love (*agape*).[5] All of these types of love are important for human welfare. But what happens if we define our identity by the love we receive from other people?

---

3   *Karl Barth* 2008, Christianity Today | Christian History, viewed 16 May 2020, <https://www.christianitytoday.com/history/people/theologians/karl-barth.html>.

4   Genesis 1:27

5   Z Kincaid 2020, *Four Types of Love*, Official Site | CSLewis.com, viewed 16 May 2020, <https://www.cslewis.com/four-types-of-love/>.

> *"The trinity is the perfect expression of community.*
> *God needs community and he knows we do."*

The problem is that the world and its people are tainted by sin. We get hurt so easily, don't we? Rejection can come from our parents, our friends, our workmates, our leaders. We can feel a bias against us because of our age, because of our skin colour, because of our marital status or even because of what we believe. Rejection is a reality and if we define ourselves by how other people see us, we are in trouble. We constantly swim in a sea of uncertainty with nothing to hold onto. The good news is that there is a very strong life raft and it's big enough for all of us. That raft is the love of God.

Look at one of the most famous verses in the Bible: 'For God so loved the world that he gave his one and only Son, that whoever believes in him shall not perish but have eternal life.'[6]

Try closing your eyes and saying this verse over and over to yourself while personalising it. For example:

For God so loved *me* that he gave his one and only son for *me* so that if *I* believe in him, *I* won't perish but *I* will have eternal life.

How amazing is God's love for each of us? That the Father would give his son to die for us and Jesus Christ would willingly sacrifice himself, so we could spend eternity with him? How

---

6   John 3:16

much would you have to love someone to be willing to be tortured and die for them?

What about this one from Romans 5? 'But God demonstrates his own love for us in this: While we were still sinners, Christ died for us.'[7]

Hang on a minute! God loved us *before* we ever did *anything* right? That blows my mind. It's not about religion or living up to any ideal. He loves us as we are. So, if ever you hear the identity-thieving liar whispering inside you that you are not good enough to be a Christian or that you have less value because of your appearance, hit that lie over the head with this truth. Boom!

There are so many things we can say about God's love for us. Love is the cornerstone of God's identity. He's not just loving – he *is* love.[8] His love is everlasting, which means – you guessed it – it lasts forever.[9] Is there any other love you know of that does that?

In Song of Songs, a book many think is an allegory of God's love for his people, it says:

> *Place me like a seal over your heart,*
> *like a seal on your arm;*
> *for love is as strong as death,*

---

[7] Romans 5:8
[8] 1 John 4:8
[9] Jeremiah 31:3

> *its jealousy unyielding as the grave.*
> *It burns like blazing fire,*
> *like a mighty flame.*
> *Many waters cannot quench love;*
> *rivers cannot sweep it away.*
> *If one were to give*
> *all the wealth of one's house for love,*
> *it would be utterly scorned.*[10]

God's love blazes for you and me like a fire that cannot be quenched. How does that make you feel? The next verse is another of my favourites. It doesn't speak directly of love, but it shows us how much we are valued by our maker:

> *For you created my inmost being;*
> *you knit me together in my mother's womb.*
> *I praise you because I am fearfully and wonderfully made;*
> *your works are wonderful,*
> *I know that full well.*[11]

Have a read of this whole psalm and see what it says about your identity. I found it transformative in that time when God was restoring my confidence. Look at those words: 'Fearfully and wonderfully made'. When my eyes were cast down by the poison of insults and rejection, this verse was the antidote that helped me realise who I really was. God had chosen to make me just as I am. I wasn't an ugly accident – I was one of his wonderful

---

10   Song of Songs 8:6-7
11   Psalm 139:13-14

works. I had to change my thinking and believe God's truth over the lies of the enemy.

> *"Love is the cornerstone of God's identity. He's not just loving – he is love."*

How about you? Can you believe you are fearfully and wonderfully made? We all need to be reminded of this because the world will always say we are lacking. We can never measure up to airbrushed supermodels and we might think we'll never be as 'good' as Mother Teresa, but God's truth is that he designed you. He formed you with great care. He held you in your mother's womb until it was time for you to be birthed into the world – and he has pursued you with his love ever since.

God made you in a way that is both *fearful* and wonderful. The word fearful here carries a sense of awe. Have you ever been in awe of something beautiful? The exquisite colours in a work of art? The view from a mountain on a clear day? What about a magnificent sunset? Or the perfect fingers and toes of a newborn babe? The angels look at *us* and are filled with the same kind of wonder. How incredible is that?

> *"The good news is that there is a very strong life raft and it's big enough for all of us."*

The truth is, we are *awe*-some and wonderful beings in God's eyes. This is our true identity. We are part of the greatest love story that's ever been told. God is our father, but his son is our bridegroom who has rescued us and will one day come to take us to be with him forever. Like every good romance, the story will have a happy ending. But until that time, we have to hold onto truth and not be cast down by lies.

Wouldn't it be amazing if we could learn to replace every one of the enemy's lies with God's word, every time we heard them? If only we could understand as we go about our lives each day that as single people we haven't missed out on love. We are not cast aside. We are not accidents of nature. We are lovingly crafted by the one true God who adores us. No matter what anyone else says or thinks about us, it's the opinion of our beautiful Jesus that matters most.

Training myself to think this way was essential to me lifting up my head and gaining confidence. I still need to do this from time to time. We have to always be on our guard against identity theft.

> *"I had to change my thinking and believe God's truth over the lies of the enemy. We are part of the greatest love story that's ever been told."*

We are Family

Not only are we loved with an everlasting love, but we are also made to 'belong'. I've already talked a lot about community and how we are not made to be an island, so I won't go over that ground again. But I'd like to focus for a moment on how this impacts our identity. We are made to belong – not just to be loved but to express love to others.

This is really important. There are a couple of identity-theft lies that weave themselves around this issue. One is that we don't belong. The other is that it is 'all about us'.

Let's look at the first of these. One of the favourite plays of the enemy is to make us feel isolated – that we don't belong. I've shared with you about the challenges I faced building new relationships inside and outside of church when I moved to Melbourne. I was slow in building relationships because of my work and became lonely. The truth is that even though I felt alone, I wasn't. God was with me and I was still part of his family.

One of the most important truths for us to remember is that no matter what happens, God is with us. If we belong to Jesus, he promises to always be with us – 'to the very end of the age'.[12] He told his disciples that he was going to send them the Holy Spirit to be with them forever.[13] That's our truth. God sent his Spirit to the church at Pentecost. He is always with us.

Let's look at Psalm 139 again:

> *Where can I go from your Spirit?*
> *Where can I flee from your presence?*
> *If I go up to the heavens, you are there;*
> *if I make my bed in the depths, you are there.*
> *If I rise on the wings of the dawn,*
> *if I settle on the far side of the sea,*

---

12 Matthew 28:20
13 John 14:15-18

> *even there your hand will guide me,*
> *your right hand will hold me fast.*
> *If I say, 'Surely the darkness will hide me*
> *and the light become night around me,'*
> *even the darkness will not be dark to you;*
> *the night will shine like the day,*
> *for darkness is as light to you.*[14]

If we belong to God, we can't escape his presence, but why would we want to if he is love? We are never alone. Even when every other person around us deserts us, he never leaves us. If we rely on other people for our sense of identity, they will sometimes let us down. The only person who will never let us down is Jesus Christ our Lord.

> *"One of the favourite plays of the enemy is*
> *to make us feel isolated – that we don't belong.*
> *One of the great metaphors for the church is family."*

Yet he knows that we need other people. One of the great metaphors for the church is family. I mentioned earlier that God puts the lonely in families.[15] We are made to live together and encourage each other. The two Greek concepts here are *storge* – the affectionate bond between family members and *philia*, which is the love of intimate friendship.[16] Paul blends these words in Romans 12:10 when he says, 'Be devoted to one

---

14 Psalm 139:7-12

15 Psalm 68:6

16 J Zadava 2018, *The 4 Types of Love in the Bible*, garymillerministries.com, viewed 15 September 2020, <https://garymillerministries.com/blogs/2018/11/3/the-4-types-of-love-in-the-bible>.

another in love.' The word here is *philostorgos* which means tenderly loving.[17] In 1 Timothy, Paul conveys the idea of *storge* when he exhorts Timothy, his protégé, to treat older men like his father, older women as mothers, younger men as brothers and younger women as sisters – with 'absolute purity'.[18]

Those last words are crucial to reflect on. I have mentioned previously that Christian singles should have friends that are both male and female, but we do need to serve each other in absolute purity. It's important to respect one another and not take advantage of each other, so we can build one another up in Jesus. We need to look out for each other in a kind and caring way, that isn't just for our benefit.

I come from a large family of ten girls and three men. We have all been there for each other as we've walked the road of life. But I have also had many Christian brothers and sisters who have been there for me as I have for them. This aspect of family is especially important for singles.

I can recall many different men and women who have helped me through the seasons of my singleness. They didn't just give me emotional support. There were brothers and sisters who helped me move to a new house, fix my car, or who looked after my garden when I was away. There have been married couples who have invited me to be part of their extended family, and others who have helped me when I was unwell. And I've done

---

17   WE Vine, MF Unger & W White, Jr. 1996, *Vine's Complete Expository Dictionary of Old and New Testament Words*, Thomas Nelson, Bath, England, pp. 1360–1361.

18   1 Timothy 5:1-2

the same for them when they needed me. That's what it means to be part of a family.

> *"Our gracious Heavenly Father fills out our adoption papers with the blood of his son and says we are his for eternity."*

If we recognise this as part of our identity, then we won't believe the lie that we are alone, nor will we heed the lie that we need to look out just for ourselves. We'll join together with others – for the long haul – celebrating life together in community. Building one another up and loving one another, as Jesus has loved us.[19]

What's in a Name?

Names are not only very important in Congolese culture, they identify you to your tribe. When someone is introduced in my homeland it is always with reference to their lineage. For example, if I had to visit the village or region my parents came from, I would introduce myself like this: My name is Mbelu Joëlle Marie – Andre Kabamba, daughter of Kabamba Andre, son of Kabamba – and so on (to the great grandfather level) – from the Baluba in the province of Kasie (Tribe), Bakwa Kalongi bena Tshimanga (the wider clan) Bena mukendi (sub-clan and village).[20] I am from the tribe of Baluba, and my father is from Bakwa Kalongi bena Tshimanga, from the Baluba clan, from the Province of Kasai Oriental in the Democratic Republic of Congo.

---

19 John 13:34

20 A Kabamba Mbikay 2002, *Family Handbook Supplement*, Brisbane, Australia.

IDENTITY THEFT

> *"You share his family name
> and the authority it brings."*

This tells people about my family lineage. In the DRC my family name and the tribe I come from define and identify me. If I went to my parent's province and did not explain who I was in this way, I would be considered a stranger with no status.

Family names can be important markers of identity. We see the same emphasis in the scriptures. In the Old Testament there are many long accounts of lineage. It was important to define who belonged to the family line. In the New Testament we have the genealogy of Christ.[21] Among other things this shows his direct lineage to King David. God had promised that the messiah would come from David's line.[22] In the Bible, your name, the name of your father and the name of your father's father matters.

Have you realised that as Christians we bear a very important family name?

When we trust in our Saviour and choose to follow him, we become part of God's family by adoption.

In Ephesians 1, the Bible clearly says that we have been adopted as sons in Christ Jesus.[23] Our gracious Heavenly Father fills out

---

21 Matthew 1:1-17. Look at how many significant women are in Jesus' genealogy.
22 Jeremiah 23:5-6
23 Ephesians 1:5.

our adoption papers with the blood of his son and says we are his for eternity.

Hang on. 'Sons? But I'm a woman.' Yes, you are, but Galatians 4:4-7 says that Jesus died so we could be adopted into God's family and have the *spirit of sonship*. I mentioned this when we looked at the scripture section in the history of women chapter. That's why Paul could say in Galatians 3:28 that there is 'neither Jew nor Gentile, neither slave nor free, nor is there male and female.' We are all one in Christ Jesus.

Ladies, we don't just carry the authority of daughters within the family. In Paul's day it was the son who had the authority. Here he is saying that everyone who is adopted into God's family carries the authority of sons. We are fully heir to all of God's power and authority working through us. We bear full rights to the family name. How about that?

We knew that anyway. Instinctively. But as we've seen in the history chapter, the role of women in both the world and the church has been limited over the years.

Women of God – don't let anyone put you down or say you cannot do something because of your gender, age, marital status or colour. People will do that, like Kelly discovered on her ministry trip to the Ukraine, where the men attended a ministry meeting to give the women their 'covering'. Girls, if you've given your life to Jesus and chosen to follow him, *he* is your covering. You share his family name and the authority it brings.

What does that do for your sense of identity?

The enemy doesn't want us to see how powerful we are as Christians, so he holds us back with lies that say we are weak, or not good enough, or 'just a woman'. We are so much more than that. We have this wonderful identity – we bear the family name.

This must give us confidence. This must give us the strength to lift up our heads and be strong in God's kingdom. But dare I say that as well as confidence there can be a cost. Bearing God's name means putting this family identity above all others.

> *"The impact we have in the world and in God's kingdom flows from our identity."*

One time, Jesus was ministering with his disciples and things became so intense that none of them had any time to eat. This caused Jesus' mother and brothers to think he was 'out of his mind' and go looking for him.[24] When they found him they tried to take him home, but he refused, saying, 'Whoever does God's will is my brother and sister and mother.'[25] Jesus was saying that there is a definition of family that is above that of biological family – membership in the family of God.

We are meant to love our families, and elsewhere in the scripture we see that Jesus looked out for his family. In John 19:26-27, Jesus entrusted his mother to the disciple John rather than his own brothers, probably because his brothers weren't members of God's family yet. In God's frame of reference, family is

---

24 Mark 3:20-21
25 Mark 3:31-35

ultimately defined by our relationship with Jesus and our willingness to follow him, not by our genetics.

If we follow Jesus and trust our lives to him, he gives us his name and his authority. But the cost may be huge. Some have chosen to follow Jesus despite rejection from their family. Some have even been killed for doing this. Yet they have followed him gladly because they know that nothing can take God's name from them – even into eternity. That's what I call trust, but that kind of confidence only comes out of being sure of our identity. Of being sure we are loved and that we have a family we can rely on. Of being sure of the name we bear no matter what our ethnicity, age, beauty, strength or marital status. Of being sure we belong to Jesus and stand in his name and authority.

As with our online information, the identity we have in Jesus can't be stolen without some kind of deception. The enemy doesn't have the authority to just take it – he needs to trick us in some way. If we partner with his lies by believing them, they will adversely affect us, but if we renounce them and close the door to them, nothing undeserved can land on us. Sometimes he persuades us to disbelieve our identity, other times he tries to coax us away from it. It's important, as sisters in Christ, that we stand together and encourage one another in the truth of our family name, so that we can all live out of this truth in confidence.

The impact we have in the world and in God's kingdom flows from our identity. Knowing who we belong to and whose name we bear, makes all the difference. If we understand that we are loved, are part of a worldwide family and represent the God of all creation, we will have the confidence to rise up and be women of influence. Yeah! Women of influence. Sounds awesome doesn't it?

Are you ready to find out more about your purpose? Let's look at this idea in greater depth.

Role vs. Purpose

Author, speaker and leadership consultant, Dr. Myles Munroe says, 'The female can only be fulfilled when she understands and submits to the purpose God first created her to be.'[26] But what is our purpose? I've heard many talks on female purpose that major on the woman's ability to have children, but how do we find our way when our singleness bars us from this? What if we don't marry and don't have children? How do we find our purpose then?

> *"Purpose goes deeper and sits at the centre of our identity."*

We've talked about the struggle many of us have with this question. It is difficult to see the way through sometimes when all we want is to have kids, but I think we have to see the difference between the roles we desire and our fundamental purpose in this world.

A role is the function we undertake. Motherhood can be a role, an office job can be a role, we can work in a role as a teacher or a doctor. We can take on a pastoral or teaching role at church,

---

[26] Twentieth Xentury 2018, *Myles Munroe: The Purpose Of Woman*, YouTube, viewed 17 April 2020, <https://www.youtube.com/watch?v=ejNuhexwtns&feature=youtu.be>.

but that is not our purpose. Roles can change depending on our circumstances, but our purpose does not change. Purpose goes deeper and sits at the centre of our identity.

Let me explain. In Luke 10:27 Jesus sums up the teaching of the Mosaic law and the prophets. He says, 'Love the Lord your God with all your heart and with all your soul and with all your strength and with all your mind.' And, 'Love your neighbour as yourself.'

There are over 600 commands in the Bible; exhortations to either do something or not do something. All of these point to this one powerful verse. The one message God wanted to convey to his people two thousand years ago, and to us today, is that our foremost purpose is to love God. He is our creator and maker.

> *"When we make loving God our purpose, this love overflows into love for ourselves."*

Do you love God? If our primary purpose is to love him, we are compelled to go deeper into this revelation so we can learn to love him more. When we spend time with him through reading his word, praying to him and worshipping him, the Holy Spirit takes us deeper into a knowledge of who God is – in a way that touches both our emotions and our thoughts.

We experience God's love in deeper ways. He is always with us but if we turn our face towards him as part of our holy purpose, we will be filled with Gods fullness.[27] We will know that we are created, wholly dependent on him for every breath, yet loved with that everlasting love I spoke of earlier. Our hearts will respond in ever deepening love for him.

Have you ever seen a pyramid of champagne glasses at a wedding? Maybe you've seen it on television or in a movie. Someone pours bubbly into a glass and it overflows, filling the glasses below. When those glasses fill up, they overflow and fill the ones below, and so on, until all the glasses are full.

> *"We need to know our worth and value before we can truly value another human being."*

When we make loving God our purpose, this love overflows into love for ourselves. When we grow in our understanding of who he is and what he has done for us, *and how important we are to him*, we have a filter through which we can view ourselves.

In my observation there are two areas we Christians need to work on in the area of loving self. The first is we sometimes love ourselves too much and put our needs and wants at the centre of our universe. The other is we hang our heads low and consider ourselves of little worth. Both of these views are wrong. When we place things in the right order – loving God first – we can love ourselves. We can be self-aware – knowing that we are not God, but we are created in his image. We can see ourselves secure in the knowledge that nothing can separate us from his love.[28] We

---

27 Ephesians 3:19
28 Romans 8:38

can rejoice as he generously adopts us and gives us the family name. Our beautiful God created us, loves us and defines us. We can raise our heads and know that we are his and he is ours. How wonderful is our God!

When we love God first, then love ourselves, the glass of love can overflow into the lives of others.

Jesus says to love others as *ourselves*. We are incapable of loving others without first loving ourselves. We need to know our worth and value before we can truly value another human being. When we realise that we reflect the image of God, we can see God's image in another person, even if they are very different from ourselves. If we try to act in our own strength because we think we 'should' help someone, we will often fail to love. We might do some superficial good, but it won't necessarily be motivated by love. If we get the order right, loving God first, then ourselves and then others, we won't get caught up in striving. The works that we do – even if they take us well beyond our zones of comfort – will be founded in the flow of our Saviour's love and resources.

Ladies, if we would like to find our purpose, we need to start here – rather than focusing on any predetermined role. People will always have their opinions as to what we can and can't do. Social structures and people's attitudes have held women back – and we've held ourselves back by limiting our vision and not recognising the authority we hold as children of God. As we pursue our purpose, we will find that we are given roles by our gracious, heavenly Father – that surprise us. God's call is always to something bigger than ourselves and our marital status.

Poised for Greatness

The purpose of today's woman is expressed in roles of influence for Christ from friends, to family, to parenthood, to ministry, to the corporate boardroom. These roles will flow from God's enabling, and our gifting. Every one of us is unique in the way God has made us. We have different strengths and different abilities. We are not all made to be brain surgeons or artists or nuclear physicists or pastors or clothing designers, but we all have the life of God flowing through us. If we make it our purpose to love God first, then love ourselves, then love others – then this purpose can flow through the roles we choose or that come our way.

> *"She also said it was essential that 'women and people of colour' have a seat at the table where the future is designed."*

However, let's be wise. The opportunities many of us have today are abundant compared with the limitations imposed upon women in history. We understand we have a great future and a place in this world, but we can sometimes feel pressed to be all things to all people. We can feel that to be a woman of purpose we have to have the corporate job as well as the family, working long hours in both spheres to the point of exhaustion.

Nobody can doubt a woman's resilience and capacity for both nurture and productivity. It has long been said: 'Give a woman a house and she will turn it into a home. Give her ingredients and she will turn it into a scrumptious meal. She is able to take a broken group of people and turn them into a loving community.'[29] But she doesn't have to burn herself out in the process.

Some women will have the capacity to manage home, family and a corporate career and some may not. But even the woman with the highest levels of energy and the greatest ability in her work, might fail to find her divine purpose if she is not centred in God's love. In the same way, the woman who chooses a simpler life can still find her purpose if her first focus is loving God.

It's important that we all become like Kelly and understand it is Christ who completes us, not our job, marital status, bank balance or street address. We don't have to do it all, or have it all, to be favoured by God. It is vital to be centred in him and live out of that place of grace and power. But when we do that, look out! Neither our singleness, our gender, our age or our colour will define us. Christ will. And he's Lord of all. Let's honour that!

We live in exciting times. God is establishing new paradigms regarding the role of women. The opportunities available for the single, modern woman are so much more than they were thirty, forty or fifty years ago, yet there is still a long way to go. While there is an increasing number of remarkable women in leadership around the globe, there are areas where women fall behind.

In an interview with David Letterman on his Netflix show, *My Next Guest Needs No Introduction*, Melinda Gates said that in

---

29 Twentieth Xentury 2018.

the USA, currently only 19% of computer science students are women, compared with 33% when she studied in the 1980s.[30] She also said it was essential that 'women and people of colour' have a seat at the table where the future is designed. We can't imagine the changes that will occur in the areas of information technology and artificial intelligence over the next thirty years. If women and people of colour are not increasingly involved in these areas, a permanent bias will be baked into the system. Melinda goes on to say that only 5% of the CEOs of Fortune 500 companies are women and that the US Congress currently consists of only 23% women.

As Christians, if we want to be agents of change for good in the world, we need to rise up in our gifting and be willing to step into these and other non-traditional roles. Our world is currently caught up in a crazy metamorphosis with shifts in trends and ideologies. We need more confident, gracious, gifted, spirit-filled women-of-purpose to rise up and change nations, breaking new ground in computer science, medicine, engineering, ethics, Christian ministry, philanthropy, finance and politics.

I recognise that there are some reading this who might come from other lands or cultures where women are limited to traditional roles. Maybe you are in a church like the one Kelly mentioned, where scriptural interpretation limits what you can do. To you I say two things. The first is to remember that purpose transcends role. You have a holy purpose and carry God's authority in whatever you do. You don't have to be a

---

30 D Letterman 2019, *My Next Guest Needs No Introduction With David Letterman | Melinda Gates*, Netflix, viewed 15 September 2020, <https://www.netflix.com/watch/81034500>.

scientist or a politician or a preacher to have influence. The second is that you never know your limits until you try. There is no greater liberator of women than Jesus Christ. He tore down cultural barriers when he walked the earth, and he can tear down our barriers now. It doesn't matter who we are. We all need to ask Jesus to make a way for us to learn, grow and lead, whatever our field of influence.

> *"There is no greater liberator of women than Jesus Christ."*

Maybe you will have effect as far-reaching as the great apostle Paul. There is no better example of a person who shifted the direction of their life, after a revelation of their true identity, than Paul. He went from being a murderer of God's people to an apostle, called by God.

When Paul introduces himself in his letter to the Ephesian church, his certainty shines through. 'Paul, an apostle of Christ Jesus by the will of God, to God's holy people in Ephesus, the faithful in Christ Jesus:'[31] Apostle means 'sent one'. In this verse, Paul declares with absolute assurance that God, who knows him by name, has chosen him and sent him to fulfil his calling.

- He knew *who* he was: Paul the apostle – no longer Saul who had murdered Christians.[32]
- He knew *whose* he was: redeemed, loved, and chosen by the King of Kings and Lord of Lords.

---

31 Ephesians 1:1
32 Acts 7:58

- He knew *what his purpose* was: to take the good news of Jesus to the church at Ephesus – and beyond.

> *"He didn't dwell in the past and disqualify himself because of the things he had done."*

I love how Paul is so confident of these things. He didn't dwell in the past and disqualify himself because of the things he had done. As Saul he'd suffered from a severe form of identity theft, where the misbelief in his own rightness led him to kill Christians.[33] Can you believe it? The one who God called to take his message to the gentile world, was an arrogant murderer. Yet when Jesus called him, Paul put his former identity behind him so totally that he could say, 'I have been crucified with Christ and I no longer live, but Christ lives in me. The life I now live in the body, I live by faith in the Son of God, who loved me and gave himself for me.'[34]

Saul was dead, now Paul lived a life totally surrendered to, and totally empowered by, Jesus.

> *"And as single ladies we can have a purpose that goes way beyond waiting for a husband."*

I believe that if we are to find our true purpose in God and live abundantly for him – whatever our sphere of influence – we all need to have this kind of revelation. If we don't know who we are – if we let our identity be stolen – we can open the door to

---

33 Philippians 3:1-14
34 Galatians 2:20

the wrong voices and lose our way in life. But if we reclaim our true identity and purpose – by dying to our old ways and being raised up by Christ – nothing can stop us. And as single girls we can have a purpose that goes way beyond waiting for a husband.

Ladies, are we understanding these truths for our own lives? Do we know:
- Who we are?
- Whose we are?
- And what we are called to do?

If not, it's time to draw close to our amazing Father in heaven and ask him to reveal the answers.

Listen! Can you hear his whisper? He's calling *your* name.

KODA-JO

My name is Koda-Jo. I am English and identify as West Indian, but I come from a very diverse ethnic background. My rich heritage includes Ghanan (escaped slaves), West African, Spanish, Welsh, Indian, Jewish, Scottish and Amerindian. I am the proud mother of three young adults that I love, respect and value very much. I always say that even if they were not mine, I would invite them to be part of my life because I am so inspired by them. They have all invited me into their lives as a friend; even now that they do not need me as a parent. I am grateful and do not take this lightly.

My first understanding of singleness was learned very early. My mother and father had a toxic marriage, where my father consistently negated his responsibilities and commitment to both marriage and parenthood. Deep inside I knew my mother was better off when he finally left. I saw her grow in confidence and capacity as she would declare, 'I have God and my five children!' She worked so hard to provide for us.

Because of my father's words and actions, I developed a sense of deep-seated rejection and abandonment. I tried to fill that space with unhealthy relationships. My attitude for most of my young adulthood, was that singleness was bad. I was ashamed of my neediness, and yet continued to engage in a series of unhealthy relationships that compromised my beliefs and values. This cycle eroded my self-confidence even further, which led to self-loathing, and so the cycle continued.

One of the things that fed my feelings of inferiority was the subtle discrimination against single people I perceived in my church: 'When are you getting married?' or 'Why aren't you married?' These constant but well-intentioned questions took on a meaning of their own because of my insecurities. I would shrug and attempt a nonchalant smile, but inside this was just another brick in the wall of my insecurity and self-hatred.

In my neediness I felt that the only way I could become an effective person was through marriage. I struggled with conflicting messages: those of my upbringing, that sexual feelings were something to be ashamed of; the message from the Bible that they weren't and should be expressed within marriage and then there was the twenty-first century focus on Eros thrown at me from every direction.

After the end of one particularly destructive relationship, I reached out for help. I attended counselling, sought prayer and completed suggested exercises as part of the healing process. I realised that Psalm 139:14 was true, 'We are fearfully and wonderfully made,' and I acknowledged that as human beings we are made for intimacy and relationship. I was at last learning my true identity is defined by my creator. I also realised afresh that there are other valid and valuable relationships which are just as important as marriage. The agape love of friendship and fellowship needs to be fostered and valued: I needed to be friends with my future husband.

From then on, I learned to become whole and healthy without a partner. There was enjoyment of life and I brought light to others just as I was. My sense of humour and warmth helped whatever the situation. The joys of singleness for me included being able to please myself and be accountable with my time, projects and finances, only to God.

I did eventually marry, and then at forty, with three children aged fourteen, thirteen and eleven, I found myself single again. The pain was crushing and at times felt like an overwhelming physical presence. I was broken and vulnerable, had low self-esteem and at one point considered suicide. However, that choice would affect my three precious blessings, so I sought help from God, my church family, friends and professional counselling. My faith was a great help along with the belief that if I got through this, I could be there for my children and perhaps help others one day. And I did get through.

In hindsight, I see that negotiating the maze of post-divorce, well-meaning advice was almost as stressful as the process of separation itself. I lost a couple of relationships with married couples because, as a single woman, I had become a threat in the eyes of the female. I found this painful as I respect marriage, even more so after my experience. I didn't let this stop me, though, from attending social events and setting out to make others laugh. On one occasion, I was given feedback stating: 'No-one would ever know what you have been through. It is so easy to have you as part of the group and we don't have to 'skip' anything around you'. Given my history, this is one of the most treasured pieces of feedback I have ever received.

My experience cemented my resolve to assist other families. This took the form of being 'Aunty' to families with younger children and encouraging other parents. I still managed moments of poor choices and self-doubt but continued to be accountable, using them as opportunities for growth instead of self-punishment.

After another relationship foundered, I decided it was important to withdraw from dating and work through my issues – to find 'me'. For the next few years I worked on myself. One of my fiercest battles was with the 'white heat of loneliness'. It was relentless, fierce and fluid, attacking at will, clinging to me like the sticky threads of a spider's web.

During this time, I heard a wonderful interview on a Christian radio station featuring the group 'Christian Singles', which further encouraged my decision. I found hosting dinner parties, prayer, reading the Bible and catching up with friends were effective. I learned a lot about self-help courses and embarked upon a journey of accountability, prayer and counselling. This helped me learn to be kind to myself and in turn, helped build my empathy for others.

I also used the time to confirm my identity. Psalm 139:13–16 is etched in my memory and has been helpful every time I observe the cruelty of gravity as well as the hairiness that is acquired with age.

My singleness allowed me to form a board for the not-for-profit organisation, 'Hope Remains Inc.', a project focused on eliminating sexual trafficking between Nepal and India. Hope Remains Inc. celebrates ordinary people, doing extraordinary things together to make a difference. I did not realise, during my time of working on this project, how much it would help me. This has been a long and difficult journey at times; however I have gained so much from this process.

Writing this story has been a reminder that singleness has been valuable to me. I have re-married and found those lessons of singleness: valuing myself; looking to God, not my husband, for fulfilment: self-reflection and speaking up when necessary, continue to enhance my relationship with my husband.

9

LET'S TALK ABOUT SEX

I once heard someone say there are three needs humans pursue with passion: sleep, food and sex. All three are God-given drives and we can't ignore them, but we certainly do need wisdom in how to navigate them if they get out of balance. Especially our sex drive.

We live in a world which says, 'If it feels good, do it.' We are bombarded with sexual images through movies, television, advertisements and social media. We can't escape them. Yet as single women we struggle. We've already seen how social trends have resulted in people marrying later, and there are a whole lot of expectations that hang around the recreational dating scene. We'd like to find a man, but we don't want the emptiness of a casual fling.

As Christians we are faced with further expectations. Churches who teach from a biblical perspective say that we should wait until we are married to have sex. That leaves many of us, in particular those who have been single for a long time, to ask how we do this. What do we do with these feelings? If God gives us these desires, is it so wrong to express them? And then, there is the battlefield of our minds to deal with.

How does a single Christian woman navigate these and other questions regarding sexuality? What about issues such as pornography, homosexuality and same-sex marriage? How do we respond when our friends in same-sex relationships ask us what we think?

I have a confession to make. When I set out to write a book on singleness, this was one chapter I didn't want to write. It's not that I'm a prude or feel embarrassed to talk about matters such as these, nor is it because I believe it's unimportant. I've been on the planet for a while now and I don't think I'm shy in discussing this topic. I also think our sexuality is a key issue for everyone, not just Christian singles. It is an area of our identity the evil one loves to target – and he does it well, hitting women anywhere from self-esteem through to overt sexual violence. Having a healthy, biblical view of our sexuality is essential to combatting the identity theft I spoke of in the last chapter.

So why was I reticent to write about this subject?

To speak about sexuality from a biblically based, Christian point of view, can feel radically countercultural.[1] I have many dear friends and colleagues who have opposing views on how sexuality should be expressed in our world. We live in a pluralistic society where belief in absolute truth and the pre-eminence of one God has been lost. Truth has become individual-centred rather than Jesus-centred. It's difficult, therefore, for anyone to speak on sexuality today without offending someone, somewhere. As a

---

1   J Hill Perry 2018, *Gay girl, good God: the story of who I was and who God has always been*, B&H Publishing Group, Nashville, Tennessee, p. 9.

society we used to be able to agree to disagree, but now it seems that if I disagree with your point of view, I must be judging you or hate you. Please know that is not my intent at all.

What I would love to do through this chapter is establish a dialogue with you, one that's been long coming. I'd like to begin the conversation rather than declare I have all the answers. Like many of you reading this, I'm walking day by day through the challenges of being a single, yet sexual, Christian woman. The main difference between me and someone who has not come to faith yet is that I'm walking this road with my hand in Jesus' hand. I believe in him, and he is the only one who can lift me back up when I make mistakes.

I do want to say that if there is anything in this chapter – or this book as a whole – that you'd like to talk about, please visit my website, www.spacebetweenpublications.com, where there will be resources and other opportunities for discussion. I don't mind if you disagree with me and would like to debate some points. What the world needs today is people who will listen to another's perspective and try to understand what they are saying, without judgement. It's important to honour one another as human beings and learn to embrace those who think differently from us. That's the only way we'll learn to love one another, and be inclusive of those different to us, as Christ said we should.

Having said that, it's time to dive in and look at these issues in detail. Let's start by looking at what God thinks about sex.

What does God Say about Sex?

Let's face it, most of us are thinking about it – or fighting not to! It's all around us. Sex is a natural part of God's design, after all, for when the time is right. But what about when the time isn't right? If we are to thrive as single women, our lives have to be built on the right foundation, and the only place I know for sure that will give us that foundation is the Bible. Let's look at some of the key ideas the Bible teaches about sex. It may be different from what you think.

The world tends to voice the lie that God doesn't think much of sex and sexuality. They say he's out to spoil our fun. But the opposite is true. It's the enemy who is trying to bring us down and devalue this beautiful gift from God.

Historically, the church has been accused of having a low view of sex. But most of the unhelpful ideas originally came from the world and the wrong expression of power, not from the Bible.

Take the Puritans for example. I've heard people say Puritans had a repressive view of sexuality, when in fact they had a healthy regard for the joy of sex within marriage.[2] It was more the early church fathers who were influenced by Greek thought, and later the neo-puritanism of the Victorian era that caused the problem.[3] It wasn't Christianity but humanistic rationalism that repressed the healthy enjoyment of sex in the nineteenth century. Reason was elevated and other functions of the body

---

2   J Boot 2013, *Sex and the History of Christianity*, Ezra Institute, viewed 4 July 2020, <https://www.ezrainstitute.ca/resource-library/articles/sex-and-the-history-of-christianity/>.

3   Boot 2013

were 'looked down upon.'[4] This pervaded culture and overflowed into the churches. The result was that sex became a 'dirty' thing people rarely spoke about.

Talk about misrepresenting the truth. Eventually societal attitudes swung in the opposite direction and now the lie is that Christianity is stuck in the Victorian era and is down on sex. Give me a break! God invented sex – he says it's a great thing.

Sex wasn't just created for the mechanics of reproduction. It was meant to be a beautiful celebration of the union of man and woman who make a covenant agreement with each other before God. We can hear the echo of that in Adam's words when he beheld Eve for the first time: 'Bone of my bone and flesh of my flesh'.[5] Can you imagine how he must have felt when he saw Eve? His overwhelming desire for her beauty, her body, her companionship? She was the same as he was, but different in all the right ways.

> *'God invented sex – he says it's a great thing.'*

We've seen how Adam and Eve's rebellion wrecked the balance of things, but in the Old Testament sexuality is still celebrated. If you have any doubt, read Song of Songs. This description of the joy of sexual love is found in our *holy* scriptures.

According to the Bible, sex is a holy thing and a reflection of God's relationship with his people. Have you realised that the

---

4   Boot 2013

5   Genesis 2:23

Bible begins and ends with marriage?⁶ From the union of Adam and Eve in Genesis, to the promise of the great marriage of Christ and his church in Revelation, God's word is a love story of intimacy and deep knowing.

While researching this topic, I found a beautiful article that expresses this perfectly.⁷ The author reflects that in the Old Testament, the most commonly used Hebrew word for 'making love' is *yada* – meaning 'to know, or to be known'. It's the word used in Genesis 4:1 when Adam lays with Eve and she becomes pregnant for this first time. *Yada* is used over a thousand times in the Old Testament, but it doesn't just refer to love making. When the Psalmist writes, 'Be still and *know* I am God,' *yada* is used to describe the 'intimate knowing' between God and his people.⁸

> *'Have you realised that the Bible begins and ends with marriage?'*

Understanding this word is important. Sex is not just a fun physical act, but it involves a deep spiritual connection between two people, a union of body, soul and spirit. We can see this in Ephesians 5:31-32, where Paul links the joining in marriage to the spiritual union of Christ and the church. That's why marriage is so important for the expression of love making. When we are sexually intimate, we join with another with more

---

6   Genesis 2:21-25; Revelation 21:1-4.

7   Holy Hen House 2014, *Sex + Intimacy with God*, Holy Hen House, viewed 7 July 2020, <https://www.holyhenhouse.com/blog/sex-intimacy-with-god>.

8   Holy Hen House 2014.

than our bodies. When we take this casually, something is lost. But when we give ourselves to someone we have committed to in marriage, we are mirroring God's covenant relationship with us in ways we cannot imagine. This is why God puts such a high value on purity and faithfulness in marriage. Marriage is meant to reflect the relationship Christ Jesus has with his church.

The world says sex can fulfil us – but only God can do that. Yes, it can give pleasure but if it occurs outside of the right context, this spiritual union is lost, and it can become very empty. Some of you who are reading this might have gone in that direction and have felt this desolation. Don't despair, there is a way back. I'll talk more about this later but if you've felt like this please know that in every aspect of life Jesus wants you to run to him rather than away from him. He is our great redeemer.

> *'Marriage is meant to reflect the relationship Christ Jesus has with his church.'*

In the same way, if your experience of marriage and sex has not been life-giving, if you have been abused inside or outside of marriage, please know that our loving God has in no way sanctioned that. Time is too limited to talk in any depth about sexual healing but if you've been wounded in this way, please seek wise counsel and run to God rather than away from him. Jesus weeps with you, and as we've just seen, he *knows* you. There is no man better able to heal you.

But if people tell you that God just wants to stop you having fun – don't believe them.

He knows we are both physical and spiritual beings and he desires the best for us. He doesn't want us to lose any part of ourselves and he wants to point us to the ultimate marriage when Jesus returns. He wants the best for us and to show his glory.

Wow, isn't' that just our God? Amazing! But hold on, what about us single ladies? While it's great to know that sex is an amazing gift, we don't have a husband yet and it might never happen. What are we to do with our desires? We're biologically wired to want to mate and the thought that cold showers can help is absurd. How do we live this life without feeling that we're missing out? It makes us wonder, does the Bible really teach purity?

The Case for Purity

One of my girlfriends once said, 'Don't judge me, okay. I like this guy even if he does not share the same core values when it comes to faith'. Although that sentence would indicate a clear lack of obedience to God, it also highlights, just because we are followers of Christ doesn't mean we are immune to the siren call of our sex-obsessed culture. Sexual images are all around us – and unless we can find a rock to hide under or can manage to weave a sound-proofed cocoon around ourselves – we can't escape them. The alluring song of sexual freedom will call to us and some of us will answer.

In recent decades I have seen many single Christian women search for sexual satisfaction outside of marriage. They say things like, 'I just wanna have fun,' or 'It's my body, I have waited this long'. 'Everyone else is doing it anyway.' Some don't realise that this isn't God's best for them, while some do know this but don't know how to address such emotions. Others do care but the yearning to be loved in this way is too strong and they get tired of waiting.

Sam Allberry in his excellent article, *Where to Find Hope and Help Amid the Sexual Revolution*, says that for many, sex has become about recreation rather than procreation. People feel they have a right to this recreation – without reproductive consequences. And marriage has moved from being seen as a life-long covenant to being little more than a flexible romantic contract. [9]

We can easily be swayed by ideas like this. We don't realise it is happening but over time our thought systems change. If sex is fun, why not indulge? And why is there so much hang up about who gets married?

> *'Sex has become about recreation rather than procreation. People feel they have a right to this recreation – without reproductive consequences.'*

The truth is, just because something seems right and feels good, doesn't mean it *is* right and *is* good for us. Proverbs 14:12 says, 'There is a way that appears to be right, but in the end it leads to death.'

---

[9] S Allberry 2018, *Where to Find Hope and Help amid the Sexual Revolution*, The Gospel Coalition, viewed 7 July 2020, <https://www.thegospelcoalition.org/article/hope-help-sexual-revolution/>.

As we've seen, in God's eyes, sex is more than just a physical thing. But the Bible has other instructions that indicate purity is his call both inside and outside of marriage.

In Hebrews 13:4 we read that the marriage bed is 'to be honoured by all' and 'kept pure'.[10] The word 'pure' is from the Greek *amiantos* which means 'undefiled' or 'free from contamination'.[11] Two of the ten commandments given to Moses on Mt Sinai speak to this. Both adultery and coveting (unhealthy desire for) our neighbour's spouse is against God's way.[12] Jesus took this further, saying that not only should we avoid acting on adulterous feelings, we shouldn't even think about someone in that way.[13]

But purity is not just about adultery. Over the whole of scripture many verses call us to avoid sexual immorality. In the Old Testament not only would an adulterous couple be killed if they were caught laying with each other but a girl could be stoned to death if she wasn't a virgin when she got married.[14] In the New Testament, when Joseph found out Mary was pregnant he was set to divorce her quietly, to spare her disgrace. But when the angel told him Mary hadn't been unfaithful, he took her as his wife.[15] And Galatians 5:19-21 is one of several passages

---

10 Hebrews 13:4

11 Vine, WE, Unger, MF & White, Jr., W 1996, *Vine's Complete Expository Dictionary of Old and New Testament Words*, Thomas Nelson, Bath, England, pp. 5198.

12 Exodus 20:14,17.

13 Matthew 5:28

14 Deuteronomy 22:20-22

15 Matthew 1:18-21

where sexual immorality is listed with other areas of rebellion, as an act of the flesh – human mind and will – that will lead to death.

My dear and precious ladies, I know this is a sensitive topic and I won't pretend I am an expert in this area, let alone pretend I have the right to point a finger of judgement at anyone whose walk is different from mine. But I believe God's word is saying that sex is meant to be confined to marriage.

Please know that God is speaking to me as well as to you as I write this. I have not always navigated this area as well as I could have. Paul says in Romans 3:23-24 that *every one of us* has done wrong things and fallen short of God's glory. Since the fall, no one has ever lived a perfect life. But if we turn around and follow Jesus, we receive a predestined antidote for our mistakes: the power of the cross. Christ forgives us and washes away the stain of sin from our spirits. That's the fantastic truth of his grace. If God doesn't condemn us no one else has the right to.[16]

If you are unsure of what God is really like, look at Jesus. Remember that Jesus spent a whole lot of his time with the people the religious leaders despised. He hung out with 'sinners' and 'tax collectors' – the ones who knew they didn't have it all together – and offended the religious establishment.[17] He let a prostitute wash his feet with her tears and wipe them with her hair.[18] This was a very intimate act to allow in public. Another

---

16 Romans 8:1
17 Matthew 9:10-11
18 Luke 7:37-39

prostitute, Mary Magdalene, was one of his inner circle.[19] It was scandalous and beautiful.

Don't get me wrong, Jesus was – and is – serious about sin but he also is serious about grace. When a crowd wanted to stone a woman caught in adultery – no one ever seems to have accused the man – Jesus asked the ones who were free from guilt to throw the first stone.[20] One by one they dropped the stones and slunk away. Jesus, the only one who was free from guilt, looked the woman in the eye and said he didn't condemn her, but that she should go and leave her 'life of sin'.[21] How amazing is his grace? We don't know what happened to her, but how could she not turn her life around after such a reprieve?

I'd like to talk in more depth about God's grace a little later in this chapter and about how we can turn around if we fall short of God's best for us, but first let's look at another reason we should keep sex for marriage.

> *'Jesus was – and is – serious about sin but he also is serious about grace.'*

Science, culture and purity

Let's take a step away from the Bible for a moment and look more broadly at the issue of abstinence. I spent many of my fifteen years of working in schools mentoring young people on this topic. I organised year-level assembly talks in human

---

19   Luke 8:1-3
20   John 8:3-11
21   John 8:11

resource education on sex topics and I have to say I was not the favourite chaplain of some of the teachers. But I did this because I believe in giving our young people an alternative. It is no longer education when we force our beliefs onto others without presenting an alternative, so they can choose.

Teenagers were being given all kinds of teaching about sex, but no one was talking about abstinence at all, let alone remaining abstinent until marriage. So, as a Bible-believing girl who was actually living the life, I took it upon myself to start the process. I found that there was also a considerable number of parents who really valued this message, as they did not want their children being encouraged to practise so-called 'safe sex' and learn about topics they weren't ready to deal with at such a young age.

> *'It is no longer education when we force our beliefs onto others without presenting an alternative, so they can choose.'*

The same popular culture that slams down the thought of abstinence as old-fashioned and irrelevant is also the one that has long been selling the message of safe sex. And while 'safe sex' has some advantages – including the prevention of unwanted pregnancies, sexually transmitted diseases (STDs) and their ongoing consequences – it won't prevent people from becoming emotionally and psychologically fractured by giving themselves to another outside of the plan of God.

You may be surprised at this but there are medical and psychological reasons we should abstain from sex outside of marriage. I'm not just referring to the act of making love but the focus of the mind as well.

Sexual Chemistry

Science has a lot to say about sexual desire and the mind. In an article called *Eros in the Brain*, Christian sexologist, Patricia Weerakoon, outlines the chemical processes in our brain that are linked with sexual desire and falling in love.[22] Desire kicks in at puberty due to an influx of testosterone (yep, even women have testosterone) but the focus of desire develops through childhood experiences due to a process called scripting. This continues to a lesser extent in our later years and is influenced by the things we choose to feed our brain. So, when the apostle Paul says we should think about whatever is 'true, noble, right, pure, lovely, admirable, excellent and praiseworthy', he is talking about neuroplasticity.[23]

'Falling in love' is a little different. Romantic love, says Weerakoon, is an emotion charged state of passionate attraction to a specific person.[24] It is fuelled by a chemical called dopamine which is part of the reward circuit in our brains. Dopamine floods the brain causing elation and euphoria. We don't eat properly and neither do we sleep well. Other chemicals are involved – serotonin decreases and noradrenaline increases – but dopamine is the main player. This phase can last 18-24 months.

---

22 P Weerakoon 2016, *Eros on the Brain*, Patricia Weerakoon, viewed 12 July 2020, <http://patriciaweerakoon.com/resources-sex-and-god/eros-on-the-brain/>.

23 Philippians 4:8

24 Weerakoon 2016

Weerakoon recommends we don't make major decisions during this period as these chemicals can flaw our judgement!

> *'Every time we have sexual relations with someone, we form this attachment with them. And when we go through a relationship break-up, that attachment is torn from us.'*

Sexual intimacy is different again. It is mediated by the brain chemicals oxytocin and vasopressin, which Weerakoon calls the 'cuddle hormones'.[25] The more you make love, the more these chemicals are released, and the more these chemicals are released, the more you make love. The result is deep attachment – the two becoming one.[26]

Let's go deeper. Our brain biochemistry agrees with the Bible by saying that sexual intimacy is not a casual thing. Every time we have sexual relations with someone, we form this attachment with them. And when we go through a relationship break-up, that attachment is torn from us. We lose a part of ourselves in the process – the emotional scars affecting the next relationship we have, and the next.

We cannot cast a blind eye to the spiritual and emotional pain that's caused when we engage in sexual relationships before the time is right. But so many do. We are surprised when it hurts – and then we shake our fists at God and blame him for our pain.

---

25 Weerakoon 2016
26 Genesis 2:24; Mark 10:8.

But this science of attachment goes beyond physical intimacy. Weerakoon says that even fantasy or virtual intimacy can be a bonding activity.[27] Oxytocin causes the person to bond with the object of orgasm.[28] This can lead to all sorts of problems including the forming of addictions.

Let's take masturbation to start with. Weerakoon says that surveys note 90% of men are said to masturbate and the other 10% are lying![29] Statistics for women are hard to come by, but it is widely practiced by both sexes. At its heart, masturbation is just the rubbing of the genitals for pleasure: The release of the chemicals of orgasm make people feel good.[30] Is this a bad thing?

Weerakoon indicates there can be problems with unchecked self-pleasuring. Masturbation can get people into the habit of being sexually selfish and not sharing the sexual journey with their partner. The other issue is that continual immediate gratification of sexual desire can limit the development of self-control – one of the fruits of the Holy Spirit – and lead to either sexual pressure in marriage or the use of pornography.[31] [32]

---

27 Weerakoon 2016

28 Weerakoon, P 2013, *It feels great to masturbate. But is it okay?*, Patricia Weerakoon, viewed 12 July 2020, <http://patriciaweerakoon.com/resources-sex-and-god/it-feels-great-to-masturbate-but-is-it-okay/>./

29 Weerakoon 2013

30 Weerakoon 2013

31 Weerakoon 2013

32 Weerakoon 2013

Habits developed in singleness can spill over into marriage so both these issues can cause future problems when a single person finds a partner. However, a pornography addiction or misplaced sexual attachment can happen any time. Also, if we fantasise about a real person, not only are we making a sexual object of that person without their consent, we are in danger of breaking the command of Jesus in Matthew 5:28, to not look at another lustfully. And if we use pornography to fuel the orgasm, we can become addicted to the use of images to arouse us. This can mess with our minds and have serious consequences for how we see ourselves – and others – sexually.

You might be saying, I'm a woman, pornography is a male thing, right? Sadly, no. In 2016, the Barna Group released a study that showed 33% of female teens or young adults in the US used porn regularly, compared with 67% of males.[33] This was a significant increase from 2008 where many girls reported accidental exposure to porn but not regular use.[34] More men than women use porn but the availability of pornography online means that many more are snared by it.

'Habits developed in singleness can spill over into marriage so both these issues can cause future problems when a single person finds a partner.'

---

[33] Barna Group 2016, *Porn in the Digital Age: New Research Reveals 10 Trends*, Barna Group, viewed 12 July 2020, <https://www.barna.com/research/porn-in-the-digital-age-new-research-reveals-10-trends/>.

[34] C McKenna n.d., *Porn: Girls Struggle Too*, Moral Revolution, viewed 14 July 2020, <https://www.moralrevolution.com/blog/Porn-girls-struggle-too>.

A 2019 survey by ABC radio's triple j station, says that 93% of young men and 58% of young women use porn.[35] While these results may be skewed by the audience of the station, they reflect a disturbing trend that the use of pornography by young women is skyrocketing. Both the Barna and triple j surveys show that many young adults don't think pornography is bad for them or for society. The truth is, pornography is very bad for us – and it's spreading like a virus.

> *'Porn isn't real – it's staged – but it can give us the wrong ideas about what good sex is like and how to treat our sexual partner.'*

It's Time We Talked, is an Australian violence prevention project dedicated to help young people who are exposed to and consume pornography.[36] This group says that while porn may seem cool or exciting, it can shape the way we think about sex and people.[37] Porn isn't real – it's staged – but it can give us the wrong ideas about what good sex is like and how to treat our sexual partner. It also can influence sexual tastes. Porn bodies are not normal, the sexual practices are not safe, and neither are they pleasurable.[38] Pornography is designed to look good, not make the actors feel good; and when young people

---

35 Triple J Hack 2019, *Here's what you told us about what porn you watch, and how often*, triple j, viewed 14 July 2020, <https://www.abc.net.au/triplej/programs/hack/heres-what-you-told-us-about-what-porn-you-watch/11442772>.

36 *Landing page* 2014, It's time we talked, viewed 15 July 2020, <https://itstimewetalked.com>.

37 *What's the issue? 2014*, It's time we talked, viewed 15 July 2020, <https://itstimewetalked.com/young-people/whats-the-issue/>.

38 *What's the issue? 2014*

try to emulate these actions in their sex lives there can be serious emotional and physical fallout. About 88% of scenes in the most popular porn shows show some kind of violence and degradation of women. The rougher it is the better it sells.[39]

Now think for a moment about the scripting I spoke of earlier. A young man or woman who becomes aroused by pornography is training their brain to like certain things. What happens when they enter into a sexual relationship and the only way a guy can enjoy sex is by hurting the girl or making her contort into a painful position. This is a recipe for relationship disaster and also for physical violence. I know from talking with friends who work with young people in this space that some terrible things happen – especially to girls who turn up at their doctor's surgery suffering from a range of serious injuries, all in the name of pornography.

> *'About 88% of scenes in the most popular porn shows show some kind of violence and degradation of women.'*

It says in God's word that the evil one masquerades as an angel of light.[40] It also says he is a thief who comes only to 'steal, kill and destroy'.[41] The young are especially vulnerable, but pornography is destructive to every age group. The enemy turns our innate sexual desire – something that is meant to be joyful and to mirror God's relationship with humanity – into an ugly

---

39 *What's the issue? 2014*
40 2 Corinthians 11:14
41 John 10:10

thing that causes despair and pain. Sorry if I burst your bubble but pornography is not cool and never will be. I hate that it's hushed up and not spoken about.

The other thing I hate about porn is that it is exploitative. I value justice and the tragic reality is that as long as people watch and consume pornography, we are advocating for and contributing to an industry that is harming millions of people. Pornography both promotes and is fuelled by sex slavery; and it objectifies both men and women. This industry is pure evil and as long as anyone consumes it, they contribute to it by creating a demand for it. We need to stand together ladies – and be our sister's – and brother's keeper.

> *'The first is that shame comes from the evil one,
> not God.'*

Right now, if you've been looking at porn, reading this may trigger two different emotions. One is shame – why am I doing this? The other is a sense of panic and despair. You've sampled porn and you know it's affected you, but you don't know how to get rid of the dark thoughts or the addiction to the images. Sexual healing is a huge subject and way beyond the scope of this chapter, as I've said, but may I encourage you in two ways?

The first is that shame comes from the evil one, not God. I previously mentioned that Jesus doesn't condemn us.[42] When we sin, we are called to acknowledge our sins and then He forgives us and calls us to stop sinning, but he never shames us.

---

42 Romans 8:1

Remember the woman caught in adultery?[43] If you are feeling shame it's from the accuser, not God.

> *'We've seen that God created sex to be a beautiful thing when expressed in the security of a loving marriage.'*

The second is that there are a lot of resources out there to help. If you are a young person and think you may have a pornography addiction, have a look at the *It's Time We Talked* support page.[44] The *Moral Revolution* site is another excellent resource for all ages.[45] Whatever you do, please don't give up on God. A problem with pornography in no way disqualifies you from God's kingdom. There is a thief who wants to destroy, but Christ loves and yearns to lead us into freedom and fullness of life.[46]

We've covered a lot of ground in this chapter so far. We've seen that God created sex to be a beautiful thing when expressed in the security of a loving marriage. We've looked at how the science of desire confirms this and how culture has led many to develop harmful sexual attachments. But we haven't yet talked about same-sex desires and relationships. This is an important issue and nowadays almost everyone has a strong

---

43 John 8:1-11

44 *Getting support* 2014, It's time we talked, viewed 15 July 2020, <https://itstimewetalked.com/young-people/getting-support/>. Resources that can help teenagers with many of the issues that surround pornography

45 *Moral Revolution* 2020, Moral Revolution, viewed 17 July 2020, <https://www.moralrevolution.com>. *Moral Revolution* aims to promote healthy sexuality by providing resources that help people live whole lives of love, honour, respect and freedom. They run courses on various aspects of sexuality including gaining freedom from addiction to pornography.

46 John 10:10

opinion on what's right and what's not, so let's take a quick look at this area.

Same-Sex Orientation

Homosexuality has long been a point of contention, both in the world and in faith communities. For centuries men and women, who are sexually attracted to their own gender, have been persecuted by both the society they belong to, and the religious establishment of many different faiths, including Christianity. Men and women have been put to death physically, or chemically castrated or otherwise mutilated because of their sexual preference. They have been bullied, rejected, subjected to demonic deliverance and made to feel sub-human.

This is true. And it makes me weep. It is my absolute belief that no human being deserves to be vilified in any way because of their gender, marital status, belief system, race, sexual preference or any other bias. When Jesus, the Son of God, walked the earth, he stood against injustice. I believe that as his follower, he calls me to take that stance today.

However, it's also my belief that God created this world. His word, the Bible, is infallible so it needs to have the final authority in how we live. God's word says some amazing things that apply no matter what our sexual orientation is. Sometimes we get so caught up in the conversations surrounding homosexuality that we forget the most important thing – our identity is founded first and foremost in our relationship with Jesus.

It doesn't matter who we are, whether we are young, old, rich, or poor. It doesn't matter what our status, race or passion in life is, or whether we are gay or straight. Looking through God's word, we are reminded Jesus is the way, the truth and the life.[47] We all aspire to 'abundant life' and that life is found when we have a personal relationship with Jesus Christ – and receive his amazing grace. Without Jesus, all of us stand guilty. Every. Human. Being. I mentioned earlier we've all fallen short of God's glory – his perfection. But because God loves us so much, he sent his son to die for us and pay the price for our sin.[48] God loves everyone *equally*. He willingly gave his life for us so we can all have life in its fullness. All we need to do is receive that free gift and follow him.

It's 'following him' that can be the sticking point. How do we work out what he wants us to do? Some Christian traditions put a high emphasis on a church authority to tell God's people how to live. Historically other denominations have emphasised scripture as our final point of authority, which is the best way to go. I love being surrounded by good church leaders who teach God's word with clarity, but it is still my personal responsibility to read, discern and choose God's way. [49]

> *'We all aspire to 'abundant life' and that life is found when we have a personal relationship with Jesus Christ – and receive his amazing grace.'*

What do we do if we love Jesus but identify as gay? I know there are believers who embrace both their practice of homosexuality

---

47 John 14:6
48 John 3:16
49 Leviticus 18:22; Romans 1:26-27; 1 Corinthians 6:9-11; 1 Timothy 1:8-11; Jude 1:7.

and their faith and I know others whose conviction is similar to mine. What I strongly recommend is that if you are gay, don't respond to this question lightly. Read the scriptures and ask the Holy Spirit for revelation. Follow the conviction he brings. Be engaged in discussions and glean ideas from those you trust, in order to gain clarity. Treat the question with the gravity it deserves and follow the wisdom God gives you.

> *'Read the scriptures and ask the Holy Spirit for revelation.'*

One of the best books on this subject is *Gay Girl, Good God*, by Jackie Hill Perry.[50] I highly recommend Perry's material if you want to explore this subject further. Her testimony as a gay woman – who fell in love with Jesus – is profound. Another authority in this area is Rachel Gilson, her book *Born Again This Way* is definitely worth reading. [51] Both of these women's story gives us insight in the complex journey that can be encountered in this space.

If you are working though this area, it's important to do so in community. As I've suggested again and again in this book, don't isolate yourself. If any of us are to find the strength to live the Christian life well, we can't do it alone. We all need one another.

---

[50] J Hill Perry 2018, *Gay girl, good God: the story of who I was and who God has always been*, B&H Publishing Group, Nashville, Tennessee.

[51] Rachel Gilson 2020, *Born Again This Way*, Good Book Company, Denmark.

> *'We need to cultivate good connections within God's family if we are to thrive as singles – connections that go beyond the surface and touch on deep issues.'*

Connection, Vulnerability & Motive

True community is characterised by three things:

- Connection
- Vulnerability
- Belonging

We need other people if we are to flourish. We need to cultivate good connections within God's family if we are to thrive as singles – connections that go beyond the surface and touch on deep issues. And we all need somewhere to belong.[52]

I'd like to suggest that as Christians, we have a great opportunity here. If God is saying that abstinence and purity are his ideal for Christian singles, whatever our sexual orientation – if he has made us with a deep need to be loved and to belong – we can help by creating a place where people from all walks of life feel welcome and connected. I'm forever grateful for my lead pastors Craig and Nadia who remain intentional about how space is created in our church so that people from all walks of life and sexual orientation can feel they belong. But this is something we can all work at. The more profound our connections and

---

52 For more information on practical living as a Christian single with a sex drive, I highly recommend the *Moral Revolution* podcast series, *Let's Talk About It*. This episode is especially relevant to this conversation. <https://www.moralrevolution.com/recommended-resources/podcast/to-all-the-singles-with-a-sex-drive>.

the deeper our friendships, the easier it will be for all of us to navigate the single journey.

As part of this, let's continue to develop spaces where we can learn to be vulnerable with one another. We sometimes find it hard to talk about sexuality with one another as Christians. It says in the Bible that the older women should teach the younger but how can this happen if we don't talk about this subject?[53] Married women sometimes stop talking about sex when single women join their discussion circle. It would be great if we could create more safe places for conversations that go beyond 'premarital counselling' and deal with the sexual issues many singles grapple with.

If we have built strong community around ourselves it can be easier to flee from temptation when it happens. Like Joseph who ran away when Potiphar's wife tried to seduce him, we do need to be wise and make good choices.[54] When our hormones are raging, should we be alone after work with that hot non-Christian colleague we know likes us? Or do we buy a pizza, go see a friend and ask them to pray with us? If we are alone in our home and we are addicted to pornography, do we give in to the urge to look at that site or do we get some girlfriends together and go out for coffee? Good community helps us make good choices.

But community isn't all we need. There is another word that is important in this discussion: *motive*.

---

53 Titus 2:4-5
54 Genesis 39:6-12

Motives are the drivers that make us do things. The stronger the motive the more we are likely to do something. If we have serious health issues, we have greater motivation to eat well and exercise than if we just want to lose a couple of kilograms to get into a new dress. In the same way, if we are to beat the various sexual pressures we face, we need to have the right motivation.

If we choose 'keeping ourselves for Mr Right' as our motivation for abstinence, what happens when we don't find him? Do we give up and do our own thing? The truth is that if the reason for our abstinence is centred on a desire for anything other than honouring Jesus – our beautiful Saviour – we can fall into trouble.

> *'We all know that purity is a radical and countercultural goal in our sex-crazed society.'*

When I was a young woman in ministry, I wasn't really interested in finding a boyfriend, but I had it in mind that if I did, he would be a virgin too. I was saving myself for this imagined 'right person'. Lucky guy – if only I could find him. Time passed and the desire deepened but I didn't meet this man. I began to realise it might not happen. I then went through a series of illnesses – including breast cancer – and had several operations. I also became isolated, as I explained earlier. My focus was on work and study and my social life suffered. Bitterness crept in. I felt an entitlement after decades of waiting and temptation began to rise. At first it was a whisper, but it became a loud shout. The result was I failed myself and took matters into my own hands.

We all know that purity is a radical and countercultural goal in our sex-crazed society. I can say from experience that if our motive for abstinence isn't iron-clad, we can easily make the wrong decision. If we base our decisions on a desire to honour a future mate, we can become weary and bitter when things don't work out how we want them to. But when our motive is to honour Jesus, lover of our soul, we are empowered to make the right choices.

In Jesus we have all love and grace and goodness, now and forever. He has given everything for us. If we choose to love Jesus by doing what he wants us to do, the best way we know how, we won't become disappointed or bitter when our earthly expectations are unfulfilled. We may still battle with our desires, but we won't have the same fuel for rebellion inside us.

Can you see the difference? One motive is temporal and situational. The other is eternal. Which is stronger? Ladies let's worship our beautiful Lord with our purity until he returns to take us – his bride, his church – to be with him. What am amazing day that will be! But what if we have made wrong decisions?

Right now, some of you are cheering me on. You're agreeing that this is the way to go. It has worked for you. But there may be others reading who want to put this book down and walk away. You like what you hear about Jesus Christ, but you haven't lived up to this ideal as a single woman. Or you are a Christian, maybe even a leader, and you've messed up big time and gone where you never thought you'd go. Or you didn't think you'd ever give in to your homosexual desires, but you did. What if people find out?

May I say that the life of faith can be tough, and it can produce scars, but it's worth the ultimate prize. Think for a moment, of a soldier going to war in their fresh, new uniform. At the end of the battle they return exhausted, wounded and ragged. What got them through? Each time they were knocked down they got up and kept fighting. They kept doing this until the battle was won. As believers, Jesus has already won the battle for us through the cross, yet the enemy hasn't stopped coming against us. The good news is that victory for us isn't about being perfect but about staying the course and keeping close to Jesus. If we get knocked down he's always ready to lift us up again.

U-turn and Restoration

One of my favourite passages of scripture is the story of the prodigal son in Luke 15:11-32. A young man asks his father for his inheritance and leaves home. The lad spends all his money on booze and women and is cheated out of the rest. He becomes destitute and starving and ends up herding pigs, unclean animals. To make things worse, he has to steal food from the pigs. He can't sink any lower so he decides to turn around and come home, hoping that his father will take him back as a servant.

Before we go further, I'd like us to imagine that we're not talking about a prodigal son but a prodigal daughter. A daughter who chooses her own way and leaves her father's house. She makes mistakes and finds herself desperate and alone. But she yearns to know the father's love again and she turns back, not knowing what welcome she'll receive.

When the father sees her in the distance. He lifts up his robes and *runs* toward her. Running was considered to be beneath the dignity of a mature Jewish man. But he races to her and embraces her and brings her back into his home with full rights as his daughter.

> *'A daughter who chooses her own way and leaves her father's house. When we choose to turn to him and come home, we are always welcomed.'*

Hence, ladies, this is what our heavenly Father does for us when we make a choice and decide to turn back to him. When we choose to turn to him and come home, we are always *welcomed*. There are no half measures in God's kingdom and no limits to his love.

Later in the story we hear the father talking to a second daughter. This daughter didn't leave home, but she lost sight of what it meant to live in the riches of her father's house. She was the older sister who always did everything right, so she thought. She became bitter when the prodigal returned home and got all the attention. When she complains to the father, he says, 'Everything I have is yours.'[55] She needed to be reminded of the rich, loving relationship she had with the father, and of the authority she carried as his daughter.

---

55 Luke 15:31

There is something in this passage for all of us. How many of us are in danger of sliding into a similar sort of bitterness? Like the older sister, year after year, you've done the right thing outwardly, but somehow lost the joy of your faith? You feel resentment toward God because he hasn't given you everything you thought you deserved and desired. Has that ever happened to you? It's not just the prodigals who need to make a U-turn. May we all 'come home' and live fully in our heavenly Father's love.

I think we all know that sin is serious, but have you noticed how we often elevate our sin above the power of the cross? We think Jesus can never accept us, or that the roof will cave in if we go back to church on Sunday after we've blown it, but we forget that God loved us so much that he gave his son to die in our place.[56] We forget the degradation Jesus willingly endured when he was falsely accused, abused and mocked – for us.[57] We forget that he willingly took the penalty for our sin as huge nails were bashed through his wrists to hold him on the crossbeam.[58] We forget that he had to haul himself up on these wrists each time he wanted to breathe – until he gave up his spirit and died – for our salvation.[59]

Yes, sin is serious. Deadly serious. It can have ongoing consequences in our lives. But I grieve at how many beautiful single people miss out on the adventure of abundant living because they feel weighed down by their mistakes.

---

56 John 3:16
57 John 19:1-3
58 John 19:16-18
59 John 19:30

*'Know that our heavenly Father,
not only welcomes us but restores us.'*

We all make mistakes. Consider the key leaders in the Bible. How many failed spectacularly at one stage or another? Peter denied Jesus, Paul helped murder Christians and Moses killed an Egyptian soldier and fled to the desert.[60] There you have it: three of the best. So, if we've made a mistake and are wondering if God will still accept us and use us, we are in great company. It doesn't matter who we are or what we've done, Jesus can turn anything around.

If it feels too hard or you think you've wandered too far away, know that our heavenly Father, not only welcomes us but restores us. He puts a ring on our finger – a ring that signifies the authority of sonship – and wraps a robe around our shoulders. How amazing is our God?

I once read a story about a traveller in Jerusalem who noticed an exquisitely beautiful building.[61] When he asked about the story of the building, he was referred to one of the oldest men in the area. The old man told the traveller about the battle to restore the property. Developers wanted to pull it down to make way for modern buildings, but he fought to gain approval for its restoration. He went on to say that the architects researched the archives and found the original drawings, then used the exact same materials for every part of the restoration and

---

60 Luke 22:54-62; Acts 7:23-26; Acts 8:1-3

61 M Munroe 2010, *Rediscovering the kingdom: ancient hope for our 21st century world*, Destiny Image Publishers, Shippensburg, pp. 69.

construction of the old house. When it was finished it was not a replica of the original, rather it had been fully restored to its original form.

Ladies, that is what God does for us when we turn back to him and place ourselves in his hands. He draws us back into his presence, broken yet loved and accepted, and breathes life and hope back into us. He renews us and rebuilds us as we were meant to be, daughters in his household, restored to full authority within his family.

> *'Sometimes we have to make the choice to return to our God, not just once, but again and again.'*

Life is to be lived once, and today he gives us grace to start again and embrace the gift of a fresh start. Today he washes our mistakes away and cleans us from the inside out. Today we realise that we were always accepted and never condemned. Today we can know with certainty how much we are loved.

Sometimes we have to make the choice to return to our God, not just once, but again and again. That's part of living and growing in God: becoming more like Jesus as we mature. For this maturity to become a reality in our lives there is one place and time we can start this journey. Not yesterday. Not one day. But right here, right now. Wherever you are sitting with this subject, whatever challenges you face, whatever temptations you wrestle with, it's time to run, and keep running, to our glorious, beautiful, gracious heavenly father. Can you see him in the distance? Look, that's him! He's running toward *you*.

Thank you and well done for staying with me on this journey through the subject of our sexuality. I know that not all of you reading this may have a Christian faith or may ever have heard of God's teaching around sex and sexuality before. Some of you may disagree with me on particular things and find my thoughts radical and countercultural. However, as a Christian I believe God's word is *the* source of truth. When faced with the revelation of God's love we must turn to him and live for him, whoever we are and whatever our situation in life. Know that whatever your current journey, God is on your side. He always wants the best for you. As a sister walking the journey beside you my intent is to empower you, not condemn you. While we still have breath, we have an opportunity for a new beginning each day, so don't lose hope.

I'd love you to visit my website and take up the opportunities for discussion there. I love encouraging other single people and enjoy learning what others think, even if it's different from my point of view. That applies to anything I've talked about in this book.

We've come a long way together over several chapters and dealt with many issues faced by singles. We've also discussed how to thrive in our circumstances. But in the next chapter I'd like to take our ability to thrive as a Christian single, further and deeper.

> *'I'd love you to visit my website and take up the opportunities for discussion there.'*

What would you say if I told you that singleness, along with all of its challenges, was a gift rather than the curse it sometimes appears to be? How would it change our outlook if we embraced this idea? How would it affect the freedom with which we worship our God?

Are you intrigued? Awesome. Let's keep going!

THE UNEXPECTED GIFT

V

EBONY

I was livid. The boys in my group were able to walk the streets of Thailand around the hidden brothels and visit a man involved in human trafficking [for the purpose of building relationship and personal education] but apparently it wasn't safe for me, a female, to be there.

I had come all this way to stay back in my room… Whatever!

With the measures in place, it felt safe enough to me. It wasn't my first time in Thailand. My introduction to the Thai community was with my grandmother when I was 16. She wanted to share her love of nations with me. Now, here I was again with a large team in southern Thailand; the nightlife had begun, and I desperately wanted to utilise every moment to study the complexities of human trafficking. I'd never felt so passionate about anything like this before. But it was the boys who got to venture outside, one even teased me over the fact that I had to stay behind.

I tried to hide my anger and jealousy, but it's etched in my memory. I politely asked our leader, 'Why can't we go? Can the girls do something too?'

The answer was, 'No,' but I could stay in the foyer and observe.

Then I had a moment of self-revelation. Instead of my gender being a problem in some situations, I realised that it might provide unique opportunities.

God said, 'Ebony, I purposed you to be a girl.'

I imagined myself sitting in a safe house with an abused, trafficked girl. She sat on the cold hard floor with her arms wrapped around her knees. I walked in. She didn't open up in conversation, but she felt safe with me. I was able to embrace her in the way a man couldn't, given her situation.

In that moment, I knew unique opportunities would arise, because of my gender.

And the irony? The boys didn't achieve what they intended. The man they went to meet wasn't available, so they played soccer with the community instead while I was having a significant moment with God.

My Thailand experience made me determined to act; not to just be moved with emotion. The following year I dedicated my 21st birthday year towards raising $21,000 by reaching 21,000 people to donate $1 each to 'The A21 Campaign'; formed to combat human trafficking and modern-day slavery. Thanks to friends and family, the financial goal was surpassed. We did it! With this donation, enslaved lives could begin to know they are loved and purposed to make a difference.

Two years on, at the age of 23, I was back in Thailand for the third time, but now my heart was torn. Life had been on track.

I'd been living in community with a diverse range of university friends, and I was enjoying church and family, but now I had again uprooted myself to go and live in Thailand. A week before I boarded the plane, I sat in the car with tears running down my face, knowing that life wouldn't be the same again. I was willing to go but the thought of missing out on everyday fun with family and friends stung. I was scared I'd be lonely and that my mental health wouldn't hold up. Mum joked that when kids move out of home, they generally move three suburbs away, not three countries. Still, I knew I had to return to Thailand. It was an incredible opportunity.

* * * * *

The cultural exchange was intense and beautiful. Living among Thai people is vastly different to living with Australians or international students. Thais are a generous people, but it seemed that everything I did was scrutinised; from eating, to hygiene, to what clothes I wore, to the things I valued. And I didn't always feel loved within the community. Curious, I asked my Thai friend Malee, how she knew she was loved. She said she didn't know.

I discovered that many parents and grandparents take a 'tough love' approach with their children. Her community tended to praise group effort rather than individual achievement. Malee wasn't encouraged or hugged as a child and she felt deep rejection when her father abandoned their family. But Malee said something that impacted me deeply. 'When you hug me, Ebony, something inside of me breaks'.

Human touch is powerful.

There were other examples. One lady told me she knew she was loved because her parents scolded her and her siblings. This helped me understand why I sometimes felt unloved in their presence. Their language of love was different to mine. I'd taken their behaviour towards me as personal indifference, but no, it was because of their culture.

While here in Thailand, I have chosen to show love, even when their perception of love is vastly different from mine. This decision to be 'me' was – and is – painful and at times I've felt paralysed: caught between wanting to be culturally sensitive, respectful and politically correct, while still being a hundred percent myself, expressing affection enthusiastically. Several people have appreciated the warmth I bring, but it requires vulnerability to demonstrate love. We experience love in different ways, but we all need community.

I have cried myself to sleep some nights. I tell myself, 'just toughen up'. But these girls don't need another hardened, protected heart. They need an empathetic and strong one, even if It's scrutinised. They too have said that they need a different way of loving. I'm aware that we're all on a journey, and with time we'll be okay.

There are other stories.

Som Wang, a prominent single Thai church leader, said she knew she was loved because God loved her, even though her family rejected her for her faith. Yet she tried to put herself in a position where she didn't need community. I've gone through my own stoicism phase where I've told myself I don't need close relationships. But I discovered that interdependence is much better than independence. God wants us to be vulnerable. Som Wang and I are on a continual pendulum of interdependence and independence. I'm learning that God created us for his pleasure and created us for each other. If either of those connections are broken, we suffer.

Then there is Suchada, a colleague who took me on her scooter to minister to children in a drug-affected community near the Thai/Malaysian border. When I told her she was amazing giving up her comfort for Christ's Kingdom purposes (taking care of children), she replied, 'If I'm so amazing, why no husband?' She laughs but there is a glimmer of truth to her statement.

However, the essence of community is that if we can't have children of our own, we can love and adore 'yours' for you.

My dreams of the future haven't been typical or traditional. I haven't envisaged finding a husband and 'settling down' with children and I haven't shopped around for this either. My great focus is on how I can connect people to God and to one another. I want to experience more of God's love, which then enables me to love and be loved by the person next to me. If the connection between God and me is out of sync – even one degree off God's purpose – I can find myself living outside of God's personal best for me, and the community I belong to suffers.

Thailand has its dangers; but I wonder if the greatest danger is a hardened heart; where God's voice is no longer a priority, where my desires are more important than meeting the needs of those around me.

Instead of searching for 'the one' to journey with, there are many 'ones' who need to be loved in my journey.

Have you seen the confidence of a girl who knows she is loved? What I've discovered is she can change the world.

You are loved!

*The names of the women mentioned above were changed to protect their privacy, however the names I chose reflect their character: Malee – 'my flower'; Som Wang – 'living up to the hope' and Suchada – 'good sister'.

10

IS SINGLENESS A GIFT?

Have you ever been given a gift that was different from what you expected? As we begin this penultimate chapter of our journey through the delightful but challenging topic of singleness, I'd like to tell you a story.

Imagine it's your birthday... one of those important ones ending in zero. Your best friend – you've known her since you were five years old – picks you up and takes you to a restaurant so you can celebrate this wonderful occasion with friends. When you get into the car you can't help noticing a large box on the back seat, wrapped in red paper and tied with gold ribbon. Excitement quivers through you. You've always loved presents. What can it be?

You can't help thinking about it as you head to the restaurant. Maybe it's that gorgeous pair of high-heeled shoes you both tried on last week? It would be an expensive gift, but your friend has just landed a high paying corporate job. Or maybe it's a set of crystal wine glasses – you saw some in a catalogue last week and they would be great for entertaining. Or it could be a huge box of Belgian chocolates. Your friends know you love chocolate, but you never buy it for yourself. Or maybe it's that book on restoring furniture by that celebrity do-it-yourself guru. You did tell your friend about it and you've wanted it for a long, long time. But no, it is the wrong shape. Maybe it's the book *plus* some chocolates – or...

It takes a while, but you manage to wrest your thoughts away from the gift. Whatever it is, you know it will be good – and beautiful. Your best friend always buys generous, lovely gifts and you know this time will be no exception.

> *"You take the gift from her with a loud,*
> *'Thank you!'"*

You arrive at the restaurant and most of your friends are already there. You sit down to many loud wishes of happy birthday, then one-by-one your friends pass you their gifts. You accept each present with a smile and a thank you, including the one from your friend. It's heavy. Maybe it's that gorgeous hand-blown glass vase you saw in that boutique shop. The vase was on sale when you went window shopping with her a month ago. Yes, that's it! That has to be it. She did ask if you liked it. It would fit in a box this size. You take the gift from her with a loud, 'Thank you!'

You long to open the presents, but you decide to wait until dessert is being served. There's nothing wrong with a bit of anticipation, although every now and then your thoughts travel to the exquisite vase in your imagination. It will be just right for the corner table in your living room. The light from the window will catch it and highlight its beauty. What a wonderful, generous friend you have.

Then it's time to open the presents. You open each one with a deep sense of gratitude. One friend gives you a small box of your favourite chocolates. Another gives you a silk scarf, another gives you a bookstore voucher. Finally, it comes to your best friend's gift. You untie the ribbon and remove the wrapper with care, all the while contemplating the designer vase inside. At last, you open the gift box to find a beautiful… Cordless power drill.

Words fail you. All your friends smile, and your friend's eyes shine. She obviously thinks she's given you the best gift ever. But you wanted that hand-blown glass vase. You had your heart set on it. You didn't want a power drill.

You force a smile and say a 'thank you' that's a little too loud. You tell yourself that it is a generous, practical present. By the time you finish dessert and coffee you've composed yourself enough to be philosophical about it, but a level of disappointment lingers within you.

> *"It's my conviction that the only way to thrive in our single status is to embrace it as a gift from God."*

When you get home after dinner you put the drill aside and wonder if you could somehow still buy that vase you wanted. You look at it online but it's not on sale anymore. You sigh inside. *Maybe one day…*

But the next morning you wake with an idea forming. You can put the voucher towards the furniture restoration book you wanted. You go to the shop, buy the book and bring it home. At once you are flooded with creative ideas. You remember there is an old chair stored in your garage. You can sand the wood back and repaint it – it will look great in the corner next to the side table.

There is one problem though. One of the legs is loose – the join needs repairing. You look for solutions online and find one. All you need is a small wooden brace and some screws and… a cordless power drill. The sense of accomplishment you feel when you fix the chair and paint it is overwhelming. The next weekend you are up early, scouring garage sales for quaint old furniture you can repair and re-purpose. Before long you are selling these pieces online at a profit and you've established a lucrative side-hustle which you *love*. Your friend visits and you thank her for the hundredth time for the unexpected, but perfect, gift she gave you.

She smiles and says, 'I knew it was what you needed.' Ladies, this story is a modern-day parable – a story that reflects a spiritual truth. We've probably all had a time where we were given a gift that was different from expected. But I'm not just talking about birthday presents – I'm speaking of a greater truth. In our lives we have all kinds of longings and expectations, and we are disappointed when those desires are not met. We feel discouraged and sometimes even devastated until we realise that the gift we've been given is exactly what we need right now to thrive.

I'm talking about singleness, of course. I know this might be hard to comprehend but it's my conviction that the only way to thrive in our single status is to embrace it as a gift from God. Just as we receive an unopened gift from someone we love, with thanks, it's vital to embrace our single status as a gift from the one who loves us most – our kind and loving Heavenly Father. Let's talk it over.

Singleness is a Gift!

Earlier in the book I mentioned the famous passage in 1 Corinthians 7 where Paul talks about marriage and singleness. It is here that Paul introduces the idea that both marriage and singleness are gifts from God.

> *"I wish that all of you were as I am. But each of you has your own gift from God; one has this gift, another has that. Now to the unmarried and the widows I say: It is good for them to stay unmarried, as I do. But if they cannot control themselves, they should marry, for it is better to marry than to burn with passion.[1]"*

How does this sit with you? I know many single women who will read this and say, maybe in the context of the desires we discussed in the previous chapter, that their gift obviously isn't singleness. 'I burn with passion, so I don't have that gift!' I've also heard people tell singles that if they desire marriage, then they obviously don't have 'the gift of singleness'.

---

1   1 Corinthians 7:7-9

> *"Singleness can lead to struggles of loneliness, deep grief, and feelings of low self-worth and rejection."*

I don't think either of these statements are correct. Jayne V. Clark of the Christian Counselling and Educational Foundation says that it is a mistake to equate the word 'gift' here in verse 7 with the spiritual gifts mentioned in 1 Corinthians 12:8-10. Spiritual gifts like prophecy and wisdom are functions focused on 'building up of the body of Christ' whereas singleness is an 'objective gift' like the gift of eternal life.[2] Singles don't use their status as singles to build up the church, they use their spiritual gifts just like married people do. However, Clark says singleness is still a gift – one we are called to receive and enjoy with thanksgiving.[3] If we are single, our singleness is a gift. If we are married, our marriage is a gift. Whatever our status, let's wear it well. God promises to be with us and give us everything we need to live for him.[4]

It is important to embrace this truth and the promise of God's sustaining power, even when things are hard. As we've journeyed through this book together, we've seen there are a whole host of challenges we can face as Christian singles. Singleness can carry a stigma in the world and sometimes even in our churches. Singleness can bring financial challenges – even throwing some into abject poverty. It can lead to struggles of loneliness, deep

---

2   JV Clark 2017, *The 'Gift' of Singleness*, Christian Counselling & Educational Foundation, viewed 1 August 2020, <https://www.ccef.org/the-gift-of-singleness/>. Clark recommends a book by Albert Y. Hsu, *Singles at the Crossroad: A Fresh Perspective on Christian Singleness* (Downers Grove, Ill.: InterVarsity Press, 1997).

3   Clark 2017

4   2 Peter 1:3

grief, and feelings of low self-worth and rejection. It can also be confronting sexually as we have just seen. While some desire singleness, many don't. When you are wracked with grief like as Kim shared in her story earlier in the book, or your husband abandons you as war rages in your country, or you are raped by invading soldiers, it is hard to see singleness as a gift.

"Ps. Maree discusses how we can realign our thoughts to the way God thinks, laying aside 'survival thinking' so we can reach our optimal potential."

I've talked about this in detail in earlier chapters, so I won't dwell on it now, but we do have to acknowledge that grief is a reality. Bad things happen to good people in this world. That's a fact and it will continue until our beautiful Saviour returns. Creation is groaning because of sin and just because we believe in Jesus doesn't mean we will have a pain-free life.[5] We know this is true. For some, like the apostle Paul, singleness is a delight. But if we are experiencing pain, how can the single life be a gift?

Shifting our Mindset

The Bible says that we need to be transformed by the renewal of our minds so that we can know God's 'good, pleasing and perfect will'.[6] That means putting the truth of things before our feelings. If we do this, we lift our eyes from the stony ground of our lives up into the loving eyes of our beautiful Saviour. Here we find the grace, goodness and power to persevere. We

---

5   Romans 8:22
6   Romans 12:2

also find the deepening of a relationship with an eternal Father who 'loves us with an everlasting love'.[7]

My senior pastor, Maree de Jong, has recently released a remarkable book on this subject. In *Think Again*, Ps. Maree discusses how we can realign our thoughts to the way God thinks, laying aside 'survival thinking' so we can reach our optimal potential.[8] All of Maree's books are great, so I definitely recommend you get hold of a copy if you want to grow in this area.

In Romans 8:28 Paul says, 'in all things God works for the good of those who love him, who have been called according to his purpose'.[9] Whatever our situation, God invites us to trust in him to work it for our good. If he says he will do this, we can trust him to do it. But we are not just talking about circumstances here. If singleness is a gift, then why not receive it in the same way you and I would receive a gift from someone who loves us? As with the gift in our parable, it's important that we hold out our hands, take the box, and say, 'Thank you,' because we trust the gift-giver. We may still have questions – God welcomes our honesty – but it's not good for us to remain stuck in our disappointment or live like prisoners of our single status. Matthew 7:11 reminds us that the gifts God gives us are good. If singleness is a gift, then it must be a good thing. And if it's been given to us, how amazing if we can embrace it, not just tolerate it!

---

7   Jeremiah 31:3
8   M De Jong 2019, *Think Again*, Life Resource International, New Zealand.
9   Romans 8:28

> *"If we wear our singleness well and lean into God's purposes, we can live a life of beauty, meaning and dignity."*

The reality is that both singleness and marriage are wonderful and distinctly unique gifts. Neither is better than the other, regardless of the fact that marriage is often espoused as the 'holy grail' of life. I might be persecuted in parts of the world for saying this! The key to thriving, be we single or married, is to embrace the situation we are given as a good gift from a good God.

Different situations bring different challenges and benefits. In the 1 Corinthians passage above, Paul says that both singleness and marriage can point us back to God. But he appreciated that his singleness let him focus on his call. We are not all called to be an apostle to the nations but if we wear our singleness well and lean into God's purposes, we can live a life of beauty, meaning and dignity: a life that God has chosen especially for us.

Consider the parable I told at the beginning of the chapter. The woman had her heart set on a beautiful vase. She knew just where she would put it in her home, but her best friend gave her a power drill, knowing that it could transform her life. The woman could have kept the drill in her laundry cupboard and sat sulking, wondering if she could somehow afford the expensive vase. Instead she had an idea, saw the possibilities of using the drill to restore the old chair, and a lucrative, satisfying hobby-business was born. It's the same with our singleness. We can sit sulking and yearning for what we don't have, or we can take the gift of our circumstances and ask our generous and wise

God how to use it. When we put ourselves in the Lord's hands, he can do amazing things in and through us. In God's eyes we are defined by far more than our single status.

> *"If we can grasp the concept that singleness is a gift and not a curse, and receive this gift by faith, then the flow-on effect will be seen in our lives."*

I named this book *The Unexpected Gift* after this chapter, because this concept is pivotal to our walk as singles. If we can grasp the concept that singleness is a gift and not a curse, and receive this gift by faith, then the flow-on effect will be seen in our lives. We will see our single status as an opportunity, not a difficulty, and God can use us to impact the world.

Can we flick the switch of our thinking and embrace our single status as a positive rather than a negative? The benefit of a positive outlook has been well documented by psychologists. In his 2014 Ted Talk, psychologist and author, Shawn Achor, says our reality is shaped by the lens through which we view the world.[10] If we can change the lens, we can increase our ability to thrive. Achor says that when he enrolled at Harvard he was delighted because he didn't expect to be accepted into that prestigious school – but he noticed within a couple of weeks fellow students were focused, not on the privilege of studying at this amazing college, but on the negative stresses of the workload. Achor says people presume that our

---

10 S Achor & TEDx 2011, *The Happy Secret to Better Work*, TEDx Bloomington, viewed 2 August 2020, <https://www.ted.com/talks/shawn_achor_the_happy_secret_to_better_work?utm_campaign=tedspread&utm_medium=referral&utm_source=tedcomshare>.

circumstances are a predictor of our happiness levels, but that's a misapprehension. It's how we look at things that's the key. In one study, switching people's thinking from a negative to a more positive mindset, improved their ability to be productive at work by 31%.[11]

> *"Our acceptance of this gift is an expression of how much we trust our Lord."*

Wow. This is significant – but we need to go deeper yet. It's great that God has given us science by which to understand the world – and it certainly is true that if we embrace our singleness as a positive life element, we will be happier, but it's not just about our happiness. It's about our relationship with God. Our acceptance of this gift is an expression of how much we trust our Lord.

Learning to Trust

I love how *The Message* translates Hebrews 11:1. 'The fundamental fact of existence is that this trust in God, this faith, is the firm foundation under everything that makes life worth living.' Trust in God needs to be our foundation for life, no matter what happens.

Charlene teaches us about this in her story. Amidst the tears and disappointment of failed relationships she trusted her heart's desires to the God who had her path. How about that? I wonder if this is the true gift of singleness. We are drawn deeper into the relationship of love and reliance on the one true

---

11 Achor & TEDx 2011.

God, because we have to trust him with our days. But when we do trust, he becomes the gift, and we are given strength for meeting the challenges of life. When things went wrong for Charlene, she focused on what she had been given. Later she says that she saw all the good things that God had given her as gifts. What a beautiful faith. She grew through her difficulties to develop resilience and confidence – a very attractive trait – as is her faith.

In the same chapter of Hebrews, it says that if we don't have faith, we can't please God.[12] Faith is the foundation of our relationship with him. When we trust each season of our lives to him, be we single, married or single again, he is thrilled. When we walk with him and let the beauty of each season impact our world, he is delighted. When we see singleness in this new light and embrace it as a gift, our Lord's eyes shine with the possibilities.

> *"Charlene teaches us about this in her story.*
> *Amidst the tears and disappointment of failed*
> *relationships she trusted her heart's desires*
> *to the God who had her path."*

When we see singleness like this – a gift from our God who loves us – and wear it well, it no longer matters how long we remain single. It stops being a burden to bear but is instead a treasure through which God can reveal his truest purpose for our lives. Some of us may remain single. For others singleness will just be a season. But how amazing it would be if we could

---

12 Hebrews 11:6

take this unexpected gift and learn to use it for however long it is given to us. Wouldn't it be great if this gift helped us not just to mend broken chairs, as in my parable, but to be God's fragrance in society – a gratitude-filled fragrance that can impact our broken world, helping to mend lives, and communities and workplaces. This gift is in our hands, ladies. Let's take it and wear it well!

Thank You

Isn't it amazing how a new perspective can bring us power and freedom? It can also lead us deeper into relationship with the giver, our precious heavenly Father. As God's creations and bearers of his identity, we are made for this relationship. As we walk with him and see his work in our lives, our hearts overflow with gratitude for his presence and his strength. We can never repay God for his goodness to us in Christ Jesus and the eternal life we have in him – we shouldn't even try. We don't repay our loved ones for giving us gifts – we express thanks. In our relationship with God one of the ways we express thanks is through worship.

> *"We don't repay our loved ones for giving us gifts – we express thanks. It opens my heart to God and lets me express my relationship with him one-to-one."*

Worship is a word we use a lot in Christian circles, but what actually is it? Just something we add into our Sunday church services, or is there more to it? And what if we are experiencing pain? How can we worship when it feels as if our lives are falling apart? Good questions! Let's see if we can find some answers.

The Power of Worship

If you've been part of a church community for a while, you'll know that the word 'worship' is often used in a way that's synonymous with praising God through music. I love this part of church life. It opens my heart to God and lets me express my relationship with him one-to-one. There is something about the act of praising God through song that allows my spirit to connect deeply with the Holy Spirit. Corporate praise can be a powerful means of centring our spirits on Christ. It can even bring a time of breakthrough. I'm not alone in having experienced moments where God has broken into my life in a new way during worship.

In John 4, Jesus tells a Samaritan woman that worship was to be in *spirit and truth*.[13] We've already discussed this passage in the context of Jesus speaking with a woman of poor reputation, but there is more to it than that. The Samaritans and the Jews didn't like each other, even though the Samaritans were an offshoot of the Jewish people. The key issue between the two rested on the location of worship. For the Jews many say it was the Temple Mount of Moriah and for the Samaritans it was Mount Gerizim. It seems like a small difference in tradition, but it led to a significant racial hatred between these two peoples. Jesus' summary of what worship really is, cut through those differences.

- Worshipping in *spirit* means we are concerned with inward spiritual realities, rather than a focus on a place, or process.[14]

---

13   John 4:4-42

14   Guzik, D 2014, *Study Guide for John 4*, Blue Letter Bible, viewed 6 August 2020, <https://www.blueletterbible.org/Comm/guzik_david/StudyGuide2017-Jhn/Jhn-4.cfm>.

It's about engaging with God heart-to-heart rather than merely following a ritual.
- Worshipping in *truth* means worshipping according to God's truth, revealed in his Word – especially the New Testament.[15] It also means that we come to God in a way that is true, not in pretence or with a false outward display.[16]

> *"Worshipping in truth means we live our lives in accordance with that truth. It means adopting a posture of reverence and fear that directs our lives as we live for God, our King."*

Both of these meanings can be applied to worship expressed in music and song – and this is a powerful thing. When a vast army threatened Jerusalem, King Jehoshaphat asked the Lord what he should do. God said they shouldn't be afraid; they wouldn't have to fight the battle. When Jehoshaphat organised his troops, he put the worshippers at the head of his army where they declared God's truth with thanksgiving: 'Give thanks to the Lord, for his love endures forever.' When they began to sing and praise, the Lord set ambushes against the invaders. The different tribes in the invading army fought and killed one another, without the tribe of Judah having to fight.[17]

Wow. The declaration of God's truth over our lives is powerful. It lifts our faith in the awesome God we serve. Let's keep worshipping in music and song!

---

15 Guzik 2014
16 Guzik 2014
17 2 Chronicles 20:1-30

But worship isn't just song. While we need to embrace this wonderful expression of our relationship with God, we do worship a disservice when we limit worship to praising him. Worshipping in truth means we live our lives in accordance with that truth. It means adopting a posture of reverence and fear that directs our lives as we live for God, our King.

> *"The truest act of worship happens when we choose to live God's way, not ours.'*

A Posture of Reverence

Recently, I learned the original Greek word for worship most often used in the New Testament is *proskynéo*, which means 'to do reverence to'.[18] Chris Hodges in his course on Christian freedom says worship literally means 'to kiss the master's hand in reverence'.[19] In the Old Testament, particularly in Proverbs, there are numerous scriptures on the 'fear' of God. 'The fear of the Lord is the beginning of wisdom,' is just one example.[20] But that word 'fear' is actually interchangeable with the word 'worship'. Fear here doesn't mean being terrified of God – it refers to a reverential awe. When God calls us to worship, it is to adore and kiss his hand in reverence and honour of him. It means offering ourselves to him and including him in all aspects of our lives.

---

18   *Strong's Greek: 4352. προσκυνέω (proskuneó) – to do reverence to* n.d., biblehub.com, viewed 6 August 2020, <https://biblehub.com/greek/4352.htm>.

19   C Hodges 2017, Freedom Course, Church of the Highlands, Alabama https://freedom.churchofthehighlands.com>.

20   Proverbs 9:10

The truest act of worship happens when we choose to live God's way, not ours. It's when we give our lives as a gift back to God in a posture of reverent surrender. It's when we no longer choose our way but let him direct our paths – dying to our agenda and leaning into his plans and purposes. But what does this actually mean for us as Christian singles? What does it look like?

Before I answer this in detail, I'd like us to consider some examples from the scriptures. One of the things I love about the Bible is that it is full of stories of ordinary people living extraordinary lives of faith. When I read these accounts, I'm inspired to live in the same way, trusting God to release his power in my life as I go. I hope you will be inspired too, and that God's truth will be echoed in your life as you take encouragement from these remarkable people.

Let's look at Esther first.

Esther

The book of Esther is the account of a beautiful young Jewish girl who becomes Queen of Persia by marrying King Xerxes, ruler of the Persian Empire. The story of her rise to this position is an amazing tale, but I'd like to focus on the key challenge Esther faced. When Esther's relative Mordecai discovers that Haman, Xerxes' viceroy, has hatched a plot to destroy all of the Jewish people in the land, Mordecai goes to Esther to ask for her help in thwarting the plot.[21] He pleads with her to go to the king for help. But Esther is scared. She knows that to go into the king's presence unannounced is an offence punishable

---

21   Esther 4:1-8

by death – unless he extends his gold sceptre and spares them. The king hadn't called her to his presence in 30 days.[22]

How terrifying for this young woman. On one hand her people could be exterminated but on the other she could die. What does she do? Mordecai insists that this situation may be the very reason she's been raised to her high position.[23] Then Esther makes one of the most beautiful declarations of surrender in the scriptures. She calls a three-day fast for the Jewish people, and says: 'When this is done, I will go to the king, even though it is against the law. And if I perish, I perish.'[24]

> *"Then Esther makes one of the most beautiful declarations of surrender in the scriptures."*

As the story continues Esther goes before the king but he is pleased with her and extends his sceptre towards her.[25] I'll leave you to read the details, but Esther's obedience leads to the deliverance of her people. Her uncle Mordecai is honoured, the hateful Haman is executed, and the Jewish people are delivered and given the right to fight their enemies.[26]

Think about those words, 'If I perish, I perish,' for a moment. This beautiful Jewish woman who has riches and status is willing to lay her life down when confronted with God's will. It's easy to read those words quickly and not feel their impact.

---

22 Esther 4:6-12
23 Esther 4:15
24 Esther 4:15-16
25 Esther 5:1-2
26 Esther 6-7

Would you do that? Would you put your life on the line, if God asked you to? Would you give up everything, leaning into God's plans and purposes, to the extent of laying down your life?

Esther's story here shows us what worship is. Her approach to the king with fear and reverence, echoes our approach to our God. The difference is our heavenly Father always extends his sceptre to us.[27] But it is more than that. It shows the power of a life surrendered to God, laying down the gifts God had given her – her life and her royal status – back to him for his purposes. It shows the power of a life of trust.

> *"Would you give up everything, leaning into God's plans and purposes, to the extent of laying down your life?"*

I loved how God delivered Esther, Mordecai and the Jewish people. Our Lord is a deliverer and he is on the side of his people. Similar stories are found all over the scriptures. It can almost seem like a recipe – worship and obey God, trust him absolutely and he will deliver you. Unfortunately, this doesn't always happen.

I love Hebrews 11. I've mentioned it before so you can tell I like this chapter. Have you ever noticed that from verse 32 onward, the writer lists a series of miracles experienced by those living by faith, including women having their dead raised back to life.[28] However the writer then lists a range

---

27 Hebrews 4:16
28 Hebrews 11:35(a)

of bad things that happened. People are tortured, flogged, imprisoned, stoned, and sawed in two – all in the name of abandoning faith.[29] They were commended for their faith but didn't receive what they wanted.[30]

We need to note this. You may not like me saying this, but we won't all get everything we want in this life. Earlier in the book I explained how social dynamics inside and outside of the church mean that there are not enough men to go around. It's easy to get a sense of entitlement that says if we serve God and worship him with abandon, he will give us a really great life partner. But what if he doesn't? What if he has other plans for us? If we have this expectation and don't get what we want, we can become cross with God and abandon him to do our own thing.

The truth is we live in a broken world and God's purposes are higher than ours. I believe he poses these questions to all of us singles today, myself included:

> *"Will you serve me no matter what?*
> *Will you worship me even if you remain single?"*

It may be that the thing you long for isn't marriage. Maybe it's the healing or salvation of a loved one. God's word to all of us is: Will you lay your desires on the altar before me, and worship me regardless of the result?

---

29 Hebrews 11:35(b)-38

30 Hebrews 11:39

I mentioned Habakkuk 3:17-18 earlier in the book and said that an attitude of rejoicing in the Lord no matter what, allows our lives to have colour amidst the delays. But it is also shows an attitude of surrendered worship. Even if everything goes wrong, God is still good and he loves us. I know this is difficult teaching, but we don't lose anything when we trust him; because our home isn't here, it's in heaven.

Look at what the writer of Hebrews says about the great people of the faith: 'All these people were still living by faith when they died. They did not receive the things promised; they only saw them and welcomed them from a distance, admitting that they were foreigners and strangers on earth.'[31] Even Enoch, Noah, Abraham and Sarah didn't receive their ultimate fulfilment in this life. God did wonderful things through them but even they were longing for a better, heavenly country.[32]

I will talk about this more in the final chapter, where we look at our singleness in the perspective of God's kingdom and eternity. I can't wait – it will be a blast – but I needed to mention this here so that you can see how the call to worship God this way sits within the context of his grace.

God doesn't abandon us on the journey. In John 16 Jesus tells his disciples, 'In this world you will have trouble. But take heart! I have overcome the world'.[33] When we walk through the valleys of uncertainty, we realise he is the one who will

---

31   Hebrews 11:13
32   Hebrews 11:16
33   John 16:33(b)

carry us through. Jesus Christ will always give us the strength to meet the challenges we face. At the end of Matthew's gospel, before Jesus ascends into heaven, he promises he will be with us to the end of the age.[34] Wow. God with us. Can we even imagine what that means?

> *"All these people were still living by faith when they died. They did not receive the things promised; they only saw them and welcomed them from a distance, admitting that they were foreigners and strangers on earth."*

In John 14:12 our Lord even says that those who believe in him – that's us – will do greater things than he did. He healed the blind and the deaf and even raised people from the dead. If we trust him, he can do amazing things through us.

Before I draw this chapter to a close, I'd like to tell you two more stories: stories of two remarkable women of God whom I hold very dear in my heart. They inspire me to lift my eyes and keep following God no matter what.

Let me introduce Elizabeth and Anna.

Elizabeth

The story of Elizabeth and her husband Zachariah takes my breath away.[35] In the first chapter of Luke we learn several things about this beautiful God-fearing couple.

---

34 Matthew 28:20(b)

35 Luke 1:1-14

They had a priestly heritage. Zachariah served as a priest as part of his role as a Levite and Elizabeth was descended from Moses' brother Aaron.[36]

They were devout. Both Zechariah and Elizabeth were 'righteous in the sight of God, observing all the Lord's commands and decrees blamelessly'.[37]

- They were very old.[38] Elizabeth was beyond childbearing age.
- They never had children. Elizabeth had never been able to conceive.[39]
- God was good to them. The child he gave them in their old age was none other than John the Baptist – the one who prepared the way for Christ.[40]

> *"This woman who devoted her life to worship was given the honour of meeting the Saviour of the world – as a baby."*

Both Elizabeth and Zechariah had a godly heritage and were following God fully, yet they hadn't received what they wanted. Childbirth was everything in this society. What did their family think? Their friends? Did they whisper behind their back that Elizabeth or Zechariah must have done something wrong to deserve this curse? In that culture it is most likely that Elizabeth would have got the blame for their childlessness.

---

36 Luke 1:5
37 Luke 1:6
38 Luke 1:7(b)
39 Luke 1:7(a)
40 Luke 1:11-17

But Luke makes it clear that while this couple hadn't received everything they wanted, they were living a life of faith and devotion. There is no bitterness mentioned here. Even in their lifelong disappointment Elizabeth and Zechariah were still serving God with abandon. How about that?

This is a beautiful picture of surrender. Elizabeth's eyes stayed on God through all those years. No matter what their circumstances were, this beautiful couple kept kissing their master's hand in reverence. Their lack of children did not paralyse their faith but led them, all the more, into worshipping and dedicating their lives to God. They left what was impossible to them, to God, and focused their energy on living for him. The God of the impossible certainly delivered – but I'm sure that if they had remained childless until the day they died they would have remained in this attitude of open-hearted worship.

> *"They left what was impossible to them, to God, and focused their energy on living for him."*

I hold the amazing Elizabeth as an example for my life. Although I have not yet received the answer I'd like in regards to my singleness – and may never do – I want to remain pliable in God's hands and have an open heart to him. I want to keep the same attitude of reverence – of kissing the master's hand – no matter what.

Let's look now at another woman I admire – the prophet Anna.

Grandma Anna

The Bible only devotes three verses to Anna's story but when I ponder her life, I'm swept away by both her persistent devotion and the goodness of God.[41] Anna was an 84-year-old prophet whose husband had died after only seven years of marriage. She must have been devastated when that happened – but instead of launching into bitterness, she devoted herself to worshipping day and night in the temple. We don't know if she had children, but we know she didn't remarry. The implication is that from this time Anna gave herself exclusively to singled out worship of the God she loved.

Look at how God's goodness touched her life. She may never have had children, but God let her see the Christ child. This woman who devoted her life to worship was given the honour of meeting the Saviour of the world – as a baby. Imagine her smile, her delight as she beheld his tiny fingers and toes. The miracle of new life – but not just any life. The Messiah had been born. There was hope for God's people. How beautiful is that? Ladies, our Lord asks us today:

> *"Are we willing to follow Elizabeth and Anna*
> *in worshipping and serving him, no matter*
> *what our circumstances? Will we choose*
> *to live like these women lived, with hearts*
> *sweet to God despite our disappointments?"*

Because that is what it means to live in surrendered worship of the living God.

---

41 Luke 2:36-38

My Cup Overflows

We can all take heart from the stories of Elizabeth and Anna. These women don't just challenge us to surrendered worship, they also show us the goodness of God. God may not give us a particular desire when we want it, but Romans 8:28 is his promise. We don't know what he will do in our lives – but if we accept our singleness as a gift and keep our heart sweet to him, he will work all things to our good. Whatever our situation, we can be a moment away from God stepping in and changing things forever. In God's economy, the gifts he gives us are so much greater than the things we originally desired.

There are a lot of things in this world that will break our hearts and leave us wounded. But while the enemy loves to steal, kill and destroy, our Saviour Jesus has come to give us abundant life.[42] One of the things I've discovered in my walk with my Lord is that when I worship in spirit and truth, the Holy Spirit realigns my life with God's truth. That truth sets me free from the things that weigh me down.[43] If we let God define us through worship, we can walk in amazing freedom.

> *"In God's economy, the gifts he gives us are so much greater than the things we originally desired."*

Letting God Define Us

I recently listened to a message by Nathan Finochio, from TheosU Chapel, regarding Jacob and his two wives, Leah and

---

42 John 10:10
43 John 8:32

Rachel.[44] Finochio drew a parallel between Jacob, who deceived his older brother out of his father's blessing, and Leah, who along with her father, deceived Jacob into marrying her instead of her sister.[45] In both cases the deception had its roots in woundedness: Jacob because he was a second son and didn't meet his father's expectations and Leah because in the world's eyes, says Finochio, she was ugly.[46]

Does something cringe inside you when you hear that word – 'ugly'? I've lost count of the number of women I've met who have a deep-seated belief that they are ugly. I wrestled with it myself when I was younger. It's one of the most significant lies the enemy can sow into our hearts as women, because it can drive us to do all kinds of things to take the pain away. In Leah's case this identity theft drove her to both deceive Jacob and strive for his love.

> "In Leah's case this identity theft drove her to both deceive Jacob and strive for his love."

Can you see the two sisters? One is so beautiful that a man will willingly work for free for seven years so he can marry her. But the other is ugly and unwanted. Leah was the older sister – it was her right to marry first – and she longed to be loved.[47] This

---

44 N Finochio 2020, *What To Do If You Are Ugly. Student Chapel August 2020*, TheosU Chapel, viewed 19 October 2020, <https://theosu.ca/programs/sq-student-chapel-august-2020-1mp4-358f1a>.

45 Genesis 29:14-35

46 Finochio 2020. Genesis 29:17 says that Leah has 'weak eyes'. Finochio says she may have been cross eyed. Either way, he says the idea is that by the world's standards, Leah was not attractive.

47 Genesis 29:26

longing led her to do a terrible thing and agree to her father's plan to take her sister's place at the altar.

Most decisions that come out of our woundedness backfire on us. Jacob married Rachel a week after Leah and the latter was forever condemned to a loveless marriage. How terrible to be shown day after day that you are not good enough. The Lord saw Leah's pain and enabled her to conceive.[48] She could bear children and Rachel couldn't – at least not for a while.[49] Leah had something to give her life meaning – but this too became part of her futile striving for love. Leah had her first three children: Reuben, Simeon and Levi, hoping against hope that this would make her husband love her.[50] But it didn't work, and she was left as the odd-one-out in an absurd love triangle.

Yet, somewhere between bearing Levi and giving birth to Judah, something changed in Leah. Instead of craving her husband's love, her focus turned to God. 'This time I will praise the Lord.'[51] I love that 'Judah' means praise. There was a shift in Leah's life – a moment of truth where she realised who she was. When Leah let God define her life, her heart and focus shifted – and the result was praise.

Do you see the freedom here? Finochio points out that when Leah stopped striving for the thing she couldn't have, she stopped giving others power to hurt her.[52] She switched the

---

48 Genesis 29:31
49 Genesis 29:32
50 Genesis 29:34
51 Genesis 29:35
52 Finochio 2020

source of her validation from a self-centred man who would never love her, to her beautiful and loving God. She gave God the gift of her worship and stopped trying to win Jacob's closed heart by giving him more children. That's huge. Imagine the weight lifted off Leah's heart, mind and soul.

> *"When Leah let God define her life, her heart and focus shifted – and the result was praise."*

Abundant Freedom

Like Leah, all of us have a space inside us that only God can fill. When we try to find acceptance from a different source, we will be let down, again and again, in a cycle of despair. Our desire to marry – in itself a good thing – can backfire if it's driven by our addiction to validation. We can be caught up in a never-ending cycle of dependence, going nowhere fast, like a hamster on its wheel. Even if we do marry, we can be disappointed when our situation doesn't live up to our expectations. But if we receive each day – and every situation we face – as a gift from our beautiful Saviour, we'll find ourselves in a different cycle – one of abundant freedom.

When we accept our circumstances, we are drawn closer to God in worship. As we worship in spirit and truth, God breaks into our lives more and more with a revelation of who he is and how much he loves us. This new understanding sets us free from circumstances and the opinion of others, which leads us to freedom from addictions and into greater worship. Just like Leah, we become caught in an upward spiral rather than a downward one.

Acceptance → worship → freedom → greater acceptance → even greater worship → even greater freedom.

Wow. What a gift! Ladies, this is so important. To live in this freedom, we need to:
- Trust God – in *all* things
- Accept singleness by faith as a gift from the one in all creation who loves us most!
- Stop striving for the things that elude us and praise God for what we have
- Worship God with our lives. Let God's truth guide our actions even if it's hard (or scary)
- Let his truth revealed in worship heal us
- Ask God how to use *our* 'power drill'.

> *"Our desire to marry – in itself a good thing – can backfire if it's driven by our addiction to validation."*

May I emphasise the last point? I began this chapter with 'the parable of the power drill' as a metaphor for the gift of singleness. May I suggest that in the next week you to take this image (or a real power drill), plus a notepad and your Bible, of course, and spend time asking God the question:

> *"How can I use this gift of singleness creatively, Lord? Help me to see where my deep joy intersects with your Great Commission."*

Write all your crazy ideas down and pray over them. See which ones have power. You don't know where this will take you if you walk with God in thanksgiving.

Note that by 'creatively', I am not meaning to limit this to what we might normally think of as creative pursuits. We are not all called to restore old furniture. However, I believe we all sit at the door of opportunity. Whether it is in our personal life, our hobby, our career or in our church life, we all have an opportunity today to not only see our singleness as a gift, but to grab it, charge it up and start creating!

What if singleness gave you the opportunity to go to bible college, study for a Master of Education, or develop a pet-sitting business? What if it gave you the free time you need to write that e-book, compose that musical or to learn accounting? The possibilities are endless.

Too often we hold ourselves back because we lack the confidence to go forwards by ourselves. Or we are afraid we'll get it wrong and maybe miss meeting 'Mr Right'. But as I said earlier, isn't it more likely that we'll meet a suitable partner when we are pursuing our passions?

Girls, I'm asking you to be brave. If you do marry at some stage, it may be harder to pursue these things as your energy will be divided, so do them now. Many of you know what you would love to do. Stop hesitating, grab hold of your singleness and go for it – worshipping our Saviour with your life; and receiving his freedom as you go. Wow. How exciting!

Do you know what else is exciting? This life we have here and now is only the beginning. There's a whole lot more to the story. The cosmos has a king and his name is Jesus Christ. When Christ walked the earth, the kingdom of God, his kingdom, began breaking into this world. One day he will return to bring all things under his rule. And we'll see the conclusion of a great love story, where a king rescues his bride and takes her to be with him forever. How amazing is that? Let's see how this works out!

> *"Write all your crazy ideas down and pray over them.*
> *One day he will return to bring all things*
> *under his rule."*

ETERNITY

11

NOW AND FOREVER

In 2008, I completed a tandem skydive near the Sunshine Coast in Queensland, Australia, as part of my local church fundraising initiative called *Hope for the Homeless*. I remember leaping into nothingness, falling through the air, with the wind raging against my face. It felt surreal to be 'flying' above everything; the view was amazing. I soared above a vast stretch of azure ocean and golden coastline – at one with this wild expanse – beholding our world from an unusual but exquisite vantage point. I didn't want it to end, but it was over all too soon. My expert parachutist guided us down safely as the ground rushed to meet us. What a blast!

A few years before (2004), I tried bungy jumping while I was on holiday with a friend in New Zealand. It was from Sky Tower, Auckland, the tallest building in that country. The view of the city and bay was amazing – the horizon stretched forever. However, on this occasion my experience was different. Fear gripped me as I stood on the edge of the building. Why was I doing this? My heart raced and I clamped my eyes shut as I jumped. But I opened them again in a moment. I had not signed myself up for this experience to do it with my eyes closed. The whole encounter was exhilarating, and I got to do it twice. Fun times!

Even though those experiences involved different kind of jumps in different places, they have similarities:
- They both lifted my horizons and let me see things a different way
- They both involved a leap of faith, in one case trusting an expert parachutist (and parachute) to keep me safe, and in the other, trusting the bungy equipment they attached to me to hold fast
- They both flashed by in what seemed like moments.

> *"When we realise our life here on earth is fleeting – we can open our eyes and make the most of the ride."*

Ladies, whether or not jumping out of planes or off buildings is for you, can you see that this analogy has a lot to teach us about the Christian life? In the last chapter we saw that singleness is a gift.
- One of the keys to embracing this gift and thriving as a single Christian woman, is to understand where we fit within God's amazing purposes. It's important to lift our horizons and see the big picture
- When we consider eternity – and realise our life here on earth is fleeting – we can open our eyes to the gift and make the most of the ride
- We can also put our trust in the only one who can keep us safe – our magnificent Saviour, Jesus Christ.

So, as we come to the end of our adventure through these pages, let's take the last ride of a lifetime. You won't have to jump out of a plane, but you might have your perspective stretched. You may also have to make a leap of faith, trusting in our beautiful Saviour, Jesus, who is surer than any parachute or bungy line. You'll also discover that no matter what happens in our lives here on Earth, marriage is part of our destiny. How super-exciting! Let's start by considering the kingdom of God.

The Kingdom of God

The Kingdom of God is one of the most important concepts in the New Testament. If we can understand what God's kingdom is and how it affects us, we can learn to flourish in our lives as God's daughters.

In the New Testament, the Greek word for kingdom, *Baselia*, appears 126 times in the Gospels and 34 times in the rest of the New Testament.[1] This means it must be an important concept that is particularly related to the coming of Jesus. When Jesus began his ministry he said, 'The kingdom of God is near.'[2] Pastor John Piper of Desiring God ministries says that word *kingdom* here is fundamentally God's kingly rule – 'his reign, his action, his lordship, his sovereign governance' – rather than about a realm or particular area of control.[3] So when Jesus says the kingdom of God – interchangeable with 'the kingdom

---

1 J Piper 2019, *What Is the Kingdom of God?*, Desiring God, viewed 25 August 2020, <https://www.desiringgod.org/interviews/what-is-the-kingdom-of-god>.

2 Luke 11:20

3 Piper 2019

of Heaven' – is near, he means that God's rule is breaking into this world.

Dr Myles Monroe in his book, *Rediscovering the Kingdom*, likens the coming of God's kingdom on Earth to the concept of colonisation where a king or ruler purposefully impacts and transforms a people into becoming an extension of their rulership.[4] The difference is that God's colonisation is a force for eternal good rather than evil.

> *"The kingdom of God is near.*
> *And everywhere the Lord Jesus went,*
> *he brought the kingdom near to people."*

We've seen it again and again through history, haven't we? One country invading another and making its people their own. I've already related what the infamous King Leopold did to the Democratic Republic of the Congo in the late 1890s.[5] So many died in slavery to Leopold's greed. Even in Australia our first nation people were often mistreated by the early British colonialists. And many indigenous people couldn't vote in Federal elections until 1962.[6]

---

4   M Munroe, M 2010, *Rediscovering the kingdom: ancient hope for our 21st century world*, Destiny Image Publishers, Shippensburg, Pa., p. 26.

5   Hochschild, A 2000, *King Leopold's ghost: a study of greed, terror, and heroism in colonial Africa*, Papermac, London, p. 1.

6   Australian Electoral Commission 2019, *Electoral milestones for Indigenous Australians*, Australian Electoral Commission, viewed 25 August 2020, <https://www.aec.gov.au/indigenous/milestones htm>.

Good News

In contrast to sinful human rule, God's rule is good news.[7] People were drawn to Christ's grace and goodness. We read in the four gospels how children, women, disciples, thieves, murderers, Pharisees, and philosophers could not stay away from Jesus as he expressed the kingdom in his ministry. Even those who didn't like him seemed to hang around him. Everywhere the Lord Jesus went, he brought the kingdom near to people.[8] The poor were uplifted.[9] People were saved, healed and set free from demons.[10] Thousands were miraculously fed.[11] God's rule triumphed over sin, evil and death. A king had come, and people were released from the things that bound them. But there is more to the story. The Bible says the kingdom of God is both present and yet to come.

In Matthew 6:10 our Lord teaches us to pray, 'Your kingdom come, your will be done, on earth as it is in heaven'. This means the kingdom didn't come in its completeness when Jesus walked with his disciples. It was like a mustard seed that would grow into a huge tree.[12] It was also a valuable treasure worth sacrificing for.[13] Christ loved the world so much he wanted to bring in God's rule everywhere, so everyone who chose him could be set free. He wanted his followers to follow God's ways and bring the good news of the kingdom to everyone.

---

7 Mark 1:15
8 Luke 17:21
9 Luke 6:20
10 Luke 10:9; Matthew 12:28
11 John 6:1-15
12 Matthew 13:31
13 Matthew 13:44; Luke 9:60-62

> *"A powerful king, with all authority, being so gentle*
> *and kind. But there is a requirement for*
> *entering the kingdom – repentance."*

But there's still more! There is a future aspect to God's kingdom where our Saviour will return in his power. Have we really understood how powerful – and fearful – Jesus Christ is? Read Revelation 5:1-14. We sometimes domesticate Jesus and make him in our image when in reality he is the 'King of Kings and the Lord of Lords' who holds all authority.[14] He is king whether we like it or not. One day every knee will bow, and every tongue will acknowledge that Jesus Christ is Lord.[15] Those who reject him will not just miss out, they will be judged for their rebellion.[16] On the other hand, those who receive him with a childlike faith, and are born again, will have every tear wiped from their eyes.[17]

Isn't this an amazing picture? A powerful king, with all authority, being so gentle and kind. But there is a requirement for entering the kingdom – repentance.[18] Repentance means turning our life around and following the Lord Jesus – rather than living our own way. Before we move on, I'd like to stop and ask you some questions:

---

14   Revelation 5:14
15   Philippians 2:9-11
16   Luke 14:15-24
17   Luke 18:16-17; John 3:3; Revelation 21:4
18   Matthew 4:7

"Have you accepted Christ's kingship?
Have you asked Jesus to be Lord of your life and had his Holy Spirit fill you?
Have you experienced the good news of the kingdom for yourself?'

Whoever we are and whatever we've done, Jesus loves us. But he wants us to come to him, trust our lives to him and choose to do what he says. He has done everything for us, and he wants God's power to work in us and through us. If you haven't ever surrendered your life to the King of Kings, then say a simple prayer like this:

- King Jesus, I want to follow you forever. Please come into my life, wash me clean and make me new. Fill me with your Spirit so I may walk in your power, authority and freedom. Amen.

Entering into God's kingdom is that simple. We have to mean it – we can't mess with God – but he is faithful and so very tender when we choose to believe and follow him. One important point: please let another Christian know if you've prayed that prayer; and also try to find a good Christian community. As I've said again and again in this book, we need one another. We weren't meant to follow Christ alone.

But if you are already a believer and have been walking with God, I'd like to ask you a different kingdom question:

"Are you walking in freedom as a Christian single?"

If Jesus is king, and the kingdom brings so much freedom, why do we sometimes feel like we are striving? We want to follow Jesus, but we end up in a dry place where we are following the rules, but there is no life.

Have you been there? The enemy loves to steal our freedom – he usually throws that in when he robs us of our identity. If he can't stop us believing, he can sometimes take away the joy and power of our faith. He accuses us, saying we are not good enough or doing enough in serving our beloved Saviour-King.

The good news – hear that phrase again – is that there is an excellent antidote to these lies of the enemy. The remedy is a fresh understanding of the truth of kingdom freedom.

Kingdom Freedom

In the last chapter we looked at the cycle of ever-growing freedom available when we flip our thinking and worship our beautiful God, no matter what our circumstances. But there is another aspect to our freedom – the freedom we have in God's kingdom when we understand his grace.

In John 8:36 Jesus says, 'If the Son sets you free, you will be free indeed.' When we give our lives to Christ we live under grace, not law.[19] We have done nothing to deserve what has been granted to us – it's a gift. We receive life in Jesus by accepting what he did on the cross. It is through faith not works that we are saved, and that faith is credited to us as

---

19 Ephesians 2:8-9

righteousness.[20] God's reign in our lives enables us to live a life of freedom and joy.

Yet sometimes as Christian singles we find ourselves striving to live for God's kingdom. We've talked about some serious issues in this book: loneliness, disappointment, sexual longings and addictions, to name a few. It is easy to think that if we are to live by God's rule, we just have to try harder to live his way. Sometimes that striving leads us to give up and walk away from God into the world. Other times we keep doing the right things but lose our joy.

> *"We have done nothing to deserve what has been granted to us – it's a gift."*

Can you recall, we talked earlier about the prodigal daughter?[21] I hope you don't mind me mentioning her again. That girl is an example of someone who strove for her own kind of freedom. She went out and lived the wild life of zero restraint and ended up eating pig food. The other daughter entered into a different kind of striving. She stayed at home and did everything right, in a bid to win her father's approval and generosity.

The truth is both women missed it. The prodigal had to learn that freedom and joy were found by living as a daughter in her father's house, and the older sister had to learn that she already had everything that belonged to her father, she just wasn't enjoying it.

---

20 Romans 3:22-26

21 Luke 15:11-32. In chapter 9 I outlined the story of the prodigal son but as this book is written to women, I changed the example to that of a prodigal daughter.

Ladies, the key to thriving in God's kingdom does involve obedience. Jesus is the King of Kings and his kingdom is a theocracy not a democracy. We don't get a vote on which commands are acceptable or otherwise. However, the Christian life is about grace not law. If God commands something, it is for our good, and he gives us the strength to live the life he wants for us – a life of joy and freedom from the sins that hold us back – when we let his Holy Spirit take control and lead us.[22]

In the last chapter I mentioned a course by Pastor Chris Rogers, on Christian freedom.[23] I love how God brings teaching that reinforces truth in my life, at a time when it will enrich me to hear it. In this course, we considered the two trees mentioned in the book of Genesis: the 'tree of life' and the 'tree of the knowledge of good and evil'.[24] Pastor Hodges explained that the tree represents the two kinds of approach we can take towards God. Living in the tree of life means living a life of grace and trust, whereas living out of the other tree means we are relying our own strength and merit.

Hodges says that if we live out of the tree of life, we are motivated by love – we want to simply know God and be close to him. The tree of the knowledge of good and evil, however, focuses on what we do. It is the 'religious path to godliness', where we strive to live for God out of duty. This tree is all about knowledge and information:

---

22 Romans 8:1-4

23 C Hodges 2017, Freedom Course, Church of the Highlands, Alabama, <https://freedom.churchofthehighlands.com>.

24 Genesis 2:8–9, 16–17.

*"Have I done enough today?
Am I better than that other person?
Do I measure up?"*

In the prodigal daughter story, the girl who returned home chose to live by the tree of life, while the older sister was living out of the tree of the knowledge of good and evil. She was judging her sister's life and her father's actions against her own set of rules. In Jesus' time the Pharisees are a great example of a group living out of the second tree. Every action had to be analysed and measured against the hoped-for outcome of pleasing God. In the process they put a burden of the law on ordinary people that caused them to feel hopeless.

*"The wow factor here is that the King calls us to intimacy by his Spirit.
Ladies, the key to thriving in God's kingdom does involve obedience. Jesus is the King of Kings and his kingdom is a theocracy not a democracy."*

Ladies, sometimes we wear our singleness better than others. In the tough times when things get to us, or we know we've not been living as we should, or we're anxious about our future, we need to run to our loving God and rest in intimacy with him. In Psalm 46:10 the Lord speaks and says, 'Be still and know that I am God.' The idea in this psalm is that when we face troubles of any kind, the place of rest is in God. The basis for this is in the second half of the verse: 'I will be exalted among the nations; I will be exalted in the earth'.[25] We don't have to fear because

---

25 Psalm 46:10

our Lord Jesus is King. Everything is subject to him. He is in control and he loved us so much he died for us.

The wow factor here is that the King calls us to intimacy by his Spirit. Hear Paul's words in 2 Corinthians 3:17-18:

> *"Now the Lord is the Spirit, and where the Spirit of the Lord is, there is freedom. And we all, who with unveiled faces contemplate the Lord's glory, are being transformed into his image with ever-increasing glory, which comes from the Lord, who is the Spirit."*

We are transformed as we spend time with Jesus and contemplate his glory. To contemplate something means to spend time gazing at that thing. It is the opposite of a quick glance. When we contemplate the beauty of the sunset or the majesty of a mountain range, we gaze at the image and drink it in. When we contemplate Christ, our king, we drink in his grace.

- He is my glorious king
- He gave his life for me
- I am loved with an eternal love
- I am forgiven and free.

Compare this to the idea of spending ritual time with God or ticking the spiritual boxes. Yep, gone to church three times this week. Prayed through my list. Memorised seven Bible verses. Gave twenty-one percent of my cash bonus to the poor... All of these things can be good in themselves if they come out of love, but if they come out of duty all they do is make us weary inside. Kingdom freedom is about love and rest, not duty.

It was great to be reminded that God wants my freedom more than I do. I was trying so hard to do the right things, yet what he wanted most was for me to draw close to him in love.
- Does this stir a longing for the kingdom life?
- Which tree are you living out of right now?

It is my prayer that our Saviour will help you recognise which tree you are living by – and that you will find rest and freedom whether your life is currently bathed in sunshine or awash with rain.

> *"Kingdom freedom is about love and rest, not duty."*

Kingdom Perspective

Think back to the beginning of this chapter and my stories about jumping out of planes and off buildings. Being up so high gave me a whole new perspective – as I could see far beyond my normal horizons. My desire is that this discussion on God's kingdom and his freedom will remind us all to see our lives from this kingdom perspective. It is my hope that this will lead us to let the kingdom of God flow through us to others.

We tend to live our lives with ourselves at the centre. We may have friends, family and occasionally workmates that we draw into this sphere but many of us live out of this hub. If our sphere is okay, then we are okay. But what of the community around us? When we consider the kingdom of God, we realise that it's not just about us, there is a whole world that needs God's grace, power and love.

As I write this book, creation is groaning. In Australia we had terrible bushfires at the beginning of the year that are probably due to our changing climate, we're in the middle of a global pandemic and injustice-fuelled race riots have scarred the face of the United States and spread like a tsunami around the globe. Humanity is struggling and the things most people trust in – like employment, social connectedness, health and freedom – are being taken away from them. I genuinely believe that Christ – and his kingdom rule – are the only hope for this world. But even if we hold this truth dear, we can still struggle at this time.

I live in Melbourne, Victoria, a state that has had a second wave of the Covid-19 virus. As I write this, we are in stage four lockdown which means that all non-essential travel is banned, church is online, and I have to work from home. But I'm a social gal. I love people and I love good hugs. I don't do well in isolation. I believe we need to control this virus as it would soon overwhelm Australia's medical system if it ran rampant, however self-care and mental health are important issues. We need one another and we need human touch. In a recent conversation during one of my supervision sessions at work, the facilitator mentioned people's interest in owning a pet had skyrocketed during the pandemic. I had been thinking about this a week before! I grew up in a home where we had dogs. I'd love to get a dog but when the lockdown lifts, a pampered pup won't fit my run-about-everywhere lifestyle. I think I'll get a bird – a parrot – so I have something to talk to when I'm home.

Even if you're reading this long after Covid-19 has been defeated, the principles apply. The reality is that in our post-modern world people are less interested in words and more interested in actions. They want love and kindness, not theory. One of the things Malee said in Ebony's story had a deep impact on me:

> *"We tend to live our lives with ourselves at the centre. When you hug me, something inside of me breaks."*

Sometimes all people need for a breakthrough in their lives is the warmth of human touch. Isn't this amazing? I admire Ebony's resolution to seek God's love before her own comfort so she can show love to others. All the ladies who have told their story in this book are remarkable women of God. They are strong and steadfast in their walk with God, but Ebony's kingdom focus, and the kingdom mentality of the Thai women she mentions, astounds me. She talks about the sacrifices she made to leave her home and live in another country, and how hard it was to translate God's love over cultural barriers. We're not all called to serve God overseas, but we are all called to live with a kingdom perspective wherever God takes us.

When was the last time you asked yourself: *Who am I called to love?*

What if the visitor you sat next to at church felt welcomed by your smile and warm conversation? What if your young friend who lost their job last week had somewhere to stay for the night? What if you offered to go to the shops for the old man next door whose wife just died? What if you felt prompted to pray for a sick person and they were healed?

Some people criticise God for allowing suffering, but he longs to bring his kingdom into people's lives and has chosen us to *partner* with him in his purposes. I put it to you that if as God's precious singles we want to have meaningful lives, we can start by bringing cups of water to the thirsty. Like Jesus, we have an opportunity to be the bearers of good news to the poor and bring some hope back into the world.

> *"In Australia we had terrible bushfires at the beginning of the year that are probably due to our changing climate, we're in the middle of a global pandemic and injustice-fuelled race riots have scarred the face of the United States and spread like a tsunami around the globe."*

Christ Jesus taught his disciples about the kingdom and demonstrated its power, then he sent them out in pairs to do the same.[26] They healed the sick and cast out demons, demonstrating the freedom that comes when God's rule breaks into people's lives. It's so easy to become stuck in a rut as singles, being worried about our status and the problems that surround it.

I believe each of us have a unique call in God. We can live safe, small lives, but we'll never have the rush of pushing through and seeing God come through in power. But if we leap forward in faith and be agents of the kingdom in our work, in our community, wherever we are placed – then we'll enjoy the dynamic of working together with the King of Kings for his

---

26 Mark 6:6-8

glory and saving lives for eternity. How significant is that? Open your eyes, single ladies, and jump into abundant kingdom living.

But the kingdom isn't the only big-picture perspective we need to grasp as Christian singles. The other key picture of God's people in the scriptures is the church. You might think that this is a humdrum topic compared with the kingdom but it's far from it. Have you realised that the church is not only a community where we can belong and grow, but it's also Christ's bride? Yep we're invited to the wedding and this time we're not the bridesmaid!

> *"The reality is that in our post-modern world people are less interested in words and more interested in actions."*

His Rockin' Church

On our 2019 church summer retreat, our guest was my former senior pastor, Wayne Alcorn, who gave a 'thought provoking' message on the importance of the church.[27] One of the things he said was that sometimes Christians think they can believe in Jesus but not be part of the church. However, that doesn't work. We can't grow and bear fruit as a floating Christian; we need to be planted firmly in good soil. Ps Wayne went so far as to say that it's offensive to God when we love his son and not the church.[28]

---

27 At the time of writing, Pastor Wayne Alcorn is the National Leader of the Australian Christian Churches.

28 W Alcorn 2020, Personal communication.

Wow, that's significant. Is it true? Is the church so important to God that we offend him by rejecting it? If it is, we need to consider this further. Let's start by looking at what the Bible says about what the church is – and isn't. Then – drum roll please – I'd like us to look, in particular, at the metaphor of the church as Christ's bride!

The word used in the New Testament for church, is *ekklesia*, which means assembly or gathering.[29] When we meet together for the purpose of following Jesus and worshipping him, we are being 'church' to one another. Jesus said that if 'two or three' gather 'in his name', he is with them.[30] It's not about the building, or having big numbers, it's about the reality of meeting together with Christ as our focus.[31] We can be the church anywhere – and anywhere we have church, Jesus is present to encourage, comfort and save.

How does this differ from God's kingdom? The kingdom is found wherever God's rule is present. If we belong to Jesus, his kingdom is within us wherever we go.[32] Church, on the other hand, happens when people meet with Jesus Christ as their focus. This is an important distinction as sometimes we Christians say we love our

---

29 G Herrick, G 2004, *8. Ecclesiology: The Church | Bible.org*, bible.org, viewed 25 August 2020, <https://bible.org/seriespage/8-ecclesiology-church>.

30 Matthew 18:20

31 D Guzik 2013b, *Study Guide for Matthew 18*, Blue Letter Bible, viewed 25 August 2020, <https://www.blueletterbible.org/Comm/guzik_david/StudyGuide2017-Mat/Mat-18.cfm>. Guzik says that to gather in Jesus name means Christ should be the focus of our meeting and that the gathering should reflect Christ's nature.

32 Luke 17:20-21

Saviour and want to live as kingdom Christians, yet we reject the idea of church. But it's important to be part of the church if we are to fulfil our potential in the kingdom.

I've heard people say they won't go to church because they've been hurt. The truth is, hurt people will hurt people. It doesn't matter if we're a new Christian or a long-term leader, we all have the capacity to wound one another. Yet despite this, Christ calls us to meet together. Our loving Saviour knows what's best for us – even if the community we belong to isn't perfect.

I find it intriguing that Christ founded the church on both himself and an imperfect man.

> *"It's so easy to become stuck in a rut as singles, being worried about our status and the problems that surround it."*

In Matthew 16:18 Jesus says to Peter, 'on this rock I will build my church, and the gates of Hades will not overcome it.' Here our Lord is using a play on words. When Jesus called Peter to follow him, he changed the disciple's name from Simon, which means 'hearer', to Peter which means 'rock'. Different people have different ideas of what this means. Is Peter the rock the church is built on or is Christ? I think it could be both.

To call Peter a rock is a word of promise over his wavering life. Peter did many imperfect things, but Jesus saw his potential.[33]

---

[33] While Peter made a few mistakes, his worst was denying Christ (John 18:15-27).

David Guzik says Peter didn't see himself as the foundation on which the church was built.[34] As the first person to confess Christ, Peter was the first rock of many that would be used to build the church. However, Christ was – and is – the cornerstone on which the church is founded.[35]

I love the idea that the church is founded on the perfect (Jesus), and initiated by the imperfect (Peter).

> *"Isn't that what we all are – imperfect beings who are following Jesus together, being transformed by him as we go?"*

Like Peter – look at our potential! But this potential can only be fulfilled if we keep gathering with God's people.

But there are some other pictures of the church that are important. Ephesians 4:11-16 says the church is Christ's body made up of different parts that need to work together if the body is to grow. If we are not part of the church, how can we grow and help others to do the same? Another wonderful image describes the church as a temple. Individually we are the temple of the Holy Spirit but we are a collective temple too.[36] The Holy Spirit doesn't just live in us as individuals, there is a unique dynamic of the Spirit's presence when people meet

---

34 D Guzik 2013a, *Study Guide for Matthew 16*, Blue Letter Bible, viewed 19 October 2020, <https://www.blueletterbible.org/Comm/guzik_david/StudyGuide2017-Mat/Mat-16.cfm>.

35 Matthew 21:42

36 Ephesians 2:19-22; 1 Corinthians 16:9.

as the church.[37] If we don't attend church we miss out on this awesome expression of God being with us.

> *"I love the idea that the church is founded on the perfect (Jesus), and initiated by the imperfect (Peter)."*

Another metaphor of the church as a family, is very dear to my heart. I've touched on this earlier in this book – we all need a family to belong to. Jesus said those who did his will were his mother and sister and brother.[38] In 2 Corinthians 6:18, God says he will be a Father to us, and we will be his children. We are members of God's household.[39] And we are to treat one another like we would treat members of our family.[40] If we don't go to church, we will risk living an isolated, empty life.

The truth is that the church includes people like you and me – and the disciple Peter – who have messed up. The flow on effect is that sometimes we don't deal with one another well. However, if we want to lean into God's purposes in the world and be kingdom daughters, we need to keep meeting with one another.[41] Whether we like it or not, Jesus has chosen the gathering of God's people to be *the* conduit for his grace and redemption.

---

37 Ephesians 6:22
38 Matthew 12:49-50
39 Ephesians 2:19; Galatians 6:10
40 1 Timothy 5:1
41 Hebrews 10:25

> *"All the pictures of the church we've considered so far look at 'the now'. The metaphor of the bride considers the perspective of eternity."*

The church is a remarkable, unique and amazing environment where divine beings choose to come and meet with us. It's a place of help, healing, growth and challenge. It's a place where the lonely can find family and where everyone can be welcome. All genders, races, and creeds are one in Christ, and it doesn't matter if we are single or married. We all are part of this amazing place that can bring order from chaos and rebirth life and hope.

But I promised you a wedding… All the pictures of the church we've considered so far look at 'the now'. The metaphor of the bride considers the perspective of eternity.

Have you ever imagined what it will be like when our Lord returns and there's a wedding in heaven? What could we possibly wear?

A Party in Heaven

When I was in my twenties I was invited to a lot of weddings. I mean a *lot*. My family used to find it amusing, when on weekends I'd often have a bag packed near the door. They'd ask me where I was going this time, a wedding or another youth camp? I went to a few of the latter too. I'm always up for a party, maybe that's why I received so many invitations. It was great at first – it's nice to be wanted and to have an excuse to dress up. But it became a problem. It was expensive. Another new outfit? More presents?

> *"Nearly every culture embraces marriage
> as a wonderful rite of passage."*

Weddings are fun, tiring and costly, but they are very important to us, aren't they? The Australian Government site, Moneysmart, says that the average Australian wedding currently costs $36,000.[42] That's a huge amount of money. Wouldn't it be better to put the cash towards a home deposit? Why do we lash out and spend so much on one day of our lives?

There are all kinds of reasons for this. Love is a powerful motivator as is our sex drive, but a wedding isn't just about desire, especially in today's secular society. Outside of our churches people can live together for years before getting married. Yet they still save up for that special day. Why?

Some of this yearning can be explained by the stories we build around it. Nearly every culture embraces marriage as a wonderful rite of passage. In the West, some young girls start dreaming of marriage from the time they can read. I have school friends who as teenagers used to keep wedding magazines under their bed. They didn't have a boyfriend yet, but they were dreaming of the beautiful dress they would wear on their special day. I thought they were crazy, of course. You've read my story earlier in this book. Back then, I wasn't interested in marriage or any of that kind of thing. But it shows how important the idea of marriage is to many of us ladies.

---

[42] https://moneysmart.gov.au/getting-married

However, I think there is something deeper going on. Marriage isn't just written into our physical or cultural DNA. It's written into our spiritual DNA. There is a reason we dream of our wedding day.

Have you realised that the Bible begins with marriage and ends with marriage? In Genesis chapter 2, God gives Adam a mate who is, 'flesh of his flesh and bone of his bone', the two becoming 'one flesh'.[43] Then in Revelation, the last book of the Bible, we find these words:

> *"Let us rejoice and be glad and give him glory!*
> *For the wedding of the Lamb has come,*
> *and his bride has made herself ready.*
> *Fine linen, bright and clean, was given her to wear."*[44]

I find it fascinating that a situation that begins with Adam and Eve, culminates with the wedding of Christ to the church. The whole Bible is about a marriage, what a story!

I've touched on this before but in the Old Testament, God refers to himself as husband to the children of Israel. In Jeremiah 3:14 God tells Israel he is married to her. The prophet Ezekiel quotes God as saying the following beautiful words:

---

43 Genesis 2:21-25
44 Revelation 19:7-8

> *"Later I passed by, and when I looked at you*
> *and saw that you were old enough for love,*
> *I spread the corner of my garment over you*
> *and covered your naked body. I gave you*
> *my solemn oath and entered into a covenant with you,*
> *declares the Sovereign Lord, and you became mine."*[45]

In the book of Hosea, we find that God was less than impressed with his bride's faithfulness. God asks Hosea to marry a prostitute, Gomer, who would be unfaithful to the prophet.[46] This was meant to parallel God's relationship to Israel who were being unfaithful to God by worshipping the pagan fertility god, Baal.[47] Poor Hosea: after Gomer leaves him, God asks him to take her back, again as an illustration of God's enduring love for his people.[48]

In the New Testament, we've noted earlier that Paul relates human marriage to the relationship between Christ and the church in Ephesians 5.[49] But I especially love the image in verses 25-27:

Husbands, love your wives just as Christ loved the church and gave himself up for her to make her holy, cleansing her by the washing with water through the word, and to present her to

---

[45] Ezekiel 16:8
[46] Hosea 1:2
[47] Hosea 2
[48] Hosea 3:1
[49] Ephesians 5:25-33

himself as a radiant church, without stain or wrinkle or any other blemish, but holy and blameless.[50]

We are part of a divine love story. Jesus Christ came to earth and gave his life to rescue his bride and make her beautiful again so he could marry her and take her to be with him forever.[51]

"The whole Bible is about a marriage, what a story! Jesus Christ came to earth and gave his life to rescue his bride and make her beautiful again so he could marry her and take her to be with him forever."

Hey amazing girls, if your desire is to find a good man and marry in this life then you desire a good thing but if we belong to Christ, know that he will one day take us to be with him forever. I know that not every one of you wants to find a man – some are settled and happy in their singleness – but many do want to marry. We long for the day we can wear a beautiful gown and walk down the aisle to meet our husband who is captivated by our beauty. This is our day. We have been chosen. We are loved! But this desire isn't just driven because we perceive a bias against our singleness, or we are subject to the hormones our bodies produce, or even because we don't want to be by ourselves. We are made for something far greater than a relationship with a man. The current, physical marriage is only a shadow of the true marriage to come.

---

50   Ephesians 5:25-27
51   Revelation 19:7-8

Oh, come on, girls, can you imagine what it will be like when Jesus comes back? What's the super-best-est wedding you've ever imagined? Look at some of the words used to describe the bride in Revelation 19:8 and Ephesians 5:27: 'fine linen bright and clean' – 'radiant, without stain wrinkle or blemish'. Think girls, we will be wearing the glorious, shining, radiant, righteousness of Christ as our dress. This 'fine linen' isn't just a reflection of our physical appearance but of our inner person looking radiant!

I have a friend who married in her forties and she said that other than the groom (of course) – and having some good friends to share the day with – what mattered most was the dress. She'd longed forever for a beautiful wedding dress. She had a lovely reception but would have been happy with a barn dance – as long as she had, *the dress*. But the truth is even if we never wear a wedding dress here on earth, if we belong to Jesus, we will have the dress-to-end-all-dresses as we rise to meet our husband-redeemer.

It's not by accident that we desire these things, because we have a groom who wants us and is coming for us. Just like my skydiving experience, the life we have here on earth will seem so brief when we look back on it from the context of eternity. Any marriage we have in this life, no matter how wonderful, will pale in comparison to being in the presence of the King of Kings.

In biblical times the bride and groom would be betrothed, which was a binding legal agreement that said this man is marrying this woman. It was like our engagement, but stronger. But then the groom would go and build onto his father's house, so he had a place to live with his bride. Tradition held that when he finished the house he would come back and surprise the bride.

I love these parallels. In John 14 Jesus tells the disciples there are many rooms in his father's house and he was going away to prepare a place for them.[52] What will this place be like? Where will you go for your honeymoon? The scriptures give us glimpses.

> *"We are made for something far greater than a relationship with a man."*

I don't know where you live but imagine that instead of asphalt and concrete, the street outside your front door is paved with gold – in fact the holy city that is Christ's bride is made of gold and the walls have gemstone foundations.[53] Can you see it? Forget the diamond in an earthly wedding ring that catches the downlights when you wiggle your fingers. Here God's glory radiates through the gems that line the streets. Can you imagine the colours as his light sparkles through jasper, sapphire, agate, emerald, onyx, ruby, chrysolite, beryl, topaz, turquoise, jacinth and amethyst? You turn around and look at your home and it's no longer a small flat but a beautiful mansion.[54] Can you see it? It's yours *forever*. The bridegroom has spared no expense for you – he didn't even hold back his life – he gave you everything so you could be here with him.

---

52   John 14:2-3
53   Revelation 21:11-12
54   John 14:2-3

But heaven isn't just a beautiful place to look at, it's a beautiful place to be. Revelation 7:9 talks about people from all nations, worshipping *together*. No longer will there be any racial discrimination or hatred. We will be as one, worshipping our King and Saviour. Pain and hunger and thirst will be gone too, and like I said earlier, God will wipe away every tear from our eyes – personally.[55] Imagine the Lord himself reaching out and wiping the tears from your face, kissing your forehead and saying it will be all right now. Oh, my, I've shed some tears in my time and I can't wait for his touch that will wipe my sorrow away for ever. The thought takes my breath away and makes me want to dance already!

And we will get to dance. Our bodies will be different – like the angels – but like the resurrected Lord we will still be able to be touched and can enjoy food.[56] That's just as well as we're all invited to a feast.[57] I'm super-excited about this too. Imagine eating all you want of the most delicious food ever, without having to count your calories or go to the gym the next day. That sounds like heaven to me. I used to do hip-hop dancing. Imagine dancing around the throne of God. Groovin' with Joseph and John and Ruth. How much fun would that be? I'm sure they'd be up for it.

It does us good to imagine these things, doesn't it? It's going to be amazing. Know this is real girls – our destination is eternity. Our life may be an incredible sky dive, but it's short in the

---

55   Revelation 7:16; 21:4

56   Luke 24:40-43; John 20:26-27; Matthew 22:30

57   Matthew 8:11

scheme of things. Read about eternity, dream about it and don't give up on it. Get ready, because our beautiful Saviour is coming for us.

Our destination is eternity.

It's a rendezvous all of us desire. So please, please, please don't miss out!

Don't Miss Out!
Jesus tells a story in Matthew 25 that we need to pay attention to.[58] There are ten young women who were waiting through the night for the bridegroom to come. They each had an oil lamp that needed to be kept filled so their flame would burn. Five of these women were foolish and five were wise. The wise girls kept the oil for their lamps in good supply, but the foolish ones were careless and let their oil run out. When they went to buy more oil, the bridegroom arrived and took the girls that were ready, with him. The foolish five were shut out of the banquet. Imagine how terrible it would be? Everyone is inside having fun, but you are on the outer, knowing you can never, *ever* go into the wedding.

This story is a clear indication that we need to be ready for when Jesus returns. We don't know when this will be, but it could be anytime. It could be today – whenever you're reading this – or tomorrow or in many years' time. God has a plan and he is holding the beginning and end of time apart so the maximum

---

58   Matthew 25:1-13.

number of people can be drawn into his kingdom. But one day time will end, and he'll come for us.

What does 'being ready' mean? It's about keeping the relationship alive. Have you ever been ghosted by someone? They are there one moment but all of a sudden, they won't answer your calls. I hate that. No relationship works well like that. Imagine having a fiancé and ghosting him – never talking to him. If we are going to spend eternity with someone, we need to walk with our Lord and talk with him. We need to learn all about him and live in communion with the Holy Spirit.

We have to stay in the relationship, even when things are tough. How tragic is it that so many single ladies get fed up with their single status to the point of leaving their faith? They say it's too hard to walk the kingdom walk so they do their own thing. Or I've tried God or church, but it is not for me. We've talked about that before, so I don't need to elaborate, but I don't want you to lose out. Please don't walk away. The very thought is painful. It's not all about the here and now.

How much better to open our eyes and live for Christ. To leap into life in tandem with Jesus – living the single life with joy and abandon – until it's time for him to take us home to be with him forever. That sounds like a much better deal to me – a lasting deal that includes being loved for eternity.

There is so much more to our existence than the here and now. There is a king calling us to make our mark and prepare for the grandest ballroom in the universe. I know which way I want to live. I want to walk with God, learn his ways and lean into his purposes. I want to be ready so that when Jesus Christ returns, I can be that kingdom girl dressed in an exquisite ballgown, dancing on the golden streets around the throne of heaven. How about you? Ready to dance, girlfriend?

Let Out Your Roar!

It is Sunday evening, the end of a beautiful day, and once again I find myself reflecting on my amazing, late maman. She was selfless, and generous with a huge capacity for love and life. She gave each of my family the gift of life and then spent all her years praying for us – and training us to be the people we are today. Most of us would have stories of gratitude towards our mothers or the mother figures in our lives.

But I am also grateful for every one of you beautiful women who have stayed with me on the journey through these pages. I am grateful for the capacity God has given each of us. He has graced us with strength and dignity to keep pouring out our lives for others even when we don't think we can do it anymore.

> *"I am grateful for the capacity God has given each of us. It's about keeping the relationship alive."*

We live in a fallen world, but we have an amazing opportunity to do great things for God. How's your imagination going so far? We've been given a canvas on which to paint something beautiful. Do you know what kind of artwork you want to make? Can you see yourself stepping into fulltime ministry or is your call in business, science or the arts? Maybe the image on your heart is to bring hope to the other women in your suburb or your village who have lost their spouse like you have, or to foster neglected children. The possibilities are endless.

"Is God only God when he gives us what we want?"

Are you willing to make a leap of faith and live an extraordinary life? There is so much more to you than you give yourself credit for. Singleness may have its challenges, but it's not the full story. Get out your paint brush and start splashing around the colour we spoke of earlier in the book, not just on your canvas, but on the lives of others. Help them to see light instead of darkness, beauty instead of shadow, and together you will thrive in God's kingdom.

That's what my maman did – and it's what I want to do too. Despite being single again and having to work hard to raise thirteen children, she brought life to others.

Her secret? She was a woman who feared the Lord. My maman reminds me of the woman in Proverbs 31. I love this description: 'Charm is deceptive, and beauty is fleeting; but a woman who fears the Lord is to be praised.'[59] The things we put our store in will fade away, but our character won't. If we fear God and put him first, the rest of life will find its right place and God will give us the things we really need.[60] Remember the prodigal daughters?

---

59 Proverbs 31:3

60 Matthew 6:33

> *"Cultivate this intimacy. Pay the cost of investing time in Christ Jesus daily."*

Some of you may be like that younger daughter, off having fun but sensing the emptiness of your life and you want to come home. Or maybe you are still in party mode and enjoying the world. Or you could be like the older sister, and you are bitter and disappointed because the dates you had decided on for marriage and having children have long since expired.

I've seen so many beautiful women lose themselves like this. If you've walked, or run, away from God – please come home to him now. If you are wearing a cloak of bitterness, cast it aside. Come home to your God and live for him. Is God only God when he gives us what we want? Isn't he the king, the ultimate authority in all of creation? He loves us but he's not just here to do our bidding. We are made to *follow him* – not the other way around – and live for the kingdom.

I don't pretend to be a perfect Christian. I've messed up lots of times. But when I do make mistakes there is one thing I do. I run back to my Saviour. I've faced all sorts of challenges. I've known heartbreak. I've lost people I love. I've battled breast cancer, had multiple operations and a tumour in my head. I've experienced prejudice because of my gender, skin colour and marital status. But in all of these things I keep getting up and moving forward. I may fall down sometimes but while there is breath in my lungs I'll keep rising up and following my Lord. I'll keep coming home!

That's what I'm calling you to do right now. Fear the Lord for it is the beginning of both knowledge and wisdom.[61] Put him first, come home to him and he will walk with you forever. Stay close to Christ.

Remember how I jumped out of a plane? I could only do that because I was strapped to an expert parachutist. Imagine if we were halfway down and I unbuckled myself from him – if I'd decided to fall through the air *my own way*. The result would not have been pretty. But because I trusted him to work the ropes of the parachute, he brought us both safely down to land.

Back in 2018 there was a scripture that kept coming back to me:

> *"I can't offer the Lord my God a sacrifice that cost me nothing (my paraphrase)."*[62]

At the time I thought it was about doing things for God and not leaving him the leftovers. But then I realised the cost was spending time in intimacy with him. I know I must relentlessly pursue this and keep it at the forefront of my life.

We can't live the single Christian life if we don't live in connection with Jesus. Our beautiful Saviour longs for us to walk closely with him so he can show us the way. Cultivate this intimacy. Pay the cost of investing time in Christ Jesus daily. Through that relationship we can have insurmountable capacity

---

61 Psalm 111:10; Proverbs 1:7.

62 2 Samuel 24:24

and influence. Anyone who walks in intimacy with the living God will be a force to be reckoned with!

Ladies, our destiny is eternity. Everything you've read in this book hinges on this and we need to live our lives in that light. My Senior Pastors, Paul and Maree de Jong, have carried a vision for decades calling us as a church to leave an echo for eternity.[63] The aim of this vision is for the generations to come to know the wonder of a God who isn't just real but wants to be part of our lives. They birthed the ministry, *Legacy*, which focuses on different ways of engaging and meeting the needs of our community.[64] Isn't that wonderful?

But what about us? We've considered many things as we've walked together through this book, but have we thought about the legacy *we* will leave on this earth?

I'd love you to take these questions and ponder them over the next days, weeks and months:

> *"What legacy can you cultivate right now that will have ripple effects in the halls of eternity?*
> *How will you be remembered at your funeral?*
> *What will the dash on your tombstone mean when people look back on your life?"*

---

[63] Paul and Maree are based in Auckland, New Zealand and are Senior Pastors and founders of LIFE, a multi-campus church with locations in Auckland, New Zealand and Melbourne, Australia.

[64] Legacy n.d., *Legacy 2020*, Legacy, viewed 1 September 2020, <https://www.legacy2020.org>.

I stir you to cultivate what's in you, so the community around you can say you are truly a woman who fears the Lord. Be unapologetic of the kingdom. Be praised and be known for your devotion. Be a kingdom girl whose name is known in both heaven and hell, because of the power of the risen Christ working in and through your life.

"A king is calling your name."

Go hard, with dignity and grace. You have nothing to lose, and everything to gain. A king is calling your name. His arms are around you – holding you fast – better than any parachute or bungy line.

It's time to say, yes, dream of the dress, leap into his purposes and live a life beyond just your status and make a mark for what matters most – eternity! Hey, wait for me. I'm coming too. What a ride!

LAST THOUGHT!

At the beginning of this book I mentioned this was not another volume about how single Christian women can find a husband. There are lots of those kinds of books out there and I longed to impart a much larger vision for our lives. It is paramount to be able to thrive as singles, *no matter what our circumstances.* Here are a few parting words of hope, especially for those who desire to marry in the near future.

I believe that the delays we are experiencing are not because God is holding out on us, it's because he wants the very best for us.

Earlier this week I was having my morning prayer time and God brought an experience back to mind. It happened a few years ago, during a time when I was feeling despondent about my singleness. I was reading the Bible and I stumbled upon this passage in Joshua:

> *"And Caleb said, 'I will give my daughter Aksah in marriage to the man who attacks and captures Kiriath Sepher.' Othniel son of Kenaz, Caleb's brother, took it; so Caleb gave his daughter Aksah to him in marriage."*[1]

---

1   Joshua 15:17-18

Have you ever had moments where God breaks into your world and crystallises truth in a fresh way? This was one of those times. As I read, it was as if God was saying that Aksah represented all of us single girls, Othniel represented single men and Caleb was a parallel of our Father God.

Aksah was poised for purpose and ready for marriage, but Caleb as a loving father didn't want just anyone to have his beloved daughter. Caleb, himself a great man of faith and bold exploits, wanted only the best for his girl. He knew she needed a man of faith and strength – a warrior and leader who could fight fearlessly – and was willing to fight for her. So, Caleb put a challenge to his men, and it was Othniel, Aksah's cousin, who stepped up and captured the land.

As I reflected on this, God spoke to my heart: *I'm not holding out on you.*

Sometimes we come to a point where we are tempted to compromise in our choice of a man, but our heavenly Father doesn't want that for us. He longs for us to have the best. He wants us to have a man of faith and character who will rise up and be bold for God's kingdom. He desires us to have someone who will fight for us and who will be strong for us, even as we are strong together. In his love for us, our father in heaven doesn't want anyone to have us until they are fit and ready for us. He wants us to have an Othniel.[2]

---

[2] In Judges 3:7-11 you can read further exploits of Othniel. He was a Judge who brought peace on the land.

What does this kind of man look like in the twenty-first century? After all, we are not all meant to wed army generals. And many of us incredible and strong sisters don't always want or need to be rescued by a man. We want to walk beside someone in God's purposes. How will we recognise a good man in our modern age?

I've pondered this for many years and have settled on the following:
- He will love God
- He will be prepared to serve you and will let you serve him too
- He will fight to protect you amidst the challenges of the day, so that no one will prey on you
- He will understand your needs and prepare to meet them. He will provide for you in the ways that matter most in your circumstances
- He will be a leader – empowering you and others towards great purpose in God's kingdom
- He won't be perfect – only Christ Jesus has that mantle – but he will grow as a man of God through the highs and lows of life.

Ladies, if you are losing hope of finding a companion as the years pass by, don't despair. God isn't holding out on us – instead he is holding onto us with his hand of protection. We are the apple of his eye, not a commodity to be forsaken. Know your worth and never settle for less than God's best.

As you live and thrive as God's glorious gal, never give up. If you desire marriage, it is my heart-felt prayer for you that God will raise up your Othniel and that together you do great things in his name. But until then, don't sit around waiting – do your own great exploits as mighty kingdom women – and live it up!

APPENDIX A

Summary of 2018 Singles Survey

In 2018, I surveyed over 50 people (men and women) aged between 20 to 62 years. I also conducted ad hoc interviews with many single Christian men and women at church and other Christian community activities.

In addition, I conducted **extended anecdotal conversations** with three sets of groups (10, 5 and 4 people). I also conducted discussion sets on singleness for my YouTube channel between 2017 and 2019. You can watch some of these conversations here: https://www.youtube.com/channel/UCuhuD9co4cbEAaSAxt-T-PQ?view_as=subscriber

Some key trends became apparent:
- **98.9 % of single women said their greatest challenge in their church was the lack of Christian men.**
- *Meeting solid single Christian guys in their 30s and up – in our society – is hard.*
- **75% of single women felt the church unintentionally focused too much on other life stage groups and for the most part left singles out.**

- *Much of today's church still structurally values families, youth, and marrieds, leaving adult singles somewhat isolated. We need more camaraderie between demographics – families need extra aunts/uncles, singles need families.*
- **In another ad hoc conversation** one woman said they would like their community: *to engage organically without always separating people in their areas of need. We need to be able to learn from different age groups and different interests not just our own.*
- **58% of single women felt the church supported the needs of singles.**
- *Church is a nicer place to be a single than anywhere else. The world understands being single, and maybe better than the church in some ways, but it doesn't understand being single and celibate.*
- *I think they are supporting it in part. I think there is a growing understanding of the dynamics of being single.*
- **In another ad hoc conversation, the women present agreed that when you are single there's a presumption that you have extra time on your hands.**
- *This means you get asked to do more projects at work or to babysit everyone's children.*

APPENDIX A

Summary of 2010 Singles Survey

In 2010 I surveyed over 100 women, aged between 18 to 50 years.

Some key trends became apparent:
- **99% of women and girls who took this survey believed they would marry one day and did not believe there was any option outside of this.**
- They said things like: *I want to die old with my husband.* And, *...well, yes of course it goes without saying – everyone would want to marry.*
- **75% of women who took the survey said they believed the advantage of being single was having time and getting to do your own thing without checking with someone.**
- *The freedom to come and go is really a great asset as a single.*
- **89% of the people surveyed admitted their friends and family were a great support to have while single.**
- *It's great to have friends who do not always want to talk about your status but get doing life and getting involved in other areas.*
- **85% of people who had broken up with their partners or become divorced said they found it difficult when their married friends stopped including them in their social settings.**
- *It is like I don't have feelings, I looked around and there was hardly anyone around. When I called, they often kept making excuses about their kids or husband.*
- **84% of singles felt that both society and their local networks put pressure on them to find a mate and stop fussing too much about it.**
- *We don't need people putting pressure on us regarding when we will meet that guy.*

THANK YOU

To my Redeemer and Saviour, defender and protector of my heart. My gratefulness and thankfulness begins and ends with you. Here is my task completed as assigned over years ago, from a prophet's mouth. Your timing is perfect and your wonder and kindness, immeasurable. May you be honoured through these pages, Saviour Jesus!

To Papa, author extraordinaire, you write like the speed of light. I admire your passion for writing. Thank you for instilling your wisdom and providing historical insight on Africa.

My beautiful large family – I love the sense of fun and life we have together. Thank you for always seeking the best in each other. Better together. Love you, *grand bisous*.

To my incredible pastors, Craig and Nadia. I am so grateful to be building his house alongside you. Thank you for adding value to this book and for always believing in God's people. Much love!

Thank you to my beautiful girlfriends who were vulnerable enough to share their journey with the world. Keep making God proud for such a time as this!

THANK YOU

To those who added value to this project through many conversations and manuscript reading: Kerry C, Vivien T, Alenta K, Chantal K, Michael K, Dr Clovis, Maman Jeanne, Katie T, Serge K and Jenny D. Also the many more who took part in the surveys, thesp_cebetwn community and those who engaged in conversations about singleness.

To my editor extraordinaire, Susan Bruce. We did it! What an appointed and divine interaction we have had with this book. You were and are God's best for this project". I am without words, *merci beaucoup!*

To my dearest Annie, amazing visual art teacher, thank you for sharing your beautiful creative input through the design of the book layout and cover. *Mille bisous!*

To Ryan thank for your flexibility and generosity, to Tamar you are an incredible blessing.

For more resources from Joëlle

The Unexpected Gift Journal
The reader's companion to the book, *The Unexpected Gift: Gods Biblical Perspective on Singleness*

Stories of Hope, inspired by the first book titled *The Chaplaincy Phenomena*.
Releasing in 2021, e-book version only

For more information:

Joëlle Marie-André Kabamba
Parcel Locker 1021607003
50 Flemington Road
Parkville Victoria 3052
Website: www.spacebetweenpublications.com
Emails: info@spacebetweenpublications.com

Social media:

- joelletheauthor   f – Joëlle M.A-Kabamba

▶ – Joëlle M.A Kabamba   in – Joëlle M.A Kabamba